US STRATEGIC INTERESTS IN THE GULF REGION

Westview Studies in Regional Security
Wm. J. Olson, Series Editor

US Strategic Interests in the Gulf Region,
edited by Wm. J. Olson

About the Book and Editor

An area vital to US interests, the Gulf has long been a volatile region. The vulnerability of Western interests is illustrated by such destabilizing influences as the political power of OPEC, the fall of the Shah of Iran, the Soviet invasion of Afghanistan, and the Iran-Iraq War. The contributors to this volume examine the causes and effects of instability in the region and US policy response, focusing on patterns of regional conflict, Soviet interests, Islamic fundamentalism, and US long-term policy for facing threats to its interests. Discussing the options open to government planners, the contributors analyze the viability of alternative political and military strategies for the Gulf in the future.

Wm. J. Olson is a regional security affairs analyst at the US Army War College's Strategic Studies Institute. He is the author of *Britain's Elusive Empire in the Middle East* and *Anglo-Iranian Relations During World War I.*

US STRATEGIC INTERESTS IN THE GULF REGION

edited by Wm. J. Olson

Westview Press / Boulder and London

Westview Studies in Regional Security

Copyright © 1987 by Westview Press, Inc.

Published in 1987 in the United States of America by Westview Press, Inc.; Frederick A. Praeger, Publisher; 5500 Central Avenue, Boulder, Colorado 80301

Library of Congress Cataloging-in-Publication Data
US strategic interests in the Gulf region.
  Westview Studies in Regional Security
  Includes index.
  1. Persian Gulf Region—Strategic aspects—Addresses,
essays, lectures. 2. United States—Military relations
—Persian Gulf Region—Addresses, essays, lectures.
3. Persian Gulf Region—Military relations—United
States—Addresses, essays, lectures. I. Olson,
William J., 1947– . II. Title: US strategic interests in the
gulf region. III. Series: Westview Studies in Regional Security.
UA830.U23 1987   355′.0330536   85-26983
ISBN: 0-8133-7119-8

Composition for this book was provided by the editor
This book was produced without formal editing by the publisher

Printed and bound in the United States of America

The paper used in this publication meets the requirements of the American National Standard for Permanence of Paper for Printed Library Materials Z39.48-1984.

6   5   4   3   2   1

To LMO & ASC and
to the memory of AMO.

CONTENTS

FIGURES AND TABLES

INTRODUCTION

In March 1985, the Strategic Studies Institute, US Army War College, hosted a two-day conference on US strategic interests in the Persian Gulf. The thrust of the conference was to take a long-term look at developments in the region that might influence US interests and to examine policy implications and make recommendations. A further theme of the conference was to look at regional events less in terms of an East-West perspective, which characterizes much of the literature on US policy in the Gulf region, and to focus more on the dynamics of the region itself. Hence, the majority of the papers in this volume stress the importance for US policy of shedding certain preconceptions and myths, and of developing responses and policies more in keeping with regional realities.

The continuing debate over the appropriate US role in any program of Gulf security, the long-term effects of a deteriorating US-Saudi relationship, the potential for radicalization in the region, the distinct possibility of a growing Soviet diplomatic presence, and the long-term potential for the continued and increased importance of Gulf oil for Western economies argue for coming to terms with the region itself, apart from an East-West confrontation.

Part of the complexity of the modern world is the emergence of alternative centers of power and a maturing of regional subsystems as critical elements in international relations. US policy, still largely preoccupied with the Soviet threat, has not taken sufficient note of nor has it adequately accommodated itself to this changing reality. Thus, the United States could embark on a program of "strategic consensus" in the Middle East designed to link the United States and regional states in an anti-Soviet consensus. The US concern was not shared by the regional states, however, who perhaps recalled a similar policy of containment—built around the Baghdad Pact—that also ignored local realities and failed ignominiously.

There are numerous bilateral concerns between the United States and the various states of the region, and among these are sufficient grounds for mutually acceptable relations. Yet, US concern for and interest in the region tends to fluctuate wildly, reflecting either a self-perpetuating naivety about the region or the episodic nature of the US-policymaking process in dealing with non-Soviet issues. Given the fact that the construction of US foreign policy requires an intricate and at times arcane mediation process among conflicting, if not mutually exclusive, interests, within a decisionmaking system that is cumbersome and self-absorbed, it may be impertinent to expect more. Certainly, however, the situation demands more, and the issues and problems that US policy must cope with are no respecters of the all-too-deliberate and short-term methodology of US responses. With this in mind, the papers in this volume take a long view of the region and suggest policies for the long term.

The papers are divided roughly into two major groups. Those dealing with thematic issues and those dealing with US political-military policies. The thematic chapters examine the nature of regional politics, ideology, and economics, and aspects of great power rivalry, looking first at sources then at types of instability. The policy-oriented sections examine US military capabilities and policies and recommend approaches for promoting and protecting US long-term interests.

Lenore Martin's chapter examines the nature and sources of regional conflict. This paper does not examine in detail the current war between Iran and Iraq, but instead looks at the characteristics of regional relations that make such conflict likely. The thrust here is not on contemporary events but on the inherent dynamics and sources of conflict that may contribute to long-term instability.

Similarly, Augustus Norton's chapter on Arab-Israeli issues looks at the consequences for the regional states and for US policy of the intractability of the Palestinian question. Norton notes that resolution of the Arab-Israeli impasse is not likely to usher in an age of peace and harmony, but he notes the deadening effect a lack of a resolution has on US policy and on regional stability.

Robert Freedman explores in detail the nature of Soviet diplomatic initiatives in the region. He provides a comprehensive survey of Soviet activities, arguing that even with considerable attention to the region, the Soviets have not reaped significant advantages for their effort. While this argument does not preclude future gains at US expense, it does show that

2

the US-Soviet rivalry in the region is not necessarily a zero-sum game, if for no other reason that there are more than two players in the game. A zero-sum mentality tends to emphasize US-Soviet confrontation at the expense of understanding the regional dynamic.

In this vein, Richard Remnek argues that the Soviet naval presence in the region has been misperceived. While he argues that the Soviet navy does pose a potential threat to US interests, he also argues that far too much has been read into their presence, particularly its military aspects. More interestingly, he illustrates the diplomatic-political nature of the Soviet presence, which is far more important than the marginal military gains to the Soviets for maintaining what can only be a highly vulnerable position in the Indian Ocean.

Jerrold Green examines some of the underpinnings of regional radicalism, in particular Islamic fundamentalism. Provocatively, he argues that Islamic fundmentalism as an ideology remains very pragmatic. It may be radical but it bases its goals on evaluating the costs and benefits of actions in relation to political and economic interests. While Dr. Green's views can be criticized for seeming to argue that because ideology is not everything it is therefore nothing, that it has no influence apart for a rational assessment of material interests, his views are an important corrective to opinions that tend to mystify Islamic fundamentalism and therefore put it beyond analysis or understanding.

Riad Ajami, more concretely, looks at the nature of the oil market in Saudi Arabia. He examines the immediate impact of declining oil revenues on Saudi Arabia, looking at the consequences for Saudi stability, but he focuses on the long-term meaning of Western oil dependency and the inescapable presence of huge reserves of Gulf oil. Many analysts tend to look only at present circumstances and fail to consider the effect on US long-term interests of short-term oil policies. Ajami argues that the United States should begin now to plan for a return of higher oil prices and Arab dominance of the oil market.

Turning from these more regional concerns, LTC Johnson details the nature of US military capabilities for contingencies in the Gulf. This study provides a handy guide to current US force structure and planning. Complementing this discussion is Michael Ryan's analysis of US security assistance for the region. He explores and explodes a number of myths about the role of US security assistance, and outlines the features of a more thoughtful, integrated, and enduring program.

Thomas McNaugher carries these analyses further by taking a sharper view of US policy in action. He argues forcefully for the need for a clear and consistent US policy for the region that is sustained and sustainable. He discusses basing problems and ways and means of ensuring adequate support for US interests without jeopardizing local security. Given the

3

delicate balancing act US policy must perform in the ambiguous circumstances that prevail in the Gulf, effecting such a policy is a challenge for a political system far less chaotic than that of the United States.

Michael Vlahos tackles one of the most perplexing problems facing US regional military policy-access. As McNaugher notes in his arguments, the US is never likely to have reliable access to bases within the region in peacetime, which complicates planning for responding to any future crisis. Vlahos accepts this reality as a challenge for US industrial innovative capabilities and proposes an off-shore, floating-island concept that would address many of the problems of a lack of regional facilities. He notes that affordable technology for building such a floating island already exists. This proposal is innovative and controversial.

The final essay proposes an alternative strategy for US political-military policy. Taking exception to the prevailing notion that if the United States is prepared to deal with the most dangerous regional scenario—a Soviet invasion of Iran—that it can deal with lesser, regional threats, this paper argues that the United States should reconsider the way it structures its forces for regional contingencies. The emphasis of such a new strategy would be on structuring forces more attuned to the nature of the most likely types of regional threats—coups, revolutions, terrorism, and interstate war. The theme of this piece, as it was with the conference, is the need to focus attention on regional affairs, to develop policies more in consonance with the interaction of US interests and local characteristics than in relation to US-Soviet rivalry. This does not mean to ignore the interpretation of international rivalry on a regional subsystem, but to argue that effective policy must be more sensitive to regional realities and less episodic.

In the course of preparing the conference and this volume I incurred numerous debts that cannot adequately be repaid by acknowledgement here. As with most undertakings, this one was no stranger to problems and unforeseen troubles. Were it not for the cooperation and support of many people, the effort would not have materialized. To all those who helped shoulder the frustration, I owe my thanks. I would particularly like to thank COL Thomas R. Stone, Director, SSI, for his support. Dr. Alan N. Sabrosky's advice was also invaluable. If it had not been for the tireless efforts of Mrs. Karen Bailey and CPT Ivan Bolden, the conference might never have happened. Dr. Jeffrey Simon also provided welcome moral support. I would also like to thank Ms. Shirley Shearer, my secretary, for her patience and effort. In addition, without the support of the US Army War College and the Department of the Army, the conference would not have been possible. Finally, I want to thank all the contributors, and Ms. Shirley Martin for her invaluable assistance.

While this volume deals with US policy, it does not, nor do any of the respective articles in it, necessarily represent the opinions of the Department of Defense, the Department of the Army, or any other government agency. The respective authors bear responsibility for the factual contents of their papers.

Wm. J. Olson
Carlisle Barracks, PA
1986

SOURCES

OF

INSTABILITY

CHAPTER 1

PATTERNS OF REGIONAL CONFLICT AND US GULF POLICY

by

Lenore G. Martin

In reaction to the Iranian Revolution, the hostage crisis, and the Soviet invasion of Afghanistan, President Jimmy Carter, in his State of the Union Address of January 23, 1980, committed the United States to the military defense of the Gulf from "external" threats. President Carter directed this doctrine most clearly at the Soviet Union. President Reagan enunciated a corollary to that doctrine after the Iranian Revolution demonstrated clear risks to the Gulf powers from "internal" threats and pledged that the United States would not permit Saudi Arabia to become another Iran.[1] These two presidential pronouncements constitute America's current Gulf policy. Through this policy the United States seeks to protect American interests in the Gulf, defined generally as securing Western energy supplies, fostering US commercial relations, and containing Soviet expansion. It is nonetheless a policy which seeks to employ the classic military strategies of deterrence and defense.

Accordingly, US policy planners should be concerned with the question of how this policy will meet the challenges of conflict in the Gulf. What then, are the sources of conflict in the region and what are the patterns of conflict that can be anticipated over the next few years?

SOURCES OF CONFLICT IN THE GULF

The patterns of regional conflicts in the Gulf arise from four principal sources of instability: territorial disputes, religious cleavages, ethnic dissension, and ideological contests. This is by no means intended as an exhaustive list. There may be, for example, conflicts arising from domestic instability within the Gulf states, such as succession crises. These may also spill over into interstate conflicts. Nonetheless, each of the four principal sources of instability have significant effects on the international politics of the Gulf.

TERRITORIAL DISPUTES

There are theoretically 21 potential loci for territorial disputes in the region, one for each of the on-shore and off-shore boundaries between the 10 states of the Gulf and Arabian Peninsula.[2] Six of these loci appear highly unlikely to produce disputes since the boundaries, off-shore and on land, between these countries have been settled, without evidence of any recent attempts to disturb the settlements. These boundaries are between the following Gulf states: Iran and Saudi Arabia, Iraq and Saudi Arabia, Iran and Oman, Saudi Arabia and the United Arab Emirates (UAE), and Saudi Arabia and Bahrain.

Eleven other Gulf boundaries, although unsettled, give no evidence of any sustained interest in settlement or active dispute, although there have been scenes of sporadic border incidents.[3] Examples of this lack of settlement include the Saudi-Oman border (which could have been settled with Saudi Arabia's resolution of the Buraymi dispute with the UAE in 1974, but was not) and the long-standing dispute between Bahrain and Qatar over the Hawar Islands and Zubara. Examples of sporadic disputes include incidents between South Yemen and Saudi Arabia over their undemarcated boundary in 1969, 1973, and 1978, as well as Omani action against Ras al-Khaymah (of the UAE) in 1977.

That leaves four territorial disputes which have been active within the past 20 years or so: Iraq-Kuwait; Iran-Bahrain; South Yemen-North Yemen; and Iraq-Iran. Each of these disputes has raised questions not merely over border adjustments but concern as well for significant loss of territory or even wholesale takeovers.

10

Iraq-Kuwait. Iraq's interest in Kuwait was expressed first by King Ghazi in the 1930s while the British still controlled Kuwait. These claims were then revived by Iraqi strongman Qasim's threat of a takeover immediately after the British withdrawal from Kuwait in 1961. Resistance first by the British then by collective action of the Arab League dispelled the threat and in 1963 the Ba'athist regime which overthrew Qasim recognized Kuwait and its frontiers. After the Ba'athist coup of 1968 in Iraq and the buildup of Iraqi forces with Soviet assistance in 1972, Iraq turned its interests to acquiring the Kuwaiti islands of Bubiyan and Warba, and some adjacent coastline, which command the entry to Umm Qasr, Iraq's only port on the Gulf. These Gulf islands became the objects of renewed disputes. A series of incidents at the Kuwaiti frontier with Iraq occurred in the 1970s. These were followed by less blatant but equally persistent Iraqi pressure for concessions from Kuwait for the use of the islands in the early 1980s.[4]

Iran-Bahrain. The Iranian pretensions to Bahrain have a long history stemming from the Bahraini rejection of Persian suzerainty in the late 18th century. These pretensions were intermittently reasserted as objections to British control in the 20th century. However, they were quieted after the British withdrawal and the Shah's determination in 1969 to permit the Bahrainis to vote for their independence. Since Khomeini's revolution, however, there has been evidence of an unofficial revival of Iranian interest in Bahrain. Ayatollah Ruhani, one of the revolutionary leaders, openly referred to Bahrain as Iran's 14th province in 1979. The Bahraini's also interrupted a planned Shi'ite coup in 1981, reportedly assisted by Iranian subversion.[5]

North Yemen-South Yemen. Unrest between the two Yemens originally stems from their imperial division under the Turks and the British at the turn of the century. Later the Imam of Yemen was unsuccessful in his attempts to expel the British from Aden and unite the two Yemens after the collapse of the Ottoman empire at the end of World War I. The Yemens, thus remained divided, with the South under colonial rule. After the British withdrawal from Aden in 1967 and the consolidation of a radical Marxist regime in the South, and after the settlement of the civil war (1962-70) which overthrew the Imamate in the North and brought to power a republican regime, the Yemens remained divided ideologically. The radical Marxist regime in the South has attempted through subversion in the 1970s to undermine the republican regime in the North, and North Yemen has aided dissidents in the south. These attempts have not succeeded, however, and both Yemens periodically espouse interest in unification.[6]

To date these unification discussions have also been unsuccessful, in part at least because of the continuing ideological differences of the two

Yemens. These differences have been further accentuated by strong Saudi support of the North and the strong Soviet support and ideological connection with the radical Marxist regime in the south. The effects of this countervailing support are uncertain since the Soviets also provide military support of the republican regime in the North. However, it is unclear what interests the Soviet Union may have in a unified Yemen. Moreover, the current turmoil in South Yemen has further complicated the situation by putting in doubt future PDRY policy, particularly that concerning improving relations with the conservative Gulf Cooperation Council (GCC) states.

Iran-Iraq. The border conflict between Iraq and Iran reaches back over 300 years. The three areas of the 730-mile-long frontier that have been pressure points for border conflict are the Kurdish areas in the north, the central area in which a projection of the Iranian border lies within less than 100 miles from Baghdad, and the Shatt al Arab waterway in the south. The Shatt is Iraq's commercial link to the Gulf and is shared by Iran. In the Algiers agreement of 1975 the parties compromised their claims over all three areas. This settlement then broke down in 1980 when Saddam Hussain initiated the current conflicts by invading Iran's oil rich province of Khuzestan. Hussain's territorial objectives were not clear. The invasion may have sought at least to have regained control over the Shatt and even to have seized Khuzestan.[7] In any event, Hussain's military initiative was timed to take advantage of what Iraq perceived as Iran's weakened state after its revolution. It also sought to counter Khomeini's appeals to the Iraqi Shi'ites to revolt and the Ayatollah's portrayal of Hussain as an infidel.

Even if the more active territorial disputes were settled, there would still be no assurance that the types of territorial claims which have given rise to these disputes would not be revived in the future. Over the years the Gulf has produced an abundance of grounds for territorial disputes. These include conflicting interests in oil, concerns over tribal fealty and grazing rights, as well as claims for renunciation of former imperial boundaries (e.g., Saudi objections to the British-Turkish demarcation of the eastern provinces) or for reassertion of imperial boundaries (e.g., Iraqi claims on Kuwait and the Iranian province of Khuzestan).

RELIGIOUS CLEAVAGES

A second source of international instability in the Gulf is created by the significant religious cleavage between Shi'ites and Sunnis.[8] In Iraq the Sunnis comprise an estimated 40 percent of the population but dominate the political system. The relatively inferior economic position of the Iraqi Shi'ites is fertile ground in which to sow the seeds of revolution. Nevertheless, despite some underground Shi'ite opposition from such groups as al-Dawah, the Hussain regime has retained the loyalty of the majority of the country's Shi'ites, as evidenced by the absence of significant Iraqi Shi'ite response to Khomeini's appeals for revolution in Iraq.[9]

In Bahrain, Shi'ites compose possibly as much as 75 percent of the population, whereas the ruling family is Sunni. The regime's pro-Western orientation and development of an atmosphere conducive for Western business has compromised some of the Islamic prohibitions concerning alcohol and dress. After the Iranian revolution, Khomeini's call for Shi'ite revolution stirred protests in Bahrain against these compromises with strict Islamic principles and Bahrain became a target for Iranian sponsored propaganda and subversion. The regime reacted in two ways. One was to increase internal security, the effects of which were demonstrated in the uncovering of a plot to overthrow the government in 1981. The other was to more strictly enforce the Islamic dress code and prohibition of alcohol. As a result, Bahrain appears to have overcome any significant shift of Shi'ite support away from the Sunni ruling family.

In Saudi Arabia the Khomeini revolution also stirred up the disaffection of the Shi'ite population which lives primarily in the Eastern Province and provides a significant number of the workers the oil fields and petroleum industry in that Province. The regime responded by forcefully putting down Shi'ite demonstrations but also by initiating economic projects to address the relatively poor economic conditions of the Shi'ites in the Eastern Province. On the other hand the most violent threat to the Saudi regime from religious disaffection after the Iranian revolution was not Shi'ite. It arose from the Sunni fundamentalist seizure of the Grand Mosque in 1979.[10]

ETHNIC DISSENSION

The third source for international instability in the Gulf is ethnic dissension which is manifest principally in the largest states of Iraq and Iran. In Iraq the Kurds remain a significant source of disaffection for the central regime.[11] In Iran, an entire perimeter of ethnic groups of different strengths and political orientations surrounds the ethnic Iranian core. The Iranian Kurds, while never as resistant to the central regime as their Iraqi counterparts, are still susceptible to encouragement in their opposition to the regime by Iraqis and Marxists within Iran,[12] and have waged a virtual civil war against the central government for over four years. The largest of Iran's ethnic groups, the Azerbaijanis or Azeris have been fairly integrated into Iranian society. However, they did host a

Soviet backed autonomous region immediately after World War II and demanded greater home rule, but not autonomy, immediately after Khomeini came to power.[13] Other groups capable of resistance to the central regime include the Baluchis on the eastern frontier with Pakistan and Afghanistan and the Qashqais in the southwest. On the other hand, the Iranian Arabs who populate the Khuzestan province are split in religious affiliation. Only one half are estimated to be Sunni and the Iranian Arabs did not succumb to Iraqi appeals to oppose the Iranian regime.

In the smaller Gulf states, the most significant ethnic force is comprised of aliens, sometimes up to 80 percent of the population as in the UAE. Except for the Palestinians in Kuwait this alien group has never organized itself for political opposition. But it nevertheless raises the possibility of labor disaffection and disruption of national economies. Furthermore the use of alien military contingents carries its own problems of control and readiness to respond to international crisis. For example the Saudis use Pakistanis to bolster their armed forces. However, when the Saudis attempted to exclude Shi'ites from the Pakistani contingents, the Pakistanis resisted and their troops were confined to barracks to quell the dissension.[14]

IDEOLOGICAL CONTESTS

The fourth source for international instability and conflict in the Gulf has been the existence of four strong ideological forces, each of which has been in contest with the others. These forces are Shi'ite fundamentalism from Iran, Ba'athism from Iraq, the puritanical Sunni orthodoxy of Saudi Wahhabism, and radical Marxism from South Yemen. Iranian fundamentalism is currently the most fervent of these ideologies. Iraq's Ba'athism has been tempered by the regime's need to retain alignments with the traditional Gulf states. Saudi Arabia's orthodoxy has been a strong conservative force for the support of the traditional Gulf Sheikhdoms and their collective resistance to radicalism and Iranian Shi'ism, most recently in the form of the GCC. South Yemen's Marxism, while it actively fueled the Dhofar rebellion in Oman in the late 1960s and early 1970s, seems focused more on subversion in North Yemen through support of the National Democratic Front (NDF). The NDF is a coalition of radical dissidents supported by tribesmen who oppose the North Yemeni regime. The effect of the recent coup, however, may see South Yemen resume support for subversion in Oman as well.

These ideological contests have had some success within Gulf states in overturning traditional regimes and reorienting the foreign policies of the regimes that have been brought to power through revolution. Thus both Iran and Iraq have undergone such radical reorientations, sometimes on more than one occasion. Iran's most radical revolution occurred in 1978-79, although less sustained changes occurred in the Mossadeq interregnum of 1951-53. Iraq's most radical revolution occurred in 1958 with the overthrow of the monarchy, but other reorientations occurred with the Ba'athist coups of 1963, 1968, and to a lesser extent with Hussain's rise to power in 1979. The traditional Gulf states now represented by the GCC have accordingly grave concerns for the security of their monarchist regimes from republican radicalism on the left as represented by Iraqi Ba'athism or South Yemeni Marxism or republican radicalism on the right as represented by religious fundamentalism.

GULF INTERNATIONAL POLITICS

The regional conflicts that result from these sources of instability are patterned for the most part by the international political environment of the Gulf. The current environment can be described as a "dynamic balance of power." The term "dynamic" is intended to focus the perception of international politics on the patterns of strategic interactions in the form of conflicts and alignments. This approach differs from the more conventional analysis of the "balance of power," which seeks to measure the relations of regional states as a function of their relative military capabilities.

To illustrate the differences of the two approaches, let us first use the more conventional "balance of power" analysis. One can observe that since the withdrawal of the British from the Gulf in the early 1970s two regional powers, Iran and Iraq, have developed military forces superior to those of the other Gulf and Arabian Peninsula states, although the current Iraq-Iran War has not demonstrated through 1986 the clear military superiority of one side over the other. Saudi Arabia, on the other hand, while clearly superior in military capabilities to the lesser Gulf states and both Yemens, still has not achieved, because of its limited population base, anywhere close to the military capability of the combatants in the Gulf War, notwithstanding the significant enhancements to Saudi capabilities from massive arms purchases from the West.[15]

Comparing these relative military capabilities, however, would miss the critical perception of a significant change in the patterns of strategic interactions in the Gulf which occurred after Khomeini's accession to power in 1979. Prior to that time and after the British withdrawal from the Trucial States/UAE at the end of 1971, there were numerous incidents of tension and even small-scale conflicts by and among many of

15

the Gulf states, major and minor. Involving the major states there was in particular the Iraq-Iran dispute over the Shatt and border areas which built up in 1974; but this was resolved by the Algiers Agreement of 1975. Involving major and minor states there were the Iraq-Kuwait border incidents in 1973 and 1976; Iranian takeovers in 1971 of the Gulf islands, Abu Musa, and the Tunbs, which were claimed by the UAE states of Sharja and Ras al-Khaymah; and Saudi occupation in 1977 of the islands of Qaru and Umm al-Maradim, claimed by Kuwait, off the Saudi-Kuwaiti coast. In addition, there were tensions and incidents between the lesser states, such as the South Yemeni support of the Dhofar rebellion in Oman until 1976; the South Yemen and North Yemen border conflict in 1979; and Omani action against Ras al-Khaymah in 1977 over border areas.

All of these incidents and tensions were, however, short-lived. Their resolutions at times produced defections from alignments (with both state and non-state allies, such as various ethnic groups) and made possible the creation of new ones. For example, the Algiers Agreement of 1975 severed the Iranian alignment with the Iraqi Kurds and allowed the diminution of Iraqi dependence on the Soviet Union for military supplies. Saudi Arabia's settlement in 1974 with the UAE of the long-standing Buraymi dispute brought Saudi diplomatic recognition of the UAE and made possible its alignment with the Saudis. Oman's suppression of the Dhofar rebellion in 1975-76 was eased by South Yemen's decision to stabilize relations with Saudi Arabia. It was also eased by the withdrawal of Iraq's support for the Dhofar rebels as a result of the Iraqi settlement with Iran in 1975.

Contrast this pattern of relatively flexible alignments and short-lived conflicts in the 1970s in the Gulf to the situation today. The Ayatollah's Iranian fundamentalism has introduced a new revolutionary ideological force into diplomatic intercourse. This ideological element has rigidified alignments in the Gulf and prolonged the prosecution of the Iraq-Iran War. That war has become a protracted one, notwithstanding Iraq's willingness to settle after being pushed back to its pre-invasion borders, primarily because of Khomeini's insistence on achieving the ideological goal of overthrowing the Hussain regime.

In response to the inability of Iraq to contain the threat of Khomeini's ideology, and to increase their internal security through collective measures, Saudi Arabia and its surrounding Sheikhdoms formed the GCC early in 1981. The GCC does not view itself as a fleeting or flexible alignment. It has the hallmarks of a NATO-like collective security organization, with joint military planning and exercises, as well as economic cooperation and a common ideological foundation in the traditional conservatism of the Gulf monarchies.[16] Nevertheless, various

GCC members have maintained their relationships with the superpowers. So, for example, to countervail possible heavy-handedness by Saudi Arabia within the GCC, Oman may look to its US connections and Kuwait to its Soviet connections. But the rigidities of alignments introduced into the Gulf by the Iranian Revolution of 1979 make it exceedingly unlikely, while Iran still seeks to export its revolution, that if Oman were threatened by a recrudescence of trouble in its Dhofar region, or if Kuwait were threatened by a resurgence of Iraqi interest in the Kuwaiti islands of Bubiyan and Warba, either Oman or Kuwait would look to Iran for assistance. Furthermore, in the face of such threats both Kuwait and Oman may be concerned that the collective security arrangement of the GCC would not have sufficient deterrent capability without their superpower connections.

How has the shift from the relatively flexible dynamic of the balance of power in the Gulf in the 1970s to the more rigid dynamic after Khomeini's revolution helped shape the patterns of conflict in the Gulf? With respect to territorial disputes, before the Iranian revolution in the 1970s the Gulf states had a strategic interest in resolving these disputes as part of the process of negotiating alliances. If the territorial disputes proved unresolvable, the Gulf states then had a further strategic interest at least in repressing territorial claims rather than letting them interfere with potential alignments. Even if boundary conflicts did erupt, they would be short-lived so as to preserve the flexibility of the combatants to negotiate future alliances.

After the Khomeini revolution alignment possibilities rigidified in the Gulf. The Gulf Sheikhdoms supported Iraq in its war against Iran and then in 1981 formed the GCC to provide for their collective security. Today the Gulf Sheikhdoms have an interest in resolving or repressing territorial disputes among themselves in order to maintain cohesion of the GCC. They have no strategic interest in letting territorial disputes between GCC members break into conflict, although the Qatari-Bahrayni dispute illustrates that confrontation remains potent. Still, compare, for example, the Saudi reactions to the Kuwaiti arms deals with the Soviet Union in the 1970s and that of 1984. When Kuwait turned to the Soviet Union for arms purchases which invited the possibility of Soviet advisors in the Gulf in 1977, the Saudis pressured the Kuwaitis to retract the invitation by occupying their disputed offshore islands.[17] In the arms deal of 1984, Kuwait appears to have been careful to limit to a handful the number of Soviet advisors it needs and Saudi Arabia refrained from an overt military reaction.[18]

With respect to the active territorial disputes, the Khomeini revolution has introduced, with the rigidification of alignments, a disinterest in quick resolution of the conflict that erupted between Iraq and Iran ostensibly over territorial claims. Contrast the relatively quick settlement of such claims at the Algiers Conference of 1975 and the impossibility of such settlement after five years of the Iran-Iraq War. In 1975 both sides viewed a territorial settlement as preferable to escalation and as a method of disrupting dangerous opposing alignments. For the Iraqis, the Iranian escalation of support for the Iraqi Kurds threatened to undermine the central state's ability not only to prosecute the border conflict, but also to integrate the Kurds into Iraqi society.[19] Settlement in 1975 also had the advantage of freeing Iraq to deal with the crisis caused by Syria's damming of the Euphrates River. For the Iranians, the escalation of Soviet support for the Iraqis threatened to introduce a new level of superpower involvement into the area.[20] The settlement also gave Iran the opportunity to repair its relations with the other Gulf states which had been damaged by the Shah's takeover of Abu Musa and the Tunbs.

With respect to the active disputes in the Gulf involving Iraq versus Kuwait and Iran versus Bahrain, the Khomeini revolution has had opposite effects. The need to retain the support of Kuwait has led Iraq to refrain from using military forces to pressure Kuwait for Iraqi military occupation of the Bubiyan and Warba islands, as did occur in the 1970s.[21] On the other hand the revival of Iran's territorial claims on Bahrain makes a Bahraini alignment with Iran unlikely. With respect to the active dispute between North and South Yemen, the rigidities created by the Iranian revolution on the eastern shores of the Arabian Peninsula have not had as much impact on those states on the western shores. Still the GCC states have shown some interest in settling or repressing disputes with both Yemens as a means of preserving their potential for alignments. This is particularly so with respect to the Yemens where potential alignments can draw them away from the Soviet Union.

The effects of the Iranian revolution on shaping patterns of Gulf conflicts deriving from religious divisions, ethnic dissension, and ideological contests, have been less clear. The reason is that these sources of instability have often been countervailing because of their tendency to be cross-cutting rather than converging. Thus, both before and after Khomeini, Kurdish separatism in Iraq has been weakened by cross-cutting ideological cleavages. The pro-Communist Kurdish parties resist alignment with the conservative Kurdish parties and various factions receive support from regimes on both sides of the border.[22] Furthermore, even after Khomeini, Iraqi Shi'ites have retained loyalties to the Hussain regime possibly because of the regime's success in vilifying the "Persian" character of Khomeini's Shi'ism. Similarly, notwithstanding Iraq's support of an Al Ahwaz (Khuzestan) liberation movement and appeals to Iranian Arabs, this ethnic group has retained its loyalties to the Khomeini regime. For some this is possibly because of their Shi'ism or due to their economic integration into Iranian society. This is similar to the experience of other groups on Iran's ethnic perimeter such as the Azeris.

The Khomeini regime through its fervent appeals to Gulf Shi'ites has attempted to create convergence among diverse ethnic groups and a common ideology. As noted before, these revolutionary appeals have achieved some successes in stirring up disaffection but only for a limited time. Generally, even before Khomeini, ideological forays across Gulf borders have not necessarily proved successful. Though somewhat due to countervailing ethnocentrism, the lack of success is also due to the tendency of the ideologies to splinter. This has even been evident in South Yemen's coups and splits between hard- and soft-liners that have affected its export of Marxism.[23] International thrusts can also be blunted because of the association of the ideology with a charismatic but unsuccessful individual, such as Nasserism, which succumbed to Nasser's defeat in the 1967 Six Day War with Israel. Thus Nasserism waned in republican North Yemen. Finally, the regimes with their own ideological orthodoxy often adopt repressive internal security measures to root out subversive opposition.

IMPLICATIONS FOR THE UNITED STATES

Current US Gulf policy, as embodied in the Carter Doctrine and the Reagan Corollary, appears to recognize the changing patterns of potential conflicts in the Gulf after Khomeini. Before the Iranian revolution, the United States looked to Iran and Saudi Arabia as twin pillars of the US policy of providing military forces to maintain security in the Gulf without clear need for US military intervention. After the fall of the Shah, Saudi Arabia was an unlikely pillar for such a policy and the need for US military intervention became more likely. The development under Carter of a Rapid Deployment Force for the Gulf and then under Reagan of the US Central Command (USCENTCOM) underlined the new Gulf policy of preparedness to resist military intervention by the Soviet Union, an overthrow of the Saudi regime, or other crises within the Gulf Sheikhdoms, all of which were viewed as possible results of the Khomeini revolution.

Events since 1981, however, have downplayed the concerns for military preparedness to protect US interests in maintaining the security of Gulf oil supplies and containing Soviet expansion. The Soviets remained embroiled in Afghanistan. The Iraq-Iran War became stalemated. And any adverse effects on Western oil supplies as a result of the Gulf war have been obscured by the oil glut since 1983-84. Still, the United States has warned against any blockage of the Strait of Hormuz by Iran in retaliation for the Iraqi strategy of interdicting Iran's Gulf oil trade. Furthermore, the United States has attempted to pressure Iran into a settlement by a "tilt" towards Iraq and by attempts to cut off allied spare parts or equipment supplies to Iran.[24] There is still concern that a desperate Iran could extend the war into the Gulf, particularly if the fortunes of war again threaten the integrity of the Iranian state.

Nonetheless, even though the Iran-Iraq War remains stalemated, we should look past the current conflict to consider other situations which can develop from the current pattern of international politics in the Gulf. I believe that four such situations can seriously jeopardize US interests in that region. Two of them, a predominant Iran and a predominant Iraq, can be viewed as developing from certain potential outcomes of the war between Iran and Iraq. The sources for the other two situations, a radicalized Saudi Arabia and a radicalized united Yemen, are not as clearly discernible from the current international political climate, but cannot be dismissed either as impossible. All four situations jeopardize US interests by creating preconditions for Soviet intervention into the Gulf as well as possibility of oil and trade embargoes which can threaten the West.

SIGNIFICANT POTENTIAL REGIONAL CONFLICTS

Predominant Iraq. This situation could arise from a collapse of Iran. For example, a succession crisis after Khomeini would pit factions of the ruling Islamic Republican Party against themselves and the weakened central regime against the ethnic groups around the Iranian perimeter that would be tempted to seek autonomy. Were the central regime to prove unable to maintain its authority over the autonomy seeking ethnic groups, or were it to engage in a protracted struggle while trying, Iran would be vulnerable to intrusions by Iraq and the Soviet Union. The Soviets might support an independent Azerbaijan, the Iraqis an independent Khuzestan. Each would be trying to succeed where it had failed earlier: the Soviet Union in 1946, the Iraqis in 1980. Whether the Soviets and the Iraqis would welcome each other's efforts would be a matter of their relations at the time. Each could assist other perimeter ethnic groups to seek autonomy in order to divert the central regime. Both could assist the Kurds, and the Soviets could encourage the Baluchis at the Afghan border.

One sign of Iraq's assertion of predominance would be an Iraqi takeover of Kuwait. This need not necessarily result from direct military aggression. Kuwait, itself, may be vulnerable to internal struggles, for example as a result of the penetration of the ruling family or military elite by left-wing or right-wing ideological forces. Such power struggles could invite intervention by Iraq, Saudi Arabia and the GCC. Even if no outright takeover by Iraq eventuates, Iraq might still be able to obtain Bubiyan and Warba as the price for its support for any faction in such power struggle.

Predominant Iran. This situation could result from civil strife within Iraq. For example an attempted overthrow of the Ba'athist regime, possibly by military coup, could initiate civil war. Iraq would then become vulnerable to intrusions by both the Soviet Union and Iran. The Soviets would seek to restore a pro-Soviet regime, the Iranians a Shi'ite one. Kurdish support for any civil war faction is a wild card in the sense that Kurdish groups would be playing for autonomy from any regime which restores central control.

A symbol of Iranian predominance would be its intervention into Bahrain, for example as a result of Shi'ite dissension. In such an event support for the regime would probably be forthcoming from Saudi Arabia and the GCC. But without assistance from Iraq or any non-Gulf powers, the Iranian forces might well succeed.

Radicalization of Saudi Arabia. This is a situation that could develop from ideological contests from the right or the left, conceivably as a result of the penetration of the royal family and/or military elite by left-wing or right-wing ideologies. There are many examples of economic and sociopolitical chains of events which would encourage radical overthrows of the regime. For instance, faltering oil revenues could trigger massive social unrest due to the dismantling of the welfare state and the widening economic gap between the elite and the population, or the disappointment of the rising expectations of the technologically trained professional class. An officers' coup or a succession crisis could paralyze the ability of the Saudi regime to respond to such social crises. Use of Saudi military resources to defend its far-flung borders or even to assist its allies in the GCC states could stretch military resources. Indeed, there may be a number of ways military actions could weaken the Saudi state as a result of military actions. Economic setbacks could further impel drastic reduction of the Saudi alien workforce upon which much of its economy depends.

The foregoing examples involve situations in which radical forces would make the monarchy a scapegoat and promise to restore the economy. A left-wing coup could attract Arab nationalist support from Iraq and possibly socialist military assistance from the Soviet Union. A right-wing coup espousing Islamic fundamentalism may seek to establish a Wahhabi republic, but it would be more isolated since it would have no republican ideological ties with any of the other GCC states and only speculative support from Iran or Pakistan.

A radicalized and resurgent Saudi Arabia, particularly one with a revolutionary message, would not be able to achieve predominance in the Gulf. It could, however, only too easily threaten its smaller neighbors, Qatar, the UAE, and Bahrain. And possibly even the GCC states of Kuwait and Oman would be threatened, notwithstanding their superpower connections.

United Marxist Yemen. The unification of North and South Yemen under a Marxist regime could result from the disintegration of North Yemen. Such disintegration could occur, for example, from civil strife involving the conservative northern tribes and the subversive leftist National Democratic Front (NDF) in the south. The regime might falter in this case particularly if it had alienated its Saudi sponsors. In such a situation Saudi Arabia might also seek to intervene but in such circumstances only to consolidate its hold over the northern conservative tribal groups. This situation might lead South Yemen to encourage subversive groups in the North, such as the NDF, to take a more active role. It would also give South Yemen more opportunity to push for a united Yemen, with the South playing a dominant role in the unified government.

A unified Marxist Yemen would be a potential threat to the Saudis. A resurgent Yemen could reassert revanchist claims for the Asir buffer region and would generally threaten the Saudi Red Sea coast, including the ideologically sensitive holy places of Mecca and Medina. Similarly, a unified Marxist Yemen would be viewed as a threat to Oman. Yemen could possibly reactivate a Dhofar rebellion which could in turn threaten the key Omani air base at Thumrait to which USCENTCOM has access.

US INTERESTS

How do the foregoing situations affect US interests in the Gulf? For one thing, each of them suggests that one faction or another contending for power might request US intervention in order to assist in the power struggle or at least to deter intervention from the Soviet Union and to contain hostile Gulf forces.

Secondly, each of these four situations heralds a significant transformation of the patterns of international politics in the Gulf. The predominance of either Iraq or Iran gives the predominant power the opportunity to achieve hegemony in the Gulf. Such predominance will therefore compel the remaining Gulf states to rally into a bloc, such as a more coordinated GCC, rather than submit to such hegemony. This will bipolarize Gulf international politics to a far greater extent than can be detected as a result of Khomeini's revolutionary ideology.

Two other situations, a left-wing radicalization of Saudi Arabia and Unification of a Marxist Yemen, do not necessarily suggest bipolarization of Gulf politics as much as they present significant opportunities for Soviet expansion in the Gulf. The ultimate result might therefore be Soviet hegemony rather than that of Iran or Iraq.

Accordingly, all four potential conflict situations raise significant risks for the aspect of US Gulf policy which is concerned with containing Soviet expansion into the Gulf. Less obviously, but equally significant should be the concern for the components of US Gulf policy seeking to support US interests in securing oil supplies for the West and the maintenance of US commercial relations with the Gulf. Consolidation of Gulf oil resources under a hegemonic Gulf power, particularly with Soviet support, would introduce a significant risk of denial of Gulf oil to the West, under certain circumstances. Furthermore, a bipolarization of the Gulf involving a protracted struggle between contending blocs or a bloc opposing a potentially hegemonial Gulf state would risk a long-term oil supply disruption for the West. Finally, a radicalized Saudi Arabia, particularly in league with other Gulf oil powers or the Soviet Union, itself would pose a threat of potential denial and disruption of oil markets. Such a radicalized regime would not necessarily require a volume of oil revenues to subsist as does the current Saudi state. On the other hand, such a regime might feel threatened and require such revenues to sustain its defense expenditures.

US POLICY PRESCRIPTIONS

Each of the foregoing potential Gulf crises of significant proportions requires a consideration of current US planning for Gulf intervention. USCENTCOM is designed as the principal instrument for the protection of American interests in the Gulf and constitutes a rapid deployment force of approximately 300 - 360 thousand personnel drawn from all branches of the US Armed Forces.[25] USCENTCOM has no bases in the Gulf, but by agreement with Oman (not all of which is public), during crises USCENTCOM is permitted access to air and naval bases built to accommodate US forces in Oman.[26] Only Marine contingents stationed on the Indian Ocean island of Diego Garcia, some 2,000 miles from the Gulf, will have the capability of a rapid response to any Gulf crisis. It has been estimated that approximately 1,800 marines could be airlifted to the Gulf within two days; and more optimistically, that up to 50 thousand marines could be delivered to the Gulf in a little more than one week.[27]

The problem with USCENTCOM planning however is that current US Gulf policy expects too much from USCENTCOM. It is supposed to undertake responses to the range of threats to the Gulf on three levels:

from Soviet invasion, to inter-Gulf war, to internal regime crises within the Gulf states. Furthermore, USCENTCOM deployment, to be effective, requires considerable support from the very Gulf states that might request it in the future, but at present deny it bases or any presence in the Gulf. Finally, in order to be assured of a welcome by the Gulf states for US intervention, obtaining the kind of military and political assistance USCENTCOM will need in times of crises will require much firmer alignments with Gulf states than are available within the current dynamic balance of power environment of the Gulf.

The solution to this problem, it is submitted, is to narrow the range of threats to which USCENTCOM will be expected to respond and to broaden the means of supporting US interests in the Gulf outside of USCENTCOM. There are a range of threats at the level of Soviet invasion or intervention for which USCENTCOM clearly cannot function as a deterrent, given the Soviet advantage from its relative proximity to the Gulf in any protracted conflict for resupply and reinforcement. Deterrence of attempted Soviet interdiction of oil supplies in Gulf chokepoints and sea lanes, while unlikely divorced from a grander strategy of Soviet intervention into the Gulf, may however be within USCENTCOM's capability. US global deterrent strategy is required to countervail a much grander Soviet design of intervention and take-over in the Gulf.

On the other hand, there are a range of crises within the Gulf states to which the GCC itself could respond, without any need for USCENTCOM deployment, although possibly with the assistance of other Middle Eastern or South Asian countries, such as the perimeter states of Egypt, Turkey and Pakistan. And the GCC itself appears to be preparing to contend with such minor crises by the development of its own rapid deployment force.[28]   USCENTCOM could therefore be dedicated to precisely those significant Gulf crises which the GCC could not handle, including all of the scenarios described above.

Such a change in USCENTCOM's military mission should be accompanied by an effective energy policy and the United States should maintain a diplomatic strategy appropriate for the dynamic balance of power environment of the Gulf.[29] Unfortunately, the Reagan Administration has publicly renounced the goal of energy independence.[30] An effective energy policy would require much more active measures be taken to decrease such dependence over the long run and increase the ability of the United States and its western allies to survive a short-term cut-off.[31] With such an energy policy the United States could risk more easily the possibility of short-term or even some potentially longer-term energy supply disruptions because of Gulf crises in which USCENTCOM would not need to become involved. Thus, the fact that USCENTCOM has been designed as a rapid deployment force should not necessarily commit the United States to a rapid reaction policy.

At the same time US diplomacy needs to recognize the limitations of the current international political environment of the Gulf. Although Khomeini's revolution has introduced a degree of rigidification of alignment patterns among the Gulf states, and particularly in opposition to Iran, the general tendency for flexible alignments within the Gulf, and particularly with their superpower connections, still obtains. While firmer alignments with GCC states can be attempted, the difficulty of their attainment should not lead to frustration. Limiting the deployment of USCENTCOM to major Gulf crises will in fact enhance US alignment opportunities since it will reassure smaller Gulf states that the United States is not preparing to use any minor Gulf crisis as a pretext to seize Gulf oil facilities.

On the other hand, the strategic use of USCENTCOM in the Gulf does require considerable local assistance. This assistance ranges from prepositioning of material and resupply facilities to early warning systems and base facilities for tactical aircraft. All such assistance depends on good relations with the local Gulf states, none of which are willing to provide permanent bases for USCENTCOM. Hence, planning for deployment of USCENTCOM without the benefit of such permanent Gulf bases while problematic, at least helps to alleviate the Gulf states' concerns that US intervention could lead to US take-overs. This is congruent with a dynamic balance of power diplomatic strategy since there is additional assurance that even after the successful resolution of any major Gulf crisis, USCENTCOM forces would be withdrawn and not tempted to stay, as with the US presence at the Guantanamo base in Cuba. Furthermore, such a dynamic balance of power diplomacy should be prepared to counter attempts by Iran or Iraq to achieve predominance in the Gulf.

ENDNOTES

1. *The New York Times,* October 7, 1983.
2. See Lenore G. Martin, *The Unstable Gulf: Threats From Within* (Lexington, MA: Lexington Books, 1984), 31-73, for a systematic examination of all territorial divisions in the Gulf.
3. These eleven are between the following states: Iran - UAE (control by Iran over the Tunbs and possibly Abu Musa, after their takeover in 1971, is still disputed); Iran-Kuwait (unsettled because of the lack of settlement or the Iran-Iraq border); Iran-Qatar (unsettled because of the lack of settlement between Qatar and Bahrain); Saudi Arabia-Qatar (unclear how affected by unpublished Saudi Arabian-UAE settlement of 1974); Saudi Arabia-Oman

(unsettled but undisputed since Saudi Arabian renunciation of Buraymi claims in 1974 settlement with UAE); Saudi Arabia-Kuwait (unsettled because of off-shore islands, which were subject of Saudi takeover in 1977); Saudi Arabia-North Yemen (unsettled, border clashes reported in oil exploration area in 1980); Saudi Arabia-South Yemen (unsettled, border clashes reported in 1978); South Yemen-Oman (unsettled, but GCC interest reported in 1982 in mediating settlement); Oman-UAE (unsettled, particularly on Musandam peninsula); Qatar-Bahrain (unsettled because of long-standing dispute over historic Zubarah and offshore Hawar islands); and Qatar-UAE (unclear if settled as a result of unpublished Saudi-UAE settlement of 1974). There are also a number of unsettled boundaries internal to the UAE beyond the scope of this article. See Martin, pp. 63-64.

4. For convenience, the various *Quarterly Economic Review* editions are referred to as "QER, [name of country]". See *QER, Kuwait* (no. 3, 1984): 5; *Foreign Broadcast Information Service, Middle East and Africa* (hereafter *FBIS*), 3 December 1984, p. C3; *Middle East Economic Digest* hereafter (*MEED*) 10 August 1984, p. 21.

5. See *QER, Bahrain, Qatar, and the Yemens* (no. 2, 1984): 11.

6. *Ibid.*, p. 23.

7. Anthony H. Cordesman, *The Gulf and the Search for Strategic Stability: Saudi Arabia, the Military Balance in the Gulf, and Trends in the Arab-Israeli Military Balance* (Boulder: Westview Press, 1984), 645-648.

8. See generally James A. Bill, "Resurgent Islam in the Persian Gulf," *Foreign Affairs* (Fall 1984): 108-127. Note that the Sunni-Shi'ite split affects almost all Gulf and Arabian Peninsula states. Not all Gulf Shi'ites, however, follow the so-called "Twelvers" beliefs of Iranian and Iraqi Shi'ites. North Yemeni Shi'ites (known as Zaidis) follow the "Fivers"' beliefs. The Sunni-Shi'ite split stems from their historical differences towards the successors of the Islamic prophet, Muhammad. Shi'ites believe that Ali, Muhammad's cousin and only son-in-law, and Ali's line of eldest male descendants, are the only legitimate successors to the prophet. These descendants, or Imams, were cloaked with infallibility and endowed with divine rights to rule in both the religious and secular spheres. The Sunni derive their name from the teachings and the life of the prophet, known as the Sunna. They believe that the successors to Muhammad, the caliphs, must be elected by consensus. They also believe that the faithful need no infallible or divinely inspired intermediary and that all have equal access to Allah.

9. There have also been reports of Shi'ite subversion in Kuwait. See *QER, Kuwait* (no. 3, 1984): 4, (Annual Supp.): 3.

10. James Buchan, "Secular and Religious Opposition in Saudi Arabia," in Tim Niblock, ed., *State, Society and Economy in Saudi Arabia*, (New York: St. Martin's Press, 1982): 122; Cordesman, *The Gulf*, 231-239.

11. See generally Stephen C. Pelletiere, *The Kurds: An Unstable Element in the Gulf* (Boulder: Westview Press, 1984); see specifically for reports of Iraqi Kurdish activity: *QER, Iraq* (no. 1, 1984): 10-11, (no. 2, 1984): 10-11, (no. 4, 1984): 10.

12. See *QER, Iran* (no. 1, 1984): 11, (no. 3, 1984): 3.

13. See the reports of Iraqi attempts to rekindle an Azeri autonomy movement in *FBIS*, 27 September 1984, p. E2.

14. *QER*, Saudi Arabia (no. 1, 1984): 8.

15. See generally Martin, *Unstable Gulf*, and Cordesman, *The Gulf*; also Thomas L. McNaugher, "Arms and Allies on the Arabian Peninsula," *Orbis* (Fall 1984): 489-526; and for specific reports of recent Saudi arms purchases or negotiations, see: *The New York Times*, 14 October 1984 (Brazil), and 18 November 1984 (USA); *QER, Saudi Arabia*, (no. 1, 1984): 7 (France) and (no. 3, 1984): 7 (UK).

16. See generally, John Duke Anthony, "The Gulf Cooperation Council," in Robert G. Darius, et. al., eds. *Gulf Security into the 1980's* (Stanford: Hoover Institution Press, 1984): 82-92; see for specific reports of GCC activities: *QER, Bahrain, Qatar, Oman, the Yemens (no. 3, 1984): 7, 9, 16; QER, Kuwait* (no. 3, 1984): 5; *QER, United Arab Emirates ["UAE"]* (no. 1, 1984): 7, (no. 2, 1984): 7, (no. 3, 1984): 7.

17. Robert Litwak, *Security in the Persian Gulf, Vol. 2: Sources of Inter-State Conflict* (Montclair, N.J.: Allanheld Osmun for the International Institute of Strategic Studies, 1981): 40; J. B. Kelly, *Arabia: The Gulf and The West* (New York: Basic Books, 1980): p.

172; Aryeh Shmuelevitz, "Gulf States," Colin Legum, *et. al.*, eds., *The Middle East Contemporary Survey* vol. 1, 1976-1977, pp. 343-344.

18. See *QER, Kuwait* (no. 3, 1984): 4; *MEED*, 17 August 1984, p. 17.

19. Richard F. Nyrop, ed., *Iraq: A Country Study* (Washington, DC: The American University, Area Handbook Series, 1979): 237.

20. Robert O. Freedman, "Soviet Policy Toward Ba'athist Iraq 1968-1979," in Robert H. Donaldson, ed., *The Soviet Union in the Third World: Successes and Failures*, (Boulder: Westview Press, 1981): 174.

21. *MEED*, 10 August 1984.

22. Martin, *Unstable Gulf*, 89.

23. *Ibid.*, pp. 102-103.

24. *Wall Street Journal*, 27 August 1984, p. 33; *The New York Times*, 17 July 1984, p. A4.

25. *The New York Times*, 10 April 1985, p. A17; 1 April 1984, p. 40.

26. *The New York Times*, 25 March 1985, pp. A1, A8, 26 March 1985, p. A8; *Wall Street Journal*, 11 April 1985, p. 34.

27. *The New York Times*, 10 April 1985, p. A17.

28. *FBIS*, 9 October 1984, p. C1, 12 October 1984, pp. C1-C2; 22 October 1984, p. C2; 23 October 1984, p. C1, 31 October 1984, p. C1; 23 November 1984, p. C3.

29. See Martin, *Unstable Gulf*, 149-151; see also William J. Olson, "An Alternative Strategy for Southwest Asia," this volume.

30. *The New York Times*, 5 October 1983, p. D24.

31. See Martin, *Unstable Gulf*, 143-149.

CHAPTER 2

THE ARAB-ISRAELI CONFLICT:
AN ENDURING DANGER TO REGIONAL SECURITY

by

Augustus Richard Norton

Since World War II dozens of serious regional conflicts have competed for global attention, but none has done so with the persistence of the Arab-Israeli conflict. No contemporary conflict has proven as intractable or has stymied as many diplomatic initiatives, and few conflicts have so shaped the political contours of a region. Indeed, the durability and the salience of the conflict have so consumed the attention of both participants and observers that other sources of instability seem scarcely to have been noticed at times.

We sometimes need to remind ourselves that the Arab-Israeli conflict is not the only one scarring the Middle East and that its settlement would not bring an end to warfare in the region. Merely the mention of Kurdish nationalism, North and South Yemen, the Western Sahara or the Gulf war evokes images of battles outside of the Arab-Israeli zone. Certainly the arms procurement programs of the Saudis, Egyptians, Jordanians, Algerians, Kuwaitis, and other Arab states arise in significant part from threats posed by Arab or Iranian adversaries rather than from Israel, although each Arab state remains keenly aware of Israeli military power.

Thus, the Arab-Israeli conflict is not the sole source of instability in the Middle East, nor is it necessarily the one that holds the most danger for regional or global peace. The region has long been marked by conflicts which have little to do with Arabs and Jews, and much of the violence of recent years—from the assassination of Anwar Sadat, the latest intercommunal battles in Lebanon, the insurrection in the Sudan, to the Gulf war—is only peripherally connected to the Arab-Israeli conflict, if at all. Even the first Arab-Israeli war was—to a notable extent—as much a conflict of competing objectives between Arab states as it was a war between the Arabs and Israelis.[1] Even if the major demands of the conflict's belligerents—the reconciliation of mutually exclusive designs for Jerusalem, the satisfaction of contending national claims of the Palestinians and the Israelis, the establishment of peaceful borders and mutual recognition, and the redress of the claims of those dispossessed of their lands—were met, it is unlikely that the Middle East would be promptly transformed into a zone of peace and tranquility.

Yet, with all the preceding caveats in mind, it is germane to note that the Arab-Israeli conflict does matter, if for no other reason than the fact that a sixth or seventh (depending on how one numbers the previous episodes) outbreak of warfare might well embroil the United States in a dangerous showdown with the Soviet Union, which like the United States asserts that its vital interests are at stake in the region. So long as it remains unresolved, the conflict will be a clear and present danger to the stability of the region, and it will pose severe potential risks for the regional interests of the United States which—like it or not—is deeply involved, even implicated in the problem. Given the increasingly intimate ties between the United States and Israel, it is fair to argue that the United States has become inextricably entangled in the Arab-Israeli conflict and may now have as big a stake in its peaceful settlement as the regional participants.

THE ARAB WORLD, ARAB UNITY, AND THE ARAB-ISRAELI CONFLICT

Since independence each of the Arab states has had to face a formidable array of challenges, ranging from combatting disease and illiteracy to raising the standard of living of its citizens. Simultaneously, each state, to one degree or another, has striven to create a locus of identity for its citizens; no easy matter, especially for the "new" states of the region that were unable to claim longstanding historical continuity, or even clearly demarcated boundaries. The natural history of the modern Arab world is one in which supracommunal identities have often been in competition with tribal, ethnic, and local ties.

This is not to argue that the Arab world is quintessentially a collection of tribes and discrete ethnic communities subsumed within artificial states; such assertions are often no more than thinly veiled racism masquerading as analysis.[2] The point is that most of the Arab states are of relatively recent vintage, and each faces differential dilemmas of modernization and social change that challenge the talents of even the best political leaders. Political modernization and socioeconomic development are no easy tasks, especially in a region where the state was long an alien concept; and like all modernizing states, the Arab ones must reconcile primordial identities with the requisites of the modern state. As such, the challenge facing the Arab states, while perhaps more difficult than that confronted by other developing states, is hardly a novel one. It is a problem of political accommodation that was aptly denoted as "the integrative revolution" by Clifford Geertz.[3] Much progress has been made, the governments of the Arab world are much more stable than they were just two decades ago, but for many Arab governments legitimacy remains an elusive goal.[4]

States led by men whose right to rule is vociferously challenged both within and without the state's boundaries are not prone to take profoundly controversial initiatives, and there is no more controversial initiative than sitting at the negotiating table with Israel. It is no accident that it was the most socially and culturally homogeneous state, Egypt, which was capable of being the exception that provided the rule by coming to terms with Israel in the historic treaty of 1979. No other Arab state, including Syria, enjoys the formidable human scale, or the self-confidence that so obviously defines Egypt. (For that matter, no other Arab state comprises as appealing an interlocutor for Israel as Egypt did.)

A dominant feature of Arab political culture is the widely shared perception that the Palestinians have been unjustly dispossessed from their homeland. The issue of Palestine has served to unify the Arabs more effectively than any other issue. But, as the record shows, Arab unity has hardly led to the end of the Arab-Israeli conflict, or, for that matter, to the resolution of the plight of the Palestinians. Instead, the Arab leaders have coalesced around a lowest common denominator stance that has emphasized unity at the expense of humanitarian concerns. In short, the Arab leaders have found it easier and safer to deny Israel than to deal with her. Consensus decision making—formalized in the charter of the Arab League—has provided the most obdurate Arab governments a veto over those who might prefer compromise over conflict. Caught on the petard of Arab unity, few Arab leaders have been willing to risk anathematizing themselves by breaking ranks.

This is not to argue that Arab unity is wholly unjustified on practical grounds. Israel's military supremacy, certainly for the past two decades, has provided strong reinforcement of the dictum that there is strength, or at least the illusion of strength, in numbers. It should be emphasized that Israel's isolation and rejection by a more-or-less unified Arab world has often been skillfully used by her leaders to justify human and materiel sacrifices that might otherwise have been rejected by Israel's populace, as well as to extract impressive amounts of military aid from major powers, especially the United States.

In short, the Arab-Israeli conflict has served Arab politicians as a rallying cry, an instrument of superficial rhetorical unity, and a demonstration of fealty to an Arab nation which would otherwise have to search for an alternative basis for solidarity. To an important degree, the quest for Arab unity has also been a quest for a secure identity by governments that remain, even today, relatively insecure. Lest we be accused of being overly cynical, it is important to emphasize the emotive resonance of the Palestinian cause—the "heart of the problem"—among the Arab people. Indeed, the justness of the quest for Palestine is generally unchallenged, even among those Arab leaders who are less than enthusiastic about those who claim the mantle of Palestinian leadership. But, more often than not, the Palestinian cause has been used as a club to enforce a negative consensus around a conviction rather than a positive consensus around a program.[5]

Unity based on a realistic appraisal of what is reasonably attainable might well be constructive, but unity based on a negative consensus has not only helped to preclude a solution, but has helped to create a fertile environment for regional thuggery and extremism. In addition, the Arabs' penchant for rhetorical excesses has fed the palpable insecurities of the Israeli people, as well as providing grist for the Arabs' pertinacious cousins in Israel. Recalcitrance feeds on recalcitrance, and the hawks on either side of the Arab-Israeli conflict are indeed allies of one another.

The gulf separating the Arab and Israeli belligerents is well illustrated by a brief consideration of a recent book by an Israeli scholar, Mark Heller. Heller, certainly not an impartial observer (by his own admission), analyzes the dilemma of Israel vis-a-vis the Palestinian question in a dispassionate cost-benefit analysis, and he comes to the relatively novel conclusion that the only feasible and suitable option open to Israel is the negotiation with the PLO of the establishment of a

Palestinian state. Heller's Palestine would only enjoy a truncated sovereignty, but it would certainly place more than a modicum of independence in the hands of the Palestinian people. Yet, what is remarkable about Heller's book is not just that it delineates a settlement that the PLO would find hard to accept, given his prescription for limited sovereignty, but that the settlement it describes would be unacceptable to mainstream Israeli politicians as well. In effect, Heller succeeds in revealing a yawning gulf, rather than a probable compromise.[6] Given the distance separating the belligerents it is clear that intransigence is its own reward.

THE TICKING CLOCK

If the shared intransigence of the belligerents merely reduced to a stable arms cease-fire, we might merely mouth some banal slogan, "there are some problems in the world that just do not have solutions," for instance, and move on to other matters. Unfortunately, as the conflict festers it spawns radicalism, and radicalism in its extremist manifestations stands as a threat to US interests in the region. Although the emasculation of extremism is not the sole reason for pursuing a reasonable settlement of the conflict, it is certainly a worthy one nonetheless. It is fair to note that the Saudis' interest in a settlement, for example, is as much a reflection of their fear of the resultant radicalism coincident to nonsettlement, as a commitment to justice for the Palestinians and the restoration of Jerusalem to Islam. In varying degrees, this pragmatic view has informed the recent actions of those Arab states customarily described as moderate, most particularly Jordan and Egypt.

Time has healed some wounds. Many of the Arab states, indeed most of them, have accepted the reality of Israel. Certainly the Fahd proposal of 1980 did in reasonably clear language, while Egypt's seal on its 1979 treaty with Israel did so explicitly, and King Hussain's statements of 1985 leave little doubt of his realistic acceptance of Israel (least of all in Israel); and even Yasir Arafat has come teasingly close to saying the magic words. In the occupied territories, the Palestinians have long acknowledged the obvious.

If some of the participants in the conflict have moderated their views, this hardly justifies claiming that the necessary conditions for ending the conflict have been established. Although Israel's leaders have consistently proclaimed their willingness to negotiate with any Arab state that acknowledges Israel's right to exist, few if any informed observers expect Israel to willingly concede the core demand of the Arabs: an independent Palestinian state. As one senior Israeli diplomat candidly admitted to me in February 1985, Israel will talk, but it will never allow an independent state of Palestine to be created. (Nor, as I was reminded by a prominent Israeli newspaper publisher, should it be glibly accepted that even the Golan Heights would be readily conceded by Israel.[7])

Even assuming that Israel will agree to the creation of a carefully circumscribed statelet—not an easy given—there is no reason to believe that those sitting on the other side of the table would rush to seize the package. The emotive significance of the plight of the Palestinians is such that any Arab politician will long hesitate before lending his imprimatur to a compromise settlement that produces a territorially abbreviated Palestinian state which enjoys only starkly circumscribed political independence. Given Israel's relative military strength, as well as the progressive integration of the occupied territories into Israel, it is unreasonable to expect much more than such a truncated sovereignty. In some circles it is considered good sport to chastise the moderate Arabs for refusing to directly negotiate with Israel, but, in fact, they might well end up risking much, with few reciprocal gains.

The passage of time may have healed some wounds, but it has caused some old wounds to fester as well as opening new ones. The four million stateless Palestinians serve as continuing evidence of the original problem, and as such they hold the Arab states hostage to their fate. Whatever the preferences of even the most cynical Arab leader, the plight of the Palestinians cannot be ignored, especially in the current climate of anti-Western agitation by militant Muslims who see the struggle for Jerusalem, the capital of Palestine, as a sacred one.

For the Palestinians, after nearly four decades of uneven struggle, success is ever more elusive. The leading Palestinian grouping, the Palestine Liberation Organization (PLO), has come to seem enfeebled. The optimism spawned by the great diplomatic successes of the 1970s, including the Arab League's 1974 recognition of the PLO as the sole legitimate representative of the Palestinian people, the unique granting of observer status to the PLO by the United Nations General Assembly, and the warm, if still tentative, diplomatic probings by the Carter Administration, are now only tattered remnants. Manipulated by the Arab states, deadened by the empty rhetoric of their leaders, and frequently dismissed in the West with calumnious adjectives, the Palestinians can certainly be excused a bleak appraisal of their political prospects. More than ever before, there is a realization that time may be running against them, and with this recognition there is a growing prospect for the increasing radicalization of Palestinian politics. As I will show, the key turning point occurred in 1982.

THE 1982 WATERSHED

The Israeli invasion of Lebanon in 1982 was an historic watershed whose significance is still not fully recognized in the West. True enough, Israel grossly misunderstood Lebanon, failed miserably in its efforts to install a malleable government in Beirut, and ended up being virtually chased out of most of south Lebanon (though it still retains a residual presence in the extreme southern segment). True enough, within Israel the war turned into a deeply unpopular one, and few Israelis were unhappy to see their country disengage from the dangerous Lebanese killing-ground in 1985. And true enough, the invasion may yet have succeeded in supplanting the *fida'i* adversary in south Lebanon with a more formidable Shi'ite adversary.[8]

Despite the preceding "truths", the invasion was an astounding short and mid-term success in one key respect: by depriving the PLO of its base in Lebanon, Israel set in gear the fragmentation and disintegration of an organization that was gaining considerable diplomatic credibility prior to June 1982. In fact, the PLO's scrupulous adherence—for 11 months in south Lebanon—to the cease-fire negotiated in 1981 by Ambassador Philip Habib was a source of enormous irritation to senior Israeli security officials who saw the PLO gaining legitimacy, and thereby enhancing its pretensions to represent the Palestinians in any international negotiations that might be organized. It was the latter possibility that Israel sought most fervently to avoid, hoping that by destroying the PLO as a political force in the region, it would thereby release other Palestinians in the occupied territories from their fealty or fear of the PLO and bring them to negotiate with Israel. On the first count, Israel has come close to realizing its goal, yet on the second, the PLO—despite its advanced dismemberment—remains the most powerful magnet for the political loyalty of the Palestinians, including the majority of those living in the occupied territories.

If the PLO retains a sizable following within the Palestinian community, that is not to assert that it enjoys the Arab world support it did prior to the Israeli invasion of Lebanon. It does not. The Palestinian resistance has been badly shattered. After being forced to evacuate from Beirut in August 1982, the PLO was then pummeled in northern Lebanon during 1983 by Syria and breakaway PLO factions, under the dissident Abu Musa, leading to Arafat's second ignominious seaborne retreat from the eastern Mediterranean.[9] Then in May 1985 the Shi'ites of Lebanon's Amal movement, acting with clear Syrian support and encouragement, began attacking the Palestinian refugee camps south of Beirut. While the 1985 battles ended close to a stalemate, in part because anti-Arafat and pro-Arafat factions momentarily joined forces, they still

35

served to demonstrate that the PLO could not safely perch where Syria's influence was writ large.

To an important degree, what has happened to the PLO is distressingly irrelevant. The depredations of the past three or four years—the massacres in Sabra and Shatila, the expulsion from Beirut, the cleaving of the PLO—have produced a growing sense of hopelessness among rank-and-file Palestinians. Absent effective political authority at the center of Palestinian politics, power has gone to the fringes, especially on the West Bank. Forlorn and alienated, many young West Bank Palestinians have begun to carry out independent acts of violence in apparent imitation of the Shi'ites of South Lebanon, thus contributing to a cycle of violence that also includes militant Jewish settlers who have shown a similar disdain for established authority. This new development was accurately described by a senior Israel officer serving on the West Bank.

> The nature of the violence [on the West Bank] is changing, making it more difficult to detect in advance . . . . Only 50 percent of the recent violence has been directed from the outside. The rest . . . was undertaken by individuals who are no longer willing to wait for the PLO to win the fight for them. They act on their own or in self-contained small groups that are very hard to penetrate.[10]

Meanwhile, Palestinian authored acts of international terrorism also are on the rise, apparently also reflecting the keen sense of frustration and alienation that mark the post-1982 Palestinian diaspora. Although Arafat attempted to distance himself—and the moderate wing of the PLO—from the incidents of international terrorism that marked 1985, by declaring that the PLO would abjure all acts of violence outside of Israel and the occupied territories, it is not clear that his hands are altogether clean.[11] In retrospect, the 1982 invasion may have succeeded in eliminating the PLO as a viable diplomatic actor, but it is quite probable that the resulting fragmentation of Palestinian politics may well stalk Israel and her supporters for some time to come. This development too may be adjudged a success, if it is believed that Israel must at all costs avoid having to meet the Palestinians on the negotiating plain. By such a rationale demonizing the PLO is good tactics, but for those who believe that the Palestinian people have legitimate rights that must be addressed—a view clearly expressed in President Ronald Reagan's September 1, 1982, proposal—such a development will only further complicate an already very complicated situation.[12] Surely, the short term benefits of ostracizing the PLO are scant in comparison with the long term dangers of creating a political body with a stake only in violence.

Despite the ominous omens alluded to above, there have been a few positive developments in the Arab-Israeli conflict. Most significantly, there has been an important bifurcation of perspectives in the Arab world; a move away from the longstanding negative unity. On the one hand, a number of Arab actors have, albeit grudgingly, spurned the negative consensus and accepted the reality of Israel. This group has, with due seriousness, attempted to find a modal framework for negotiating with Israel. Perhaps most noteworthy in this regard is the effort of King Hussain to come to a working agreement with Arafat. Arafat, ever the political tightrope walker, backed away from his February 11, 1985, statement with Hussain, after he failed to gain the support of the PLO Executive Committee for his agreement with the monarch to work toward the creation of a confederation between a state of Palestine and the Kingdom of Jordan. Yet the agreement is still an important and constructive benchmark (Arafat has not repudiated the agreement). As one knowledgeable observer has noted, the February 11 agreement constituted both realism and progress.

> Realism because it accepts, in fact, President Reagan's negotiating scenario expressed in his speech of September 1, 1982, and best characterized in the phrase "territory for peace." Progress because it recognizes, in fact though not completely in form, that a separate Palestinian state between Israel and Jordan is not a feasible possibility, however just or rational it may appear to many on the Arab side and their friends. A separate Palestinian state is one obstacle too many in the jungle of assumptions, assertions and fixed positions taken by the parties concerned. Both the PLO and the Jordanians appear to recognize that; hence the formula of February 11, 1985.[13]

On the other hand, nonsolution has served to reinforce the perspective of those who see no feasible solution short of erradicating Israel *qua* Zionist entity. The result is a deadly dialectic of violence that has already claimed too many victims. To date, both sides—extremists and moderates—have proven profoundly impotent. The extremists can make life difficult for others, but they have little prospect of effecting their program of destruction. The moderates, often diffident to a fault toward their adversaries, have nothing to show for their explorations save an increase in risks.

Whatever the mistakes and missteps of the cobelligerents, it is unfair and unreasonable to expect full-blown magnanimity from those caught in the web of the Arab-Israeli conflict. Each party must serve a demanding and contentious constituency that severely limits the freedom of action of any of the respective leaders. Unless forward steps are reinforced by meaningful outside actors, as President Carter did during the negotiations that led to the historic Camp David Agreement, any hope of solution is ill-placed.

IMPLICATIONS FOR THE UNITED STATES

It is not hard to understand why Washington might not, in early 1986, feel compelled to assume more than low profile diplomacy in the Arab-Israeli conflict. The Reagan Administration was badly stung by the failure of American efforts to retrieve a significant victory from Israel's invasion of Lebanon.[14] Having once seen its efforts prove futile, even counterproductive, the administration is understandably tentative toward any invitation for a more activist role. The international economic crisis, spawned in part by the heady increases in the price of oil following the 1973 Middle East War, has now passed. The price of oil is down, there is a glut of oil on the world market and OPEC seems to be in the throes of a drastic loss of market control and influence. Despite the setbacks the United States has suffered, the Soviets have not been very successful in capitalizing on American misfortune, although the Soviet Union has managed to increase its diplomatic representation in the Gulf. International terrorism, increasingly indiscriminate and steadily more anti-American in its focus, effectively distracted the US government for long periods of time during 1985, while at the same time fortifying those who argue that the only true friend of the United States in the Middle East is Israel (this sometimes being an implicit assertion that the United States should not apply diplomatic pressure on Israel). The PLO, which has not succeeded in avoiding at least the appearance of a conspiratorial role in such outrages as the seizure of the *Achille Lauro* cruise ship, has seen its abysmal credibility further eroded.

In short, while the United States will certainly not ignore the Middle East, there does not seem to be any reason why the United States can't just sit on the sidelines of the Arab-Israel conflict and see what game the participants choose to play. Furthermore, for those engaged in the policy process in the United States, it is always hard to avoid taking the short view—focusing on the latest epiphenomenon—rather than tackling issues at their roots. Until the red lights start blinking, there are just too many other issues screaming out for attention. This last factor is well described by Philip Stoddard:

> In the absence of a crisis, or a dramatic initiative taken by someone else, administrations are very reluctant to take initiatives. Rather than seize opportunities that may only be dimly perceived, they tend to sit back until they have to do something; that has been the record in the past. If we do not see a crisis or a dramatic initiative, persuading the administration to take the risks of involvement becomes much more difficult, especially if the issue is of low priority.[15]

No one can assert with total assurance that the time to move is 1986 or any other year, at least not unless speaking retrospectively. Nonetheless, at mid decade there are strong clues to indicate that with a few strong nudges, and a decisive shove or two from influential extraregional actors, such as the United States, it might just be possible to get things moving in a constructive direction. During 1984 and 1985, Israel, Jordan, Egypt, and even the PLO took pains to emphasize that they wish to pursue a negotiated settlement, and each seemed acutely aware that time is hardly their ally. Within the region there are troubling dynamics in process, and without progress on the peace front the situation may well get much worse. This is no time to be standing on the sidelines.

The United States is in an influential position to encourage Arab and Israeli leaders of moderate persuasion, but to succeed on both fronts the United States must avoid appearing so sensitive to Israeli concerns and demands that the moderate Arab states seem—to their domestic opponents—to be serving Israel's interests rather than their own. The key seems to be that while the United States engages in partiality toward Israel, it should not so favor Israel as to forget its other relationships. It is not as if there is a precise formula, but there is certainly a precise problem if the United States is seen as losing all balance in its Middle East policy. Sadly, many of the closest Arab friends of the United States believe that the United States is in danger of ignoring their reasonable interests in deference to its friendship with Israel.[16]

Whatever good the United States does in the Middle East, without a solution to the Arab-Israeli conflict the United States will be haunted by its deadly by-products. The Palestinian cause is too deeply rooted in the political culture of the region for it to disappear, despite glib predictions to the contrary. In addition, it is crucial that the viability of the PLO not be confused with the durability of the issue that the PLO represents. The Arab-Israeli conflict presents the United States with a set of problems that will neither go away, nor become any easier to solve in the foreseeable future. Indeed, there are already indications that the situation in the region is deteriorating.

Israel's renowned senior statesman Abba Eban has cogently emphasized the urgency of American involvement in seeking an end to the Arab-Israel conflict.

> We have reached a stage in which American passivity would amount to active intervention against a possible era of reconciliation. There is no way of testing the temperature of the water without plunging in. It will not become any warmer or more inviting after further delay.[17]

Prognostication is a hazardous business when it comes to the Middle East, but even so there is one prediction that is well supported by the tragic experience of several decades, and that is that today's opportunities are usually not recognized until tomorrow, and tomorrow's opportunities are likely to make us nostalgic for yesterday's. The Arab-Israeli conflict will not wither away; it will continue to shape the political environment in the Middle East until it is put to rest. However well intended the policy of the United States, without a solution to this conflict the United States will continue to be haunted by nonsolution. There are no guarantees that US involvement will pay off, but it is a virtual certainty that the situation left untended will only get worse, producing further terrorism, instability and bloodshed.*

ENDNOTES

1. See Barry Rubin, *The Arab States and the Palestine Conflict* (Syracuse: Syracuse University Press, 1981).

2. This style of presentation is found in Yoram Ettinger and Benyamin Calvary, "How Politics Works [sic] in the Middle East," *Focus*, published by the Britain/Israel Public Affairs Committee, September 1985; and, James R. Kurth, "American Perceptions of the Israeli-Palestinian Conflict and the Iranian-Iraqi War: The Need for a New Look," *Naval War College Review*, 38 (January-February 1985): 75-86.

3. Clifford Geertz, "The Integrative Revolution: Primordial Sentiments and Civil Politics in the New States," in Clifford Geertz, ed., *Old Societies and New States: The Quest for Modernity in Asia and Africa* (New York: The Free Press, 1963), 105-57.

4. The pursuit of legitimacy is the theme of Michael Hudson, *Arab Politics: The Search for Legitimacy* (New Haven: Yale University Press, 1977).

5. Malcolm Kerr, "Regional Arab Politics and the Conflict with Israel," in Paul Y. Hammond and Sidney S. Alexander, eds., *Political Dynamics in the Middle East* (New York: American Elsevier Publishing Co., 1972), 31-68, see esp. 60-63.

6. Mark A. Heller, *A Palestinian State: The Implications for Israel* (Cambridge, Mass.: Harvard University Press, 1983). For a review by Augustus R. Norton, see *American Political Science Review* 79 (June 1985): 581-82.

7. One well informed Israel notes, "Israel is very reluctant to withdraw from the Golan Heights, possibly even in lieu of a peace agreement, while Syria apparently refuses to sign a full peace agreement with Israel even if she regains the Golan." Moshe Ma'oz, "Israel and the Arabs: The Challenge of Peace," a speech delivered at Georgetown University on 20 March 1985, reprinted in *American-Arab Affairs* 14 (Fall 1985): 158-61.

8. See Augustus R. Norton, "Making Enemies in South Lebanon: Harakat Amal, the IDF, and South Lebanon," *Middle East Insight* (January/February 1984) 13-20.

9. Arafat, the ultimate survivor, has demonstrated a peerless instinct for survival, but it is precisely this overdeveloped instinct that may preclude innovative policy shifts. In other words, the very traits that explain his durability may also explain his pathological inability to escape the trap of lowest-common-denominator politics.

10. Quoted in Thomas L. Friedman, "The Palestinian-Israel Fight: Arab Lands Now Spectators," *The New York Times*, 3 October 1985.

---

*The author would like to thank his colleagues, Charles S. Ahlgren, George C. Edwards III, and Daniel J. Kaufman for their thoughtful and penetrating comments on this chapter, and to absolve them of any responsibility (or blame) for the finished product, for which the author alone is responsible. Moreover, the views and arguments presented herein do not purport to represent the position of any agency or institution of the United States Government.

11. Arafat's statement was broadcast on the Cairo domestic service, 7 November 1985, and is translated in *Foreign Broadcast Information Service: Middle East and Africa*, 8 November 1985, pp. D1-D2.

12. Address by Ronald Reagan, "A New Opportunity for Peace in the Middle East," 1 September 1982, reprinted in *American-Arab Affairs* 2 (Fall 1982): 149-54.

13. Robert G. Neumann, "The Middle East Peace Process: Stuck Once More?" *American-Arab Affairs* 14 (Fall 1984): 26-37, quote taken from p. 26.

14. See Philip H. Stoddard, "US Policy and the Arab-Israeli Conflict: Observations on the Current Scene," *Annals* 482 (November 1985): pp. 19-39.

15. *Ibid.* p. 33. Also see Robert G. Neumann, "Middle East: America's Next Steps," *Foreign Policy* 59 (Summer 1985): 106-22.

16. See the interview with King Hussein in *The New York Times*, 15 March 15, 1984. Also see Hassan Bin Talal [Crown Prince of Jordan], "Return to Geneva," *Foreign Policy* 57 (Winter 1984/85): 8-13.

17. Abba Eban, "No Choice but Activism," *Foreign Policy* 57 (Winter 1984/85): 3-7, quote taken from p. 7. For a thoughtful and informed analysis of how the negotiating process might be enlivened see Harold H. Saunders, "Arabs and Israelis: A Political Strategy," *Foreign Affairs* 64 (Winter 1985/86): pp. 304-25.

CHAPTER 3

SOVIET POLICY TOWARD THE PERSIAN GULF
FROM THE OUTBREAK OF THE IRAN-IRAQ WAR
TO THE DEATH OF KONSTANTIN CHERNENKO

by

Robert O. Freedman

In analyzing Soviet policy toward the Persian Gulf since the outbreak of the Iran-Iraq War, there are two major points to keep in mind. In the first place, Soviet policy toward the Gulf can best be understood as part of Soviet policy toward the Middle East as a whole. Second, the Iran-Iraq War has been a major blow to Soviet policy in the Middle East and for this reason Moscow has been trying, albeit unsuccessfully, to bring the war to an end since its inception in September 1980.

In order to understand Soviet policy toward the Persian Gulf and, in particular, its key states Iran, Iraq, Saudi Arabia and Kuwait, it is necessary to deal first with the problem of determining Moscow's goals in the Middle East as a whole.

There are two major schools of thought on Soviet goals in the Middle East.[1] While both agree that the Soviet Union wants to be considered as a major factor in Middle Eastern affairs, if only because of the USSR's propinquity to the region, they differ on the ultimate Soviet goal in the Middle East. One school of thought sees Soviet Middle Eastern policy as being primarily defensive in nature; that is, as directed toward preventing the region from being used as a base for military attack or political subversion against the USSR. The other school of thought sees Soviet policy as primarily offensive in nature, as aimed at the limitation and ultimate exclusion of Western influence from the region and its replacement by Soviet influence. The policy implications of this debate are clear. If Moscow is basically defensively oriented in the Middle East, then it is not only possible but actually desirable for the United States to work with the USSR to bring about settlement of such conflicts as the ones between the Arab states and Israel, and between Iran and Iraq. Conversely, if Moscow's goals are seen as offensive in nature, then it is undesirable to try to bring Moscow into the peace process because the Soviet leaders would only exploit the opportunity to weaken the position of the United States. It is the opinion of the author that Soviet goals in the Middle East, at least since the mid-1960s, have been primarily offensive in nature; and in the Arab segment of the Middle East, the Soviet Union appears to have been engaged in a zero-sum game competition for influence with the United States.

In its efforts to weaken and ultimately eliminate Western influence from the Middle East, and particularly from the Arab world, while promoting Soviet influence, the Soviet leadership has employed a number of tactics. First and foremost has been the supply of military aid to its regional clients.[2] Next in importance comes economic aid; the Aswan Dam in Egypt and the Euphrates Dam in Syria are prominent examples of Soviet economic assistance, although each project has had serious problems. In recent years Moscow has also sought to solidify its influence through the conclusion of long-term Friendship and Cooperation treaties such as the ones concluded with Egypt (1971), Iraq (1972), Somalia (1974), Ethiopia (1978), Afghanistan (1978), South Yemen (1979), Syria (1980), and North Yemen (1984), although the repudiation of the treaties by Egypt (1976) and Somalia (1977) indicate that this has not always been a successful tactic. Moscow has also attempted to exploit both the lingering memories of Western colonialism and Western threats against Arab oil producers, and the USSR has, as in the case of the assassination of Indira Gandhi, deliberately used "disinformation" to discredit American policy.[3] The USSR has also sought influence through the establishment of ties between the CPSU (Communist Party of the Soviet Union) and such Arab ruling political parties as the Syrian Ba'ath and the Algerian FLN. Yet another tactic aimed at gaining influence has been the provision of security infrastructure assistance to countries like South Yemen and Ethiopia. Finally, Moscow has offered the Arabs aid of both a military and diplomatic nature against Israel, although that aid has been limited in scope because Moscow continues to support Israel's right to exist; both for fear of unduly alienating the United States with whom the Russians desire additional strategic arms agreements and improved trade relations, and because Israel serves as a convenient rallying point for potentially anti-Western forces in the Arab world.[4]

  While the USSR has used all these tactics, with a greater or lesser degree of success over the last two decades, it has also run into serious problems in its quest for influence in the Middle East. The numerous inter-Arab and regional conflicts (Syria-Iraq; North Yemen-South Yemen; Ethiopia-Somalia; Algeria-Morocco; Iran-Iraq, etc.) have usually meant that when the USSR has favored one party, it has alienated the other, often driving it over to the West. Secondly, the existence of Middle Eastern Communist parties has proven to be a handicap for the USSR, as Communist activities have, on occasion, caused a sharp deterioration in relations between Moscow and the country in which the Communist party has operated. The Communist-supported coup attempt in the Sudan in 1971, Communist efforts to organize cells in the Iraqi army in the mid and late 1970s, and the activities of the Tudeh party in Khomeini's Iran, are recent examples of this problem.[5] Third, the wealth which flowed to the Arab world (or at least to its major oil producers) since the quadrupling of oil prices in late 1973 has enabled the Arabs to buy quality technology from the West and Japan, and this has helped to weaken the economic bond between the USSR and such Arab states as Iraq. Fourth, since 1967 and particularly since the 1973 Arab-Israeli War, Islam has been resurgent throughout the Arab world, and the USSR, identified in the Arab world with atheism, has been hampered as a result, particularly since the Soviet invasion of Afghanistan in 1979 where Moscow has been fighting against an essentially Islamic resistance force. As the Ayatollah Khomeini, the leading Islamic fundamentalist in the Middle East currently in a position of political power, has noted:

> We are fighting against international communism to the same degree that we are fighting against the Western world devourers led by America, Israel and Zionism. My dear friends, you should know that the danger from the communist powers is not less than America . . . Once again I strongly condemn the dastardly occupation of Afghanistan by the plunderers and occupiers of the aggressive East. I hope that the Muslim and noble people of Afghanistan will as soon as possible achieve true victory and independence and be released from the grip of these so-called supporters of the working class.[6]

Fifth, in the diplomacy surrounding the Arab-Israeli conflict, Moscow is hampered by its lack of diplomatic ties with Israel, a fact which enables the United States alone to talk to both sides of the conflict. Finally, the United States, and to a lesser extent, France and China, have actively opposed Soviet efforts to achieve predominant influence in the region and this has frequently enabled Middle Eastern states to play the extra-regional powers off against each other and thereby prevent any one of them from securing predominant influence.

To overcome these difficulties, Moscow has evolved one overall strategy—the development of an "anti-imperialist" bloc of states in the Arab world. In Moscow's view these states should bury their internecine rivalries, and join together, along with such political organizations as the Arab Communist parties and the PLO, in a unified front against what the USSR has called the "linchpin" of Western imperialism in the Middle East—Israel. Under such circumstances it is the Soviet hope that the Arab states would then use their collective pressure against Israel's supporters, especially the United States. The ideal scenario for Moscow, and one which Soviet commentators have frequently referred to, is the situation during the 1973 Arab-Israeli War when virtually all the Arab states supported the war effort against Israel, while also imposing an oil embargo against the United States. As is well known, not only did the oil embargo create domestic difficulties for the United States, it caused serious problems in the NATO alliance, a development that was warmly welcomed by Moscow. Unfortunately for the USSR, however, this "anti-imperialist" Arab unity was created not by Soviet efforts, but by the diplomacy of Egyptian President Anwar Sadat and when Sadat changed his policies and turned toward the United States, the "anti-imperialist" Arab unity sought by the USSR fell apart. Nonetheless, so long as Soviet leaders think in terms of such Leninist categories of thought as "united fronts" ("anti-imperialist" Arab unity, in Soviet parlance, is merely another way of describing a united front of Arab governmental and nongovernmental forces) and so long as there is a deep underlying psychological drive for unity in the Arab world, Moscow can be expected to continue to pursue this overall strategy as a long-term goal.

MOSCOW AND THE GULF FROM THE 1973 ARAB-ISRAELI WAR TO THE OUTBREAK OF THE IRAN-IRAQ WAR

In the aftermath of the 1973 Arab-Israeli War the Soviet position in the Gulf, and in the Middle East as a whole, sharply deteriorated. Egypt moved from the Soviet camp into the American camp as Henry Kissinger mediated the Sinai I and Sinai II Egyptian-Israeli accords, and Egypt abrogated its Treaty of Friendship and Cooperation with the USSR; Syria reestablished diplomatic relations with the United States and pulled away from the Soviet Union as Kissinger secured a Golan Heights agreement, and Assad came into conflict with the PLO in Lebanon as Syria invaded that country in 1976. Meanwhile, Iraq, which had been heavily dependent on the USSR for weaponry to combat both Iran and an internal uprising by the Kurdish segment of its population also began to move away from Moscow. A 1975 treaty with Iran lessened the threat on Iraq's eastern borders; the Kurds were suppressed; and Iraq made use of its new oil wealth to buy extensively in Western Europe, Japan, and the United States as it embarked on a major development program. The Iraqi government also cracked down on the Iraqi Communist Party, a process that intensified following the Communist seizure of power in Afghanistan in 1978.[7]

Indeed, despite the Communist coup in Afghanistan, by 1978 Moscow's position in the Gulf, and in the Middle East as a whole, seemed weaker than at any time since the 1973 war. The United States could count among its allies the key states in the region, Egypt, Israel, Saudi Arabia, and Iran, which together combined both military and petrodollar power, and effectively served to keep Soviet influence in the region limited. The links between Egypt and Saudi Arabia, and Egypt and Iran, and Israel and Iran, plus improving relationships between Egypt and Israel and Saudi Arabia and Iran helped strengthen this tacit pro-American alignment. Fortunately for Moscow, two events later that year were to severely weaken the American position in the region and thereby, given the zero-sum game view Moscow holds of Soviet-American rivalry in the Third World, strengthen the Middle East position of the USSR.

The first key event to cause the United States difficulty was Camp David. While US President Jimmy Carter had successfully mediated the Camp David agreements between Israel and Egypt in September 1978, he was unable to secure Arab support for the accords. Indeed, an anti-Camp David Arab alignment emerged at the Arab summit in Baghdad in November 1978, which excluded Egypt. Rapprochements between Syria and Iraq, and between Jordan and the PLO, preceded the summit, and the strongly anti-Camp David resolutions adopted by the Baghdad conference could only have encouraged Moscow, as did the anti-Egyptian measures that were carried out by a second Baghdad conference in March 1979, following the signing of the Egyptian-Israeli treaty, measures that effectively isolated Egypt and the US-supported Camp David peace process. The Baghdad meetings also severed the once close ties between Saudi Arabia and Egypt, thus further weakening the

US position in the Arab world. Moscow may also have entertained the hope that the anti-Egyptian grouping at Baghdad might provide the basis for the "anti-imperialist" Arab unity the USSR had long sought.[8]

The second major blow to the United States in the region came with the collapse of the Shah of Iran's regime in late 1978 and his subsequent flight into exile in early 1979. The Shah had been the American "policeman" of the Persian Gulf, and, in accordance with the Nixon Doctrine, had been heavily supplied with arms. When the Shah's regime collapsed and the short-lived Bakhtiar government gave way to the Islamic fundamentalist regime of Ayatollah Khomeini, the strategic situation in the Gulf changed. Declaring Iran's neutrality, Khomeini pulled Iran out of CENTO, ended American use of telemetry stations for monitoring Soviet missile tests, pulled its troops out of Oman, and broke off relations with both Egypt and Israel. At the same time the confused US response to the events in Iran—dispatching and then recalling three days later a naval task force to the Gulf—seemed to indicate that the Carter Administration was unsure of itself. The US position both in the Gulf and the Middle East as a whole deteriorated further when its embassy was seized in Tehran in November 1979 and the United States seemed helpless to do anything about it. All of this stood in sharp contrast to apparent Soviet gains; as the fall of the Shah, the emergence of an anti-Camp David Arab coalition, and the rise to power of pro-Soviet regimes in Ethiopia and Afghanistan seemed to tilt the regional balance of power toward the USSR.

Nonetheless, the period of Soviet ascendancy in the Middle East proved to be short lived, as the Soviet invasion of Afghanistan alienated most of the states of the region. Iran sharply criticized the Soviet invasion and the two leading candidates for the Iranian Presidency, Hassan Bani Sadr and Foreign Minister Saddeg Ghotbzadeh, both attacked the USSR in campaign speeches, with Bani Sadr accusing Moscow of wanting to divide Iran and push to the Indian Ocean.[9] At the January 1980 Islamic Conference, the Iranian representative joined in the general denunciation of Soviet policy and urged the conference to demand the withdrawal of Soviet forces from Afghanistan. For his part Khomeini cracked down on the Tudeh and other left-wing political organizations in Iran while also pledging support for the Muslim insurgents fighting the Soviets in Afghanistan.[10] Secondly, the Soviet invasion of Afghanistan both alarmed and alienated many of the Arab states Moscow had been courting, a number of which begin to turn toward the United States, despite Camp David, as a counterbalance.[11] In addition, the Soviet invasion seemed to split the anti-Camp David unity of the Arab world, a unity that had already been weakened by the reemergence of tension between Syria and Iraq following Saddam

Hussain's accession to power in Iraq in July 1979. As a result the Arab world split into three major groupings. On one end of the spectrum was the so-called Front of Steadfastness and Confrontation composed of Syria, Libya, South Yemen, the PLO, and Algeria. These nations opposed Camp David and, with the exception of Algeria, backed the Soviet action in Afghanistan. On the other end of the spectrum was the Egyptian camp, made up of Egypt and its allies, the Sudan, Somalia, and Oman. This grouping supported Camp David while opposing the Soviet invasion of Afghanistan. In the middle of the Arab spectrum were the so-called Arab Centrists. These Arab states, Saudi Arabia, Jordan, Kuwait, North Yemen, Iraq, the United Arab Emirates, Bahrain, Qatar, Morocco, and Tunisia opposed both Camp David and the Soviet invasion of Afghanistan. From the point of view of Soviet diplomacy, the goal was to bring the Centrist Arabs and the Steadfastness Front back together again, much as they were at the Baghdad conferences following Camp David. Unfortunately for Moscow, the outbreak of the Iran-Iraq War made this task almost impossible.

MOSCOW AND THE OUTBREAK OF THE IRAN-IRAQ WAR

When, after increasing border tension, the Iraqi army invaded Iran in September 1980, Moscow had little choice but to remain officially neutral because an almost equally good case could have been made in the Kremlin for assisting either Iran or Iraq.[12] On the one hand, Moscow was linked to Baghdad by a Treaty of Friendship and Cooperation and the Soviets had long been Iraq's main supplier of military weaponry. In addition, Iraq had been a leading foe of the US-sponsored Camp David agreements and, as a nation with pretensions to leadership in the Arab world, could one day become the focus of the "anti-imperialist" Arab unity which Moscow sought. Indeed, by its leadership at the two Baghdad conferences, Iraq demonstrated a potential for just such a role. Yet another argument for aiding Iraq that could have been made in the Kremlin was the fact that such aid would be a demonstration to the Arab world that Moscow was indeed a reliable ally (some Arab states had questioned this, despite Soviet aid to the Arab cause in the 1973 war). From the point of view of the Soviet economy, aid to Iraq would help assure the continued flow of Iraqi oil to the USSR and its East European allies.

Soviet opponents of aid to Iraq could point to the continued persecution of Iraqi Communists, and to Iraq's clear move away from the USSR since their treaty was signed in 1972, as typified by its condemnation of Moscow after the invasion of Afghanistan, its February 1980 Pan-Arab charter which called for the elimination of both superpowers from the Arab world, and the growth of its economic and military ties with France and other West European nations. On balance, however, since the Russians saw Iraq as "objectively" a major anti-Western force, there was a good argument for aiding the Iraqis.

On the other hand, there was a very good case for aiding Iran. First and foremost, the Khomeini revolution had detached Iran from its close alignment with the United States, thereby striking a major blow to the US position in the region. In addition, by holding onto the American hostages, the Khomeini regime carried on a daily humiliation of the United States, a factor which further lowered American prestige. Consequently, any major Soviet aid effort to Iraq contained the possibility of ending the hostage impasse, or of even moving Iran back toward the American camp because of Iran's dependence on US military equipment. Given Iran's large population (three times that of Iraq) and its strategic position along the Persian Gulf and at the Straits of Hormuz, such a development would clearly not be in Moscow's interest. Another strategic factor that the Soviet leadership had to take into consideration was that Iran, unlike Iraq, had a common border with the USSR, as well as with Soviet-occupied Afghanistan. While Iranian efforts on behalf of the Afghan rebels had thus far been limited, one could not rule out a major increase in Iranian aid to the rebels should Moscow side with Iraq, as well as a more pronounced effort on the part of Khomeini to infect the USSR's own Muslims with his brand of Islamic fundamentalism. Finally, as in the case of Iraq, there was an important economic argument. While Iran had cut off gas exports to the USSR, the signing of a major transit agreement between the two countries just before the war erupted may well have seemed to Moscow to have been the first step toward the resumption of natural gas exports; given Iran's large available gas reserves, Moscow may have wished to encourage the supply relationship as a hedge against its own natural gas and oil reserves.[13]

Soviet opponents of aid to Iran could have pointed to the Islamic fundamentalists' treatment of the Tudeh (although Tudeh members were not yet as brutally treated as were Iraq's Communists),[14] as well as to its treatment of Iranian minorities, such as the Kurds, with whom the USSR hoped to cultivate a good relationship. Here again, however, Iran's treatment of its Kurds seemed no worse than Iraq's. Finally, opponents of aid to Iran could have pointed to Iran's leading anti-Soviet role in Islamic conferences, although again there may not have been too much choice between Iran's and Iraq's anti-Sovietism. The main factor in the Soviet evaluation of both countries was that they seemed far more anti-American than anti-Soviet, and both contributed to the weakening of the American position in the Middle East. For this reason, Moscow needed a good relationship with both and could not afford to alienate either, and as a result, adopted a position of neutrality at the start of the war and suspended arms sales to Iraq.[15]

Yet, as Moscow remained essentially neutral during the first two years of the conflict, the fallout from the war negatively affected its Middle East position. In the first place, while Syria and Libya backed Iran, both the Centrist Arabs and the Egyptian bloc of Arab states backed Iraq, with Egypt selling Iraq large amounts of weaponry. Under the circumstances, and as the Iraqi invasion first bogged down and then collapsed, a certain amount of rapprochement between the Centrist Arabs, who feared Iran, and Egypt became almost inevitable. This momentum accelerated after the formation of the Gulf Cooperation Council (GCC) in 1981—a group of five Centrist Arab states (Saudi Arabia, Kuwait, Bahrain, Qatar, and the United Arab Emirates) and one Arab state in the Egyptian camp, Oman.

A second negative result of the conflict for Moscow was the strengthening of the US position in the Gulf. The stationing (and eventual sale) of US AWACS aircraft and the positioning of ground radar personnel in Saudi Arabia following Iranian threats to close the Straits of Hormuz seemed to demonstrate American willingness to help defend Saudi Arabia and other Arab states in time of need, a development that made the major American military buildup in the Indian Ocean, which had occurred as a result of the hostage crisis, more diplomatically acceptable, thereby refuting Moscow's charge that the US buildup was a threat to seize the oil of the Arab world. Indeed, the AWACS move appeared to reverse the decline in Saudi-American relations caused by both Camp David and US inactivity during the fall of the Shah, and Moscow became concerned that Saudi Arabia might even be enticed to join the Camp David process. About the only positive element Moscow might see from the war that was it seemed to keep oil prices high, at least through 1981, since oil sales were one of the chief sources of hard currency earnings for the USSR. On balance, however the war had very negative repercussions for Moscow's position in both the Gulf and the Middle East as a whole, and the Soviet leadership was not slow in trying to change the situation.

SOVIET POLICY TOWARD THE GULF FROM THE OUTBREAK OF THE IRAN-IRAQ WAR UNTIL THE ISRAELI INVASION OF LEBANON IN JUNE 1982

Moscow's reaction to the outbreak of the war took several forms. In the first place, in addition to proclaiming Soviet neutrality, the USSR repeatedly called for the rapid end to the war from which it said "only the imperialists benefited." Secondly, seeking to contain the military and political gains made by the United States in the Gulf as a result of the war, and reflecting Soviet fears that Washington might obtain military bases as a result of the conflict, Brezhnev called for the neutralization of the Gulf during a visit to India in December 1980:

> We propose to the United States, other Western powers, China, Japan, all the states which will show interest in this, to agree on the following mutual obligations:
> — Not to establish foreign military bases in the area of the Persian Gulf and adjacent islands; not to deploy nuclear or any other weapons of mass destruction there;
> — Not to use and not to threaten with the use of force against the countries of the Persian Gulf area, not to interfere in their internal affairs;
> — To respect the status of nonalignment, chosen by Persian Gulf states; not to draw them into military groupings with the participation of nuclear powers;
> — To respect the sovereign right of the states of the region to their natural resources;
> — Not to raise any obstacles or threats to normal trade exchange and the use of sea lanes that link the states of that region with other countries of the world.[16]

Nonetheless, the Soviet leader received at best a mixed reception to his call, and Moscow was to encounter yet another Middle East problem in mid-January 1981. At that time, just as the inauguration of the outspokenly anti-Soviet US President Ronald Reagan was taking place, the American hostages were released from Iranian custody, thanks in part to the aid of Steadfastness Front member Algeria, which played an important mediating role. Moscow used disinformation in a futile attempt to continue the hostage crisis as a barrier to any improvement in Iranian-American relations.[17] The hostages were freed despite a major Soviet propaganda effort that tried to convince the Iranians that the United States was using the hostage negotiations as a cover for a military attack on Iran.

Perhaps as a result of the failure of this ploy, at the 26th Soviet Communist Party Congress, in February 1981, Brezhnev offered—for the first time—to combine discussions of the Afghanistan situation with that of the Persian Gulf, although he made it clear that Afghanistan's internal situation (i.e. its Communist government) was not a matter for discussion, and that the USSR would not withdraw its forces from Afghanistan until the "infiltration of counter-revolutionary bands" was completely stopped, and treaties were signed between Afghanistan and its neighbors to ensure that no further infiltration would take place.[18] As far as the Iran-Iraq War was concerned, the Soviet leader at the congress once again called for its immediate termination, and stated that the Soviet Union was taking "practical steps" to achieve that goal. Interestingly enough, the Soviet leader also made note in his speech of two related Middle Eastern phenomena to which the USSR was having difficulty in adjusting its policies: the Khomeini revolution in Iran and

52

the rise of fundamentalist Islam. As far as Iran was concerned, Brezhnev noted that "despite its complex and contradictory nature, it is basically an anti-imperialist revolution, although domestic and foreign reaction is seeking to alter this character." Brezhnev also offered Soviet cooperation with Iran (no mention was made of Soviet-Iraqi relations in his speech, and the failure of an Iraqi government delegation to attend the congress indicated the chill in Soviet-Iraqi relations caused by the war), but only on the grounds of "reciprocity," perhaps a reference to continuing anti-Soviet speeches and activities in Iran including the brief seizure of the Soviet Embassy in Tehran on the anniversary of the Afghan invasion, an action which was both tolerated and justified by the Iranian leadership.[19] In discussing Islam, Brezhnev acknowledged that "the liberation struggle could develop under the banner of Islam," but also noted that "experience also indicates that reaction uses Islamic slogans to start counterrevolutionary insurrections."

Following the CPSU Congress, Moscow sought to woo Kuwait, a key Centrist Arab state that was also a member of the GCC, in an effort to prevent the Centrist Arabs and the GCC from moving toward the Egyptian camp. Kuwait, whose deputy premier Sheik al-Sabah visited Moscow on April 23, was a key target of Soviet diplomacy. As the only state in the GCC at the time with diplomatic relations with Moscow, it was also the most "nonaligned" and the Soviet leaders evidently hoped to use Kuwait's influence within the GCC (it is the second most important country after Saudi Arabia) to prevent that organization from committing itself too closely to the American side.[20] For its part Kuwait had been carefully cultivating a relationship with the USSR since 1975, the last time Sheik Sabah had journeyed to Moscow.[21] Then, as in April 1981, Kuwait's regional problems made it seek protection. In 1975, Kuwait was confronted with territorial demands by Iraq; in 1981, while relations had improved with Iraq, a far more serious problem lay on its border with Iran whose warplanes were occasionally bombing and strafing Kuwaiti territory because of Kuwaiti aid to the Iraqi war effort. Under these circumstances, the Kuwaitis evidently felt they needed support not only from the United States, whose ability and willingness to aid Kuwait may have come into question during the collapse of the Shah's regime, but from the Soviet Union as well; and the Kuwaiti deputy premier, who was also his country's foreign minister, went a long way toward meeting his host's diplomatic needs during his visit to Moscow.[22] Thus not only did he denounce Camp David, he also came out in favor of an international conference on the Middle East, thereby supporting a cardinal Soviet goal. In addition, he announced Kuwait's opposition to the creation of foreign military bases in the Persian Gulf, thus supporting yet another central Soviet foreign policy goal. Finally, he joined Moscow in calling for an international conference on the Indian Ocean aimed at turning it into a "zone of peace," thereby supporting another Soviet diplomatic ploy to eliminate the US military presence from the region.[23]

To be sure, there were areas of disagreement during the talks, which *Pravda* reported as a "detailed exchange of views on the situation in the Persian Gulf."[24] Probably the most important issue of disagreement was Afghanistan (Kuwait continued to oppose the Soviet presence in Afghanistan) of which no mention was made in the formal communique. Nonetheless, on balance it was a most successful visit as far as Moscow was concerned since it was able to obtain Kuwaiti support for a number of major Soviet Middle East policies.

Soon after Sheik Sabah's visit came an incident which Moscow may well have hoped would serve to rebuild its strained ties with Iraq (the cessation of Soviet arms sales had been strongly criticized by Baghdad) and possibly rally the Arabs back into a common anti-Israeli stand—the Israeli bombing of Iraq's nuclear reactor on June 9, 1981. As might be expected, Moscow moved quickly to try to exploit this situation, not only condemning the Israeli raid but also pointing to the fact that the Israeli action was carried out with American-supplied aircraft and that it took place despite—or indeed because of—the US AWACS radar planes operating in Saudi Arabia.[25] President Reagan's decision to postpone shipment of additional F-16 fighter bombers to Israel because of the attack was deprecated by Moscow, which sought to exploit the Israeli action by using it to focus Arab attention on the "Israeli threat" to the Arab world (rather than the "Soviet threat") and to undermine the American position in the region while at the same time improving Soviet-Iraqi relations.[26]

Moscow may have also seen the Israeli raid as undercutting Egyptian efforts to reenter the Arab mainstream through aid to Iraq, since it took place only four days after a summit meeting between Israeli Prime Minister Menachem Begin and Egyptian President Anwar Sadat.[27] Since the outbreak of the Iran-Iraq War, Egypt had sold Iraq thousands of tons of Soviet ammunition and spare parts to assist its war effort—something noted with displeasure in Moscow, which worried about Sadat's lessening isolation.[28] Fortunately for Moscow, the Israeli raid did serve, albeit only briefly, to slow the Iraqi-Egyptian rapprochement, despite Sadat's denunciation of the Israeli action.

Moscow, however, was less successful in exploiting the Israeli raid to undermine the US position in the Arab world, and in particular to improve Soviet ties with Iraq. While there had been calls in the Arab world to embargo oil to the United States because of the raid, the Reagan Administration's decision to join with Iraq in a UN Security Council vote condemning Israel seemed to deflate any such Arab pressures.[29] Indeed, the Iraqi-American cooperation at the United Nations seemed to set the stage for improved Iraqi-American relations, as Iraqi President Saddam Hussain, on the ABC television program, "Issues and Answers," stated his interest in expanding diplomatic contacts with the United States and announced that he would treat the head of the American interests section in the Belgian Embassy in Baghdad as the head of a diplomatic mission.[30]

In taking this posture, Iraq appeared to be trying to both improve its ties with the United States as Iraq's position in the Iran-Iraq war deteriorated[31] and also to drive a wedge between the United States and Israel, which was very unhappy with the US vote in the UN. On the other hand, Moscow may have seen that the United States was seeking to drive a diplomatic wedge between the USSR and Iraq. In any case, Soviet-Iraqi relations had been declining for a number of years and they were not helped by Moscow's position of neutrality in the Iran-Iraq war. A further deterioration in Soviet-Iraqi relations had come at the February 1981 CPSU Congress when the head of the Iraqi Communist Party, Aziz Mohammed, denounced the Iraqi government for its acts of repression against the Iraqi Communist Party and the Iraqi Kurds, and also condemned the Iran-Iraq war and demanded the immediate withdrawal of Iraqi troops from Iran.[32] As Soviet-Iraqi relations were deteriorating, the United States moved to improve relations with the regime in Baghdad. Secretary of State Haig noted the possibility of improved Iraqi-American relations in testimony to the Senate Foreign Relations Committee in mid-March 1981 (Iraq was seen as concerned by "the behavior of Soviet imperialism in the Middle Eastern area"),[33] and followed this up by sending Deputy Assistant Secretary of State Morris Draper to Iraq in early April.[34] To improve the climate for the visit, the United States approved the sale to Iraq of five Boeing jetliners.[35] While nothing specific came out of Draper's talks, Washington continued to hope that because of Iraq's close ties with Jordan and Saudi Arabia, the regime in Baghdad might move toward peace with Israel, while continuing to improve ties with the United States. Indeed, Saddam Hussain himself, in his ABC interview, gave some hints about just such a move. It was perhaps to prevent any further move by Iraq toward the United States that Moscow resumed arms shipments to Iraq in the fall.[36]

While Moscow sought, albeit unsuccessfully, to exploit the Israeli attack on the Iraqi nuclear reactor to weaken the US position in the Middle East, it also tried to follow the same policy during the upheavals in Iran, which witnessed the ouster and escape to Europe of Iranian President Bani-Sadr, the assassination of his successor Mohammed Ali Rajai along with a number of key Iranian Islamic Republican Party leaders such as Ayatollah Beheshti, and a series of additional bombing and other attacks directed against the fundamentalist Khomeini government by the opposition Mujahidin.

The central Soviet concern in its policy toward Iran was a fear that after the hostage release, the United States and Iran might move toward a rapprochement, particularly because of Iranian military requirements. Fortunately for Moscow, anti-Americanism remained a central foreign policy theme of the Khomeini regime during 1981 as it had been the previous two years, and the regime's enemies were usually branded American or Zionist agents. Given Moscow's previous displeasure with Bani-Sadr, his departure was no loss, but the Soviet leadership was quite unhappy with the assassination of Beheshti whom *Pravda* characterized on July 3 as "one of the most consistent proponents of an anti-imperialist, anti-American policy."[37] The bombings at the end of June and at the end of August, while eliminating a number of top Iranian leaders, gave Moscow the opportunity to try to reinforce Tehran's suspicions that the CIA was behind the incidents.[38]

Moscow also sought to link US aid to the Afghan rebels (early in 1981 Reagan had announced publicly that the United States was aiding the Afghan resistance) with US aid to the opposition in Iran in an effort both to discredit the Afghan resistance in Iran and to further alienate Iran from the United States.

Yet, while Iranian-American relations remained highly strained, it did not appear as if Moscow was making much headway in improving its own position in Iran—a pattern that was to continue into 1985. Iranian leaders remained suspicious of Moscow both for its centuries-long record of hostility toward Iran and because of suspected ties between Moscow and Iranian ethnic minorities fighting for independence, such as the Kurds. Indeed, Moscow may well have been placed in a difficult position when in late October 1981 the Kurdish Democratic Party of Iran, led by Abdul Rahman Gassemlou, joined the opposition front headed by Bani-Sadr and Mujahidin leader Massud Rajavi.[39] Moscow and Gassemlou had long maintained friendly ties and the formation of the opposition front once again posed a difficult problem of choice for the USSR.

Yet another irritant in the Soviet-Iranian relationship was Tehran's unhappiness that Moscow had taken only a neutral position on the Iran-Iraq War in the face of "flagrant Iraqi aggression," as the late Iranian Prime Minister Mohammed Ali Rajai told Soviet Ambassador Vladimir Vinogradov on February 15,[40] a message repeated in October by the Iranian Ambassador Mohammed Mokri, during an Iranian delegation's visit to Moscow.[41] A third area of conflict was Iranian unhappiness with the Soviet intervention in Afghanistan, despite Soviet efforts to tie the CIA to the resistance movement in both Iran and Afghanistan. Finally, the Islamic fundamentalist regime increased its pressure on the Communist party and its ally, the majority faction of the Fedayeen guerrillas, as Iranian Prime Minister Hussain Mousavi declared that Iran would execute members of the Tudeh and majority Fedayeen who, if they joined the revolutionary guards or other fundamentalist organizations, failed to state their (Communist) party affiliation.[42]

Soviet-Iranian relations continued to decline in 1982, although Moscow welcomed the visit of Iranian Energy Minister Hasan Ghafurifard in February and his statement at a news conference that Iran regarded the Soviet Union as a friendly country and that his visit had laid the basis for greater Soviet-Iranian cooperation.[43] Nonetheless the Ghafurifard visit, during which a protocol on accelerated economic and technical cooperation in the construction of two gas-fired power plants was signed, was to be the high point of Soviet-Iranian relations in 1982. Less than a month later, senior *Pravda* Middle East correspondent Pavel Demchenko issued the strongest Soviet criticism of the Khomeini regime since Alexander Bovin had personally criticized Khomeini himself in September 1979.[44] While noting the increase in Soviet-Iranian trade, and the fact that the USSR was assisting Iran in the construction of a number of industrial projects, including the Isfahan Metallurgical Works, Demchenko openly complained that Iran's "unilateral acts" had damaged Soviet-Iranian relations in a number of spheres in the period since the Khomeini regime took power.[45] These included the reduction of the diplomatic staff of the Soviet Embassy in Tehran, the closing of the Soviet consulate in Resht, the refusal to grant entry visas to Soviet newspaper correspondents, and the closing of the Iranian Society for Cultural Relations with the USSR (where Russian was taught), along with the Russian-Iranian Bank and the branches of the Soviet Insurance Society and Transport Agency. In addition, Demchenko complained of an atmosphere of "greatly intensified anti-Soviet propaganda" and of anti-Soviet demonstrations outside the Soviet Embassy in Tehran, and he blamed these activities on "conservative groupings" around Khomeini.

It is not clear whether the *Pravda* article merely reflected growing Soviet frustration or whether it served as a warning to Iran over its anti-Soviet activities. If the latter, it was not particularly successful, as Soviet-Iranian relations continued to deteriorate in the spring and summer despite the dispatch of a new Soviet Ambassador, V.K. Boldryev, who had extensive experience in Iran.[46]

While Moscow may have drawn some consolation from the arrest and subsequent execution of former Iranian Foreign Minister Sadegh Ghotbzadeh, since he had been the most anti-Soviet of the Iranian secular leaders,[47] it was very unhappy with a number of other Iranian developments. These included the Khomeini regime's increasing crackdown on the Tudeh party and the banning of its publication, "Ittihad-i Mardom"; its continued refusal to export natural gas to the USSR unless it received a much higher price; the expansion of its economic ties with Pakistan, Turkey, and Western Europe, which meant a lessened economic dependence on the USSR (indeed, an Iranian-Turkish natural gas pipeline deal, signed in September, may have caused concern in Moscow that Iran was seriously considering a permanent redirection of its natural gas sales from the USSR to Western Europe);[48] its continued opposition to Soviet policy in Afghanistan; and, perhaps most of all, its continued prosecution of the war with Iraq and its refusal to seriously consider mediation efforts to end the war.[49] As mentioned above, the continuation of the war frustrated Moscow. It reinforced the divisions in the Arab world and, particularly after Iran again went on to the offensive and threatened Iraqi territory in May 1982, and helped reinforce the American military and diplomatic position in the Persian Gulf, while accelerating a rapprochement between Egypt and a number of Centrist Gulf states.

While Moscow was having difficulty in its relations with both Iran and Iraq in the period before the Israeli invasion of Lebanon, it was also not making much headway in trying to improve its ties with Saudi Arabia. In many ways Moscow was ambivalent about the Saudi regime. On the one hand, as the leading Centrist Arab state opposed to Camp David, Saudi Arabia pursued a Middle Eastern policy which Moscow also strongly supported. On the other hand, as a leading opponent of Soviet policy in Afghanistan and as a nation with close military ties to the United States and as a nation which had sought to use its financial power to pry several Arab states out of the Soviet camp, Saudi Arabia was a leading anti-Soviet force in the Arab world. Moscow's ambivalent position toward Saudi Arabia was especially apparent in 1981. In April 1981, Moscow warmly welcomed both Saudi Arabia's rebuttal of US Secretary of State Haig's call for an anti-Soviet alliance during Haig's visit to the Middle East, and Saudi Foreign Minister Saud al-Faisal's statement that Israel, not Moscow, was the main threat to the Arabs.[50] Indeed, one month later, a key article in *Literaturnaya Gazeta*, written by Soviet commentator Igor Belyayev, noted, in discussing the failure of Haig's visit:

Arab politicians, even the conservative ones, have never refused Soviet assistance in the struggle against their real enemy—the Israeli expansionists. The Arabs will hardly become accomplices in an anti-Soviet crusade under the aegis of the U.S.[51]

On the other hand, in late August, Moscow's chief oil analyst, Reuben Andreasyan, bitterly noted Saudi Arabia's unwillingness to act against

US interests during an OPEC meeting to set oil prices, as he complained that despite the Israeli raid on the Iraqi nuclear reactor and the attack by US Air Force planes on Libyan aircraft, "on the very day the OPEC meeting opened," there was no agreement on prices.[52]

In many ways, the AWACS debate in the US Congress seemed to be a turning point in the Soviet view of Saudi Arabia. Moscow's central fear was that congressional approval for AWACS would cement the Saudi-American relationship to the point that Saudi Arabia might be persuaded both to support the Camp David agreements and also provide facilities for the American Rapid Deployment Force "in direct proximity to the extremely rich Persian Gulf oil fields,"[53] a fear that was even more openly expressed after the US Senate approved (by failing to vote down) the AWACS agreement. *Pravda*, on October 30, noted that Saudi Arabia would now become a bridgehead against the Arab world. That day Moscow Radio Peace and Progress went even further in its criticism, asserting that the AWACS deal was "aimed at transforming the Wahhabi Kingdom into a source of threat to the entire Islamic world."[54]. Thus Moscow took an increasingly dim view of Saudi Arabia, and the Soviet leadership must have become even more concerned when, following the assassination of Anwar Sadat, the new Egyptian leader, Hosni Mubarak, actively sought to improve Saudi-Egyptian reactions.

In sum, the period from the outbreak of the Iran-Iraq War in September 1980, until the Israeli invasion of Lebanon in June 1982, the Soviet position both in the Gulf and in the Middle East as a whole deteriorated. Soviet neutrality in the Iran-Iraq War alienated both countries, and Iraq began to move toward the United States despite Moscow's resumption of arms sales, while Moscow's ties with Iran went from bad to worse. The AWACS sale reinforced US-Saudi relations and made Soviet efforts to improve ties with Saudi Arabia ineffectual. Only with Kuwait did Moscow score some gains, but even this was not sufficient to prevent the gradual rapprochement between the Centrist Arab states and Egypt, a development caused in large part by the success of the Iranian offensive against Iraq. This process gathered momentum after the assassination of Sadat, and continued even after the Israeli invasion of Lebanon, which Hosni Mubarak strongly condemned.

SOVIET POLICY TOWARD THE GULF FROM THE ISRAELI INVASION OF LEBANON TO THE DEATH OF CHERNENKO

The Israeli invasion of Lebanon was, at least initially, to cause further problems for Moscow both in the Gulf and elsewhere in the Middle East. In the first place, because its frequent warnings to the United States and Israel during the course of the war proved to be ineffectual, Soviet

59

credibility suffered a major blow.[55] Indeed, Moscow's failure to aid Syria and the PLO during the fighting raised questions about Moscow's value as an ally, much as the US failure to aid the Shah had raised questions about US credibility. Second, the overwhelming victory of US-supplied Israeli weapons over the military equipment supplied by Moscow to Syria called into question the quality of Soviet military equipment and, to a lesser degree, the quality of Soviet training. Finally, the Soviet leadership had to deal with a situation where the United States, having mediated the PLO withdrawal from Beirut, had the diplomatic initiative and sought to exploit it by means of the Reagan plan. Proclaimed on September 1, 1982, the plan called for a stop to Israeli settlement activity on the West Bank, declared US refusal to accept any Israeli claim of sovereignty over it, and called for a fully autonomous Palestinian entity linked to Jordan.[56] Moscow worried that the plan would gain Centrist Arab support[57] and, following the publication of an Arab peace plan at Fez,[58] Morocco, a week later, Moscow came out with its own peace plan which, in many ways, incorporated much of the the Fez plan in an effort to attract Arab support.[59] Nonetheless, by the end of 1982, with both King Hussain and Yasir Arafat expressing qualified support for the Reagan plan, the new Soviet leader, Yuri Andropov, who succeeded Leonid Brezhnev in November 1982, faced considerable difficulties as he sought to rebuild the Soviet position in the Middle East.

As the Soviet Middle East position worsened during and immediately after the Israeli invasion of Lebanon, Moscow responded with a "tilt" toward Iraq in the Iran-Iraq War. As soon as Israel invaded Lebanon, Saddam Hussain had offered to end the war with Iran so that all Muslim support could go to fight the Israelis—an action approved by Moscow. Iran rejected this ploy, however, and sought to embarrass Saddam Hussain by sending approximately 1,000 "volunteers" to Lebanon. The Iran-Iraq War continued with Iran very much on the offensive. Under these circumstances, Soviet and Syrian calls for an oil embargo against the United States during the Israeli siege of Beirut fell on deaf ears,[60] since the Arab oil producers of the Gulf, particularly at a time of an oil glut, were unlikely to impose an oil embargo on the United States one day if they foresaw the need to call on the United States for help against Iran the next.

Andropov learned the need for a more active Middle East policy when an Arab delegation, headed by King Hussain, arrived in Moscow in early December to discuss the Fez plan. While *Pravda* gave page one coverage to the talks and to the significance of the Arab delegation's visit, its report that the discussions took place in a "businesslike and friendly atmosphere," and that there was "an exchange of opinions," reflected the fact that the Soviet leader was unable to get the Arab leaders to either criticize the Reagan plan or to agree to Moscow's peace plan.[61]

At least one positive result of King Hussain's visit for Moscow was the fact that Soviet Foreign Minister Gromyko had a meeting with Saudi Foreign Minister Prince Saud al Faisal, who was the first Saudi official to visit the USSR since the 1930s.[62] Nonetheless, following the visit, Saudi Information Minister Mohammed Abd ul-Yamani stated that Saudi Arabia was not considering diplomatic relations with the USSR because "the time was not ripe for such links."[63] In addition, the fact that Moscow subsequently invited a delegation from the Popular Front for the Liberation of Bahrain—an anathema to Saudi Arabia—to an anniversary celebration in Moscow was an indication that the USSR did not foresee any rapid improvement of relations with the Saudis.[64]

Meanwhile, Moscow faced yet another negative Middle Eastern development—the resumption of the momentum for a reconciliation between Egypt and the Centrist Bloc, which the Israeli invasion of Lebanon temporarily interrupted. Indeed, the visit of Iraqi and United Arab Emirates military delegations to Cairo in December 1982,[65] and the calls by both Arafat and Iraqi Deputy Prime Minister Tariq Aziz for Egypt to reenter the Arab world without having to renounce Camp David,[66] seemed to signal a quick end to Egypt's isolation in the Arab world. Under these circumstances, as its Middle East position continued to deteriorate, it was not surprising that Moscow decided to send the highly sophisticated SAM-5 surface-to-air missile system to Syria, a move apparently aimed at reinforcing Soviet ties to Syria before the Syrians might opt for the United States.[67] Moscow also increased its shipments of arms to Iraq,[68] although Iraqi leader Saddam Hussain in late November publicly complained that Iraq's Treaty of Friendship and Cooperation "has not worked" during the Iran-Iraq War.[69] The Iraqi President also asserted that the USSR, like the United States, opposed an end to the war because both superpowers were allowing weapons to flow to Iran. Perhaps in an effort to gain increased Soviet support for Iraq's war effort, a top level Iraqi delegation composed of Taha Yassan and Tariq Aziz journeyed to Moscow in December for a meeting with Gromyko and Boris Ponomarev which, reportedly, was more successful than the visit of Tariq Aziz who had journeyed to the Soviet capital on June 4, the eve of the Israeli invasion of Lebanon.[70] In any case, despite its increased arms shipments to Iraq, Moscow was not pleased with Iraq's growing rapprochement with Egypt, or with the repeated gestures for improved relations with the United States.

Nonetheless, as Moscow tilted to Iraq by stepping up shipments of such weapons as T-72 tanks and MIG-25 aircraft, Soviet relations with Iran got worse. In February 1983, the First Secretary of the Tudeh,

Nureddin Kianuri, and a number of other top party leaders were arrested on charges of espionage.[71] Moscow vehemently denied the charge in a *Pravda* article on February 19, blaming the arrest on the increased activity of "reactionary conservative forces in Iran which are trying to deal a blow against the progressive patriotic forces and at the same time damage Iranian-Soviet relations." *Pravda* went on to list the areas in which the Soviet Union had aided Iran since the fall of the Shah, and pointedly cited the comments by the late Soviet Party Secretary Leonid Brezhnev on the need for reciprocity in the Soviet-Iranian relationship. If the *Pravda* article and its call for reciprocity was intended to deter the Khomeini regime from moving further against the Tudeh, it failed.[72] On April 30 Kianuri made a public confession on Iranian TV of spying for the Soviet Union.[73] Four days later Iran expelled 18 Soviet diplomats and dissolved the Tudeh party, declaring that "any activity on behalf of the party is now illegal."[74] Slogans as "Britain is bad; America is worse than Britain; and the Soviet Union is worse than both of them," added to the anti-Soviet atmosphere in Iran.[75]

The Soviet response came in a *Pravda* editorial on May 6 which not only denied that the Tudeh members had spied for the USSR, but also asserted that their confessions resulted from torture. In addition, the editorial noted that the USSR had lodged a "resolute protest" against the Iranian government's "arbitrary" and "groundless" expulsion of the Soviet diplomats. Nonetheless, it was still in Moscow's interest to preserve some ties with Iran, lest Iran begin to gravitate toward the West, a possibility noted by the *Pravda* editorial. For this reason, Moscow's counteractions against Iran were limited to (1) editorial denunciations of the Iranian authorities as a whole, without mentioning Khomeini by name; (2) a more sympathetic treatment of the Iraqi position in the Iran-Iraq war, which Moscow continued to deplore as it had since the war erupted in 1980; and (3) the expulsion of three Iranian diplomats from Moscow.[76] Gromyko, however, reiterated Moscow's displeasure with Tehran in a foreign policy speech to the Supreme Soviet in mid-June:

> We have relations of friendship with Iraq. We are for normal relations of friendship with Iran as well. The USSR would like to continue to see it as an independent state and has always striven for good neighborly relations with it. Regrettably, actions like those recently taken by the Iranian side with regard to a group of employees of the Soviet mission in Iran by no means contribute to the development of such contacts between our countries. In short, the USSR will be guided in its actions by whether Iran wants to reciprocate its action or whether it has different intentions.[77]

Meanwhile, increased Soviet shipments of arms to Iraq did not seem to be paying Moscow many political dividends, since France also stepped up sales to Baghdad. Indeed, armed with new French Super Etendard fighter bombers and Exocet missiles, Iraq threatened to destroy Iranian oil export capabilities, which elicited an Iranian counterthreat to close the Straits of Hormuz if Iraq disrupted Iranian oil shipments.[78] The crisis had a number of negative implications for Moscow. In the first place, the Iranian threats forced such Arab states as Saudi Arabia and Kuwait to look to the United States for protection against Iran.[79] Indeed, an *Izvestia* article on October 24 noted that, "the aggravation of the situation in the Persian Gulf is seen as a convenient reason to expand the range of US activities in the Middle East." In addition, as the Iraqi position worsened, Baghdad appeared to turn to the West for support. Iraq signed a major oil-for-arms deal with France, and in January 1983, in a *Le Monde* interview, Iraq's Foreign Minister Tariq Aziz stated that France was Iraq's "main political, economic, military, and trading partner," a comment that could only have angered Andropov.[80] In addition, Iraq moved to improve ties with the United States by moderating its position on Israel. In early January Saddam Hussain, in a major policy change, publicly indicated that, "it was necessary to have a state of security for the Israelis" in any peace settlement.[81] Then, in May, Iraqi Foreign Minister Aziz met US Secretary of State Shultz in Paris for what the Iraqi leader later said were "useful talks."[82] Despite continuing US-Iraqi friction over the presence of Palestinian terrorist Abu Nidal in Iraq, Iraqi-US relations continued to improve as an Iraqi Foreign Ministry representative visited Washington in early September and the new US Middle East envoy, Donald Rumsfeld, visited Baghdad in December, and the United States extended agricultural credits to Iraq.[83]

As Franco-Iraqi and US-Iraqi relations improved, the USSR moved to improve its relations with Iraq to counterbalance the Iraqi move to the West. Thus, while continuing to both maintain official neutrality in the Iran-Iraq War and to call for as rapidly as possible an end to the conflict, from which it claimed "only the imperialists" benefited, Moscow stepped up its arms shipments to Iraq and began to openly criticize Iran for continuing the war. Praising Iraq's ceasefire proposal of June 1983, a *Pravda* commentary by Yuri Glukhov on November 14 criticized Iran's rejection of it, blaming Tehran for "chauvinistic attitudes." Moscow also heavily publicized a visit by Tariq Aziz to the Soviet Union in late November, during which the USSR again called for a rapid end to the Iran-Iraq War and stated that Moscow would continue to work for a political settlement of the conflict.[84] A *Pravda* report describing the talks as having taken place in a "frank and friendly atmosphere," with "an exchange of views" on the situation in the Middle East and on Soviet-Iraqi relations, clearly indicated, however, continuing disagreement on a number of issues.

Soon after the Iraqi Foreign Minister's visit, however, Moscow may have expected its Middle Eastern fortunes to change dramatically as the US position in Lebanon collapsed. Although the United States had successfully mediated a troop withdrawal between Israel and Lebanon, signed on May 17, 1983, Syrian opposition to the agreement, the inability of the United States to mobilize the support of other Arab states such as Saudi Arabia on behalf of the accord, and major political mistakes by Lebanese President Amin Gemayel, who alienated both the Lebanese Shi'ites and the Druze and drove them into the arms of Syria, doomed the Lebanese-Israeli agreement. For its part, the United States by strongly supporting Gemayel, became a party to the renewed Lebanese civil war and by September found itself in a military confrontation not only with the Druze and Shi'ites but with Syria as well. The September crisis, precipitated by the Israeli withdrawal from the Chouf Mountains, ended in a ceasefire before a direct military conflict between Syria and the United States took place. But the attack on the US Marine headquarters in October increased Syrian-American tension, and in early December led to a military confrontation during which Syrian antiaircraft fire shot down two American Navy planes.[85]

Interestingly, during this entire period, Moscow kept a very low profile, as it indicated it wished to avoid a superpower conflict over Lebanon which, by itself, was only tertiary to Soviet interests.[86] Moscow sought, nevertheless, to exploit the Syrian-American confrontation by tying the US attack on the Syrian positions in Lebanon to the strategic cooperation agreement concluded between Reagan and Israeli Prime Minister Yitzhak Shamir a week earlier, and claimed that the attack forfeited the US role as an "honest broker" in the Middle East.[87] Moscow also appealed for Arab unity on an "anti-imperialist" basis in an attempt to exploit the Syrian-American clash to slow the rapprochement between the Centrist Arabs and the pro-American Egyptian camp in the Arab world.

Two months after the Syrian-American confrontation the US position in Lebanon collapsed, a development signaled by the "redeployment" of US Marines to their ships in the Mediterranean. The perception throughout the Middle East, including the Gulf, was that Syria, Moscow's principal Arab client, had won a major victory, while the United States, and the Reagan plan as well, had suffered a major defeat. The US redeployment followed shortly by the other members of the multinational force, coincided with American naval shelling of antigovernment positions in the vicinity of Beirut, although the Reagan Administration never clearly explained the rationale for this. Indeed, the general course of US policy during this period seemed confused at best, and whatever mistakes the United States had made in backing the

Gemayel government up to this point, the hurried exodus of the Marines from Beirut coupled with what appeared to be indiscriminate US Naval gunfire into the Lebanese mountains hurt the US image, not only in Lebanon, but in the Middle East as a whole, something Moscow clearly welcomed and exploited, despite the death of Andropov in February.

Syria achieved another success for its Lebanese policy when Amin Gemayel, now virtually bereft of US military support, turned to Syrian President Assad for help in staying in power. Assad, at least in the short term, proved willing to help—for a price. The price was the abrogation of the May 17 Israeli-Lebanese agreement, and Gemayel announced its abrogation on March 5. Yet even as Moscow hailed this development (Soviet commentators called it a major blow to the entire Camp David process), a number of Middle Eastern problems confronted the new Soviet leader, Konstantin Chernenko, despite the collapse of the US position in Lebanon. In the first place, Syria remained in diplomatic isolation in the Arab world, while Egypt continued to improve its ties to Centrist Arab states. Arafat's surprise visit to Cairo, after his expulsion from Lebanon in December 1983 as a result of a Syrian-inspired split within Fatah, reinforced Egypt's rapprochement with the Centrist Arabs. The decision of the Islamic Conference to readmit Egypt to its ranks in mid-January, a development Moscow attributed to the "pressure of conservative Muslim regimes," further highlighted the Egyptian-Arab rapprochement.[88] The fact that Libya, Syria, and South Yemen walked out of the conference indicated the continuing isolation of Moscow's closest Arab allies, and the USSR had to be concerned about the possible formation of a new Arab front that would reincorporate Egypt into the Arab League and revive the Reagan plan. Soviet concern with such a development could only have increased with Mubarak's visit to King Hassan of Morocco—the first official visit to an Arab country by the head of the Egyptian state since the 1979 peace treaty, as Moscow TV unhappily noted[89]—and by Mubarak's meeting with King Hussain in Washington in mid-February as the two Arab leaders prepared for talks with President Reagan.

Meanwhile, as Egypt's relations with Centrist Arab nations improved, Syria, despite its victory in Lebanon, remained isolated. Not only was its influence insufficient to prevent the Islamic Conference from readmitting Egypt, it was again in isolation when the Arab League Foreign Ministers, in a meeting in mid-March, which Syria and Libya boycotted, took a strongly anti-Iranian position, condemning Iran for its continuing "aggression against Iraq," and warning Iran that the continuation of the war would force the Arab states to reconsider their relations with it.[90] Indeed, one of the main obstacles preventing Moscow from exploiting the US failure in Lebanon was the situation in the

Persian Gulf. Iran had launched another major offensive against Iraq, threatening the key southern Iraqi city of Basra, while at the same time repeating threats to close the Straits of Hormuz if Iraq, using its newly-acquired Super-Etendard fighters, interfered with Iranian oil exports. Moscow worried that the United States, which had again pledged to keep the Straits open, and which had increased the size of its fleet near the Gulf, would exploit the Iranian threats to reinforce its position in the Gulf, and thereby divert attention from its failure in Lebanon. As *Kraznaya Zvezda* noted on March 4, 1984, "Washington is trying in (the Persian Gulf) to compensate at least somehow for its political and military errors in Lebanon."[91] In a counter to the stepped up US deployment near the Gulf, the Soviet government denounced US activity in the Gulf as a "grave threat to peace and international security," and stated that the USSR would not abide by any restrictions imposed by the United States in the Gulf region.[92]

Moscow also moved to exploit the sudden chilling of US-Iraqi relations resulting from US accusations in March 1984 that Iraq had used poison gas. In addition to denying reports of Soviet supply of chemical weapons to Iraq, and castigating the Iranian government for spreading the rumors,[93] Moscow sought to strengthen its ties with Iraq by signing an intergovernmental agreement on economic and technical cooperation which involved Soviet assistance in the construction of two major projects in Iraq: a heat and power station and a hydroelectric complex.[94]. A month later, Iraq's Deputy Prime Minister Taha Ramadan was invited to Moscow for talks. The fact that in addition to meeting with Prime Minister Tikhonov, Ramadan also met with both Soviet Deputy Defense Minister and Chief of Staff, Nikolai Ogarkov, and the Chairman of the State Committee on Foreign Economic Relations, Yaacov Ryabov, who was responsible for foreign arms sales, appeared to mean that the Iraqi leader was interested in more arms from the USSR.[95] Subsequent reports of increased Soviet arms shipments indicate that Ramadan may well have been successful in his quest, although it is interesting to note that while the *Pravda* description of the talks stated that Ramadan had criticized US "imperialist intrigues,"[96] the Iraqi news agency description cited no such statement.[97] Iraq clearly had no wish to unnecessarily alienate the United States, as Iran, whose February offensive had scored some costly gains, prepared yet another major offensive.

Another purpose of Ramadan's visit may have been to alert the USSR to Iraq's plan to wage a war of attrition against Iran's oil exports. Having proclaimed a 50 mile air and sea blockade around Iran's main oil export terminal on Kharg Island in February, Iraq now began to attack oil tankers and other vessels that entered the zone. Iran responded by using its air force to attack Kuwaiti and Saudi tankers, and the Gulf war escalated further. Moscow's concern that the United States would exploit the situation to improve its ties with the Gulf states was confirmed in the case of Saudi Arabia.[98]

As a result of Saudi unhappiness over US policy in Lebanon, the increasingly close US tie with Israel, the US Congress's opposition to the sale of Stinger antiaircraft missiles to Saudi Arabia, and the possible move of the US Embassy in Israel to Jerusalem, Saudi-US ties had cooled considerably by April 1984;[99] and such incidents as the Saudi decision to consider purchase of a $4.5 billion air defense system from France rather than the United States, and the invitation of Soviet Ambassador Anatoly Dobrynin to a dinner at the Saudi embassy in Washington were cited in some quarters as evidence of Saudi Arabia's move away from the United States.[100] Nonetheless, the Iranian attack on a Saudi oil tanker in mid-May quickly reversed this trend. Two days after the tanker attack, Saudi Ambassador Bandar Bin Sultan met with US Secretary of State George Shultz, reportedly to obtain a US commitment to come to Saudi Arabia's aid in case a crisis occurred.[101] The United States responded quickly. President Reagan sent a letter to King Fahd reportedly reaffirming US support for the kingdom and US support for freedom of navigation in the Gulf, and stating that the United States would back up its commitment with military power if requested to do so by friendly nations in the area.[102] Reagan, citing the demands of "national security" (which obviated the need for congressional approval), then sent 400 Stinger missiles and 200 launchers to Saudi Arabia along with a KC-10 tanker aircraft to augment the three KC-135 tankers already there. This enabled Saudi F-15s and the Saudi-based US AWACS to stay in the air for longer periods; and thereby, in the words of the State Department spokesman Alan Romberg, "to lower the risk of a broader conflict by providing a deterrent against hostile activities."[103] Thus strengthened, the Saudi leaders sent up their F-15s against Iranian F-4s hunting for oil tankers near the Saudi coast, and in June 1984 shot down one Iranian plane while driving off a number of others. The fact that the Saudis had acted with US AWACS assistance, and that more American assistance was on the way in the form of extra fuel tanks for the F-15s, along with more advanced AWACS capable of detecting slow moving ships and aircraft,[104] clearly indicated improved US-Saudi relations; and the Saudis reciprocated soon afterwards by freeing many of the Americans held in Saudi jails, as part of a general amnesty.[105] The Saudi-US relationship improved still more in August when the United States promptly responded to Saudi requests to clear the Red Sea of mines which, apparently laid by Libya, hampered not only maritime trade in the Red Sea and through the Suez Canal, but also the Hajj which

Saudi Arabia, as the keeper of the Holy places of Mecca and Medina, took great pride in hosting.

While Moscow could do little about the US success in exploiting the escalation of the Iran-Iraq War to improve ties to Saudi Arabia, it worked energetically to prevent a similar development in US-Kuwaiti relations. As the most neutral of the Gulf Cooperation Council states, and the only one to have diplomatic ties and a military purchase relationship with the Soviet Union, Kuwait, as mentioned above, occupied a special place in Soviet strategy toward the GCC. Moscow had long feared that the GCC, both because of the invasion of Afghanistan and because of Iranian victories in the Iran-Iraq War, might gravitate to Egypt and to the United States for protection; and the Soviet leadership had sought to cultivate Kuwait's neutral leanings, and its basically anti-American press, to prevent such a development. On the eve of the escalation of the tanker war in mid-May, a Kuwaiti delegation headed by the Undersecretary of the Foreign Ministry Rashid ar-Rashid visited Moscow for discussions on the Gulf war and to arrange the visit to Moscow of Kuwaiti Defense Minister, Sheik Salem as-Sabah.[106] The delegation also met with Yaacov Ryabov, possibly for a preliminary discussion on new arms sales, and also signed an agreement on cultural cooperation. Then, however, came the attacks on Saudi and Kuwaiti tankers, and members of the elite in Kuwait questioned the desirability of a nonalignment in the face of the Iranian threat. Possibly noting that President Reagan had been willing to face congressional opposition to quickly send Stinger missiles to Saudi Arabia, the Kuwaiti Foreign Minister, Sheikh Sabah al-Sabah, also asked for the missiles.[107] Unfortunately for Kuwait, however, its refusal to accept an American ambassador the year before because of his previous service in the US Consulate in East Jerusalem, and the generally anti-US tone of the Kuwaiti press, did not particularly endear the Kuwaitis to President Reagan, who clearly had no desire to alienate Congress further by sending Stingers to Kuwait. Other arguments against the sale were the relatively small US stockpile of Stingers for export and US fears that the Stingers might wind up in the hands of terrorists.[108] Thus, the United States announced, in the words of State Department spokesman John Hughes, that while "no final decision had been made on the sale, we do not contemplate a sale at this time."[109] The United States, however, did offer to improve the quality of the US-made Hawk antiaircraft missiles that Kuwait already possessed (a US team which had made a survey of Kuwait's defense needs had recommended this) while also offering to share with Kuwait the information gathered by US AWACS based in Saudi Arabia. On the eve of the trip to Moscow by its Defense Minister, Kuwait made no formal response to the US offer to improve the Hawks, although the Kuwaiti Foreign Minister did announce that Kuwait was already making use of the AWACS-gathered information.[110]

Under these circumstances Sheik Salem as-Sabah, the Kuwaiti Defense Minister, journeyed to Moscow in early July. The Soviet leadership, noting that the Kuwaitis had been denied the weapons system they really wanted, and had been embarrassed in the process (the Kuwaiti Foreign Minister, after being privately denied the missiles, had made a public appeal to the US Congress, going so far as to say that the missiles were only for defensive purposes and "not to declare war" against Israel),[111] moved to demonstrate that the USSR could treat a client far better than the United States. The Soviets, besides reportedly offering a wide variety of weapons,[112] took Sheik Salem on visits to Leningrad, Tbilisi, Sevastopol, Tashkent, and Samarkand, invited him to witness live-fire exercises (including a combined land, air, and naval exercise), and also showed him a number of archaeological sites and Soviet museums.[113] The Soviet leadership seemed to go out of its way to demonstrate warm hospitality to the Kuwaiti official, and while the result of the visit appears not to have been the $347 million arms deal initially rumored, the Kuwaiti Defense Minister ultimately did agree not only to purchase Soviet air defense missiles[114] but also to invite a small number of Soviet advisers to Kuwait—the first time this had ever happened—to train Kuwaitis in their use.[115]

Nonetheless, despite the decision to buy the weapons from Moscow, Kuwait maintained its ties to Washington, and in the fall of 1984 concluded an agreement to train 150 Kuwaiti pilots in the United States and to establish a pilot training school in Kuwait.[116] At the same time, the Kuwaiti government gave red-carpet treatment to the new US Ambassador to Kuwait, Anthony Quinton, and also toned down the usually anti-US Kuwaiti press.[117] Finally, during the hijacking of a Kuwaiti plane to Iran, the Kuwaiti government stood firm and refused to free the imprisoned terrorists accused of the attacks on the US and French Embassies in December 1983, as demanded by the hijackers, thereby earning warm praise from President Reagan.

While the escalation of the Iran-Iraq War, somewhat paradoxically, led to an improvement in Kuwait's ties to both the USSR and the United States, on balance Washington gained more—much to the displeasure of Moscow, which continued to see the Arab world as a zone of zero-sum competition with the United States. Moscow must have been heartened by the fact that the GCC, thanks at least in part to Kuwait's opposition and to a lessened fear of Iran because of a prolonged postponement of the expected Iranian offensive, did not move to establish a joint defense treaty or even a joint air defense system at its meeting in late November 1984, although its constituent members did agree to earmark troops for a

GCC Rapid Deployment force.[118] As *Literaturnaya Gazeta* commented on December 5: "this means that the GCC will remain an economic organization as its founders intended and will not become a military organization, a kind of defensive pact, over which the United States seeks to gain control."[119]

While Moscow proved unable to move Saudi Arabia away from the United States, and had only limited success in reinforcing Kuwait's neutralist leanings, it remained frustrated by the Iran-Iraq War, and, in particular, by the Khomeini regime. Moscow's relationship with Iran had reached a new low on the eve of 1984, as shown by an extensive article in *Pravda* which, in addition to criticizing the regime for arresting 8,500 Tudeh members, noted that the anti-Soviet circles in Iran were trying to entice the Iranian government "onto a path of blind fanaticism" and warned the Khomeini regime to stop the "filthy campaign of slander" against the USSR.[120] Similarly, a feature article in *New Times* analyzing the first five years of the new Iranian government complained that the political revolution did not develop into a social revolution and blamed Iran for the continuation of the war. It also noted the growing trade ties between Iran and the United States and other NATO members and the antisocialist hostility which "the conservative wing of the Iranian religious and political leadership has always harbored." The article also condemned Iran for its support of "Afghan counterrevolutionaries" and for arresting and imprisoning Tudeh members as terrorists.[121] Interestingly, both the *Pravda* and *New Times* articles also appealed to Iran for improved relations, much as Moscow previously did at times of Soviet-Iranian conflict.

If Soviet-Iranian ties were strained, US-Iranian relations (except in the area of trade which had risen to $1 billion in 1983) seemed far worse. The United States blamed Iran for the terrorist attack on the Marine Corps Headquarters in Lebanon in October 1983 and officially classified Iran as an exporter of terrorism, thus necessitating a close scrutiny of all exports to Iran,[122] and possibly making Iran a target for a US retaliatory strike. Nonetheless, as in the past, a hostile relationship with the United States did not drive Iran any closer to the USSR, as, despite Soviet warnings, Iran announced the execution of ten Tudeh members in late February.[123] Moscow grew increasingly angry as Iran renewed its the offensive against Iraq the same month, fearing, as mentioned above, that such a development would push the Gulf Arabs toward the United States. *Kraznaya Zvezda* noted in its review of the war on April 21, that the escalation of the war created "a pretext (though a false one) for a further build-up of the US military presence in the Gulf."

The outbreak of the tanker war however, and a possible split in Iran's ruling elite over the desirability of Iran's continuing its go-it-alone policy, may have caused Iran to partially change its policy toward the USSR in June. In the first major diplomatic gesture to Moscow since the expulsion of 18 Soviet diplomats the year before, Tehran sent Seyed Mohammed Sadr, the director general of the Iranian Foreign Ministry to Moscow on June 6 where he met with Soviet Foreign Minister Gromyko.[124] In commenting on the trip, Iran's newly reelected speaker of Parliament, Hashemi Rafsanjani, stated that the visit was "unrelated to the war" but that it helped improve relations. He also observed that Iran did not want its relationship with the USSR to become "darkened."[125] Following that visit, a thaw seemed to set in as there were reports that Moscow's allies, Bulgaria, Czechoslovakia, and North Korea, had stepped up their shipments of arms to Iran,[126] and on June 21 the Soviet Union's Deputy Power and Electricity Minister, Aleksei Makukhin, led a delegation to Iran, the highest level Soviet delegation to visit in over a year. Moscow's purpose, in addition to reciprocating the visit of the Iranian Foreign Ministry official, was to use its economic relationship in hopes that this would form the foundation for improved political relations. One of the central themes of Moscow radio's Persian language broadcasts to Iran since the Khomeini regime took power had been the benefits that would accrue to Iran from increased trade with Moscow (one broadcast went so far as to urge Iran to allow the rebuilding of the bridges on the border rivers "which were built in the early years of World War II and are now old"[127] —as if the Iranians might have already forgotten how the bridges were used to facilitate Soviet occupation of Northern Iran at the time). Another goal of the Soviets may have been to try to save the lives of imprisoned Tudeh leaders, as a Persian language broadcast to Iran on the eve of the Soviet delegation's visit cited the appeal of the Arab Communist and workers parties to free the Tudeh members.[128]

While moving to improve its ties with Moscow somewhat, however, Iran made gestures to the West as well, with the visit to Tehran in late July of Hans Dietrich Genscher, the West German Foreign Minister, who said after his visit—the first by a European Economic Community Foreign Minister since the fall of the Shah—that the Iranian government had expressed a "clear wish" to gradually reestablish contacts with the West.[129] In addition, despite the fact that France sold arms to Iraq and harbored many exiles opposed to Khomeini, Rafsanjani was quoted as saying that, "not all doors with France were closed."[130]

In the following months, the central difficulties in Soviet-Iranian relations continued: the persecution of the Tudeh party; anti-Soviet propaganda in Iran; continued Iranian aid to the Afghan mujahidin; and, especially, the continuation of the Iran-Iraq War. The Soviet press, in describing the fifth anniversary of the outbreak of the war in

September 1984, continued to call for the war's end as soon as possible since the conflict "only benefits the imperialists."[131] Dmitry Volsky, writing in *New Times*, summarized Moscow's unhappiness with the conflict:

> The protracted war between Iran and Iraq has upset the fragile military-political balance throughout the vast area from the Atlantic to the Indian Ocean and served as a catalyst of the religious and national strife dating back to the Middle Ages which had seemed to have become a matter of the past. More, the new seat of war became something of a connecting link between the zones of older local conflicts, primarily the Arab-Israeli and Indian-Pakistani conflicts. It gave added impetus to the adventurism of the Tel Aviv rulers, who saw their chance in the growing division in the Arab world owing to the Iranian-Iraqi war and hastened to take advantage of this to invade Lebanon. On the other hand, the Gulf War fanned Moslem extremism, which is capitalized on in the undeclared war against Afghanistan . . .[132]

Moscow itself was to suffer from this extremism not only in Afghanistan, but in Lebanon, where Islamic fundamentalists fired a grenade at the Soviet Embassy in Beirut, and in the Red Sea where the shadowy Islamic "Holy War" group took credit for laying mines in August.[133] This latter action was directly counterproductive to Soviet strategy since not only were the United States and other Western nations called in to help clear the mines—thus shoring up ties with Saudi Arabia and Egypt—but also because the USSR itself depended on the Red Sea for its seaborne trade and Soviet ships and those of its Warsaw Pact allies were also at risk because of the mines. The Iranian leadership seemed to be at cross purposes over the mining, with Tehran Radio praising the mining (while saying Iran was not involved), while Khomeini condemned it several days later.[134]

As Moscow was encountering difficulties with Iran, and the fundamentalist Islam which had been encouraged by the Khomeini regime, it could at least draw comfort from the fact that US-Iranian relations appeared to worsen, especially after the US-Iranian claims panel suspended meetings after two Iranian judges physically attacked a Swedish Judge whom they accused of pro-American bias,[135] and the Iranian Foreign Minister Ali Akhbar Velayati, noted in an interview that he saw no hope of improving ties with the United States.[136] In addition, possibly in a gesture to Moscow when Iran was undertaking a minor offensive against Iraq, Velayati also stated "our relations with the USSR are exactly what relations between two neighboring states should be. The Tudeh party is an internal problem for us that had absolutely nothing to do with any foreign government."[137]

If the Soviet leadership could perhaps take some small comfort from the words of Velayati, it was less positively inclined towards developments in Iraq. Despite increased Soviet shipments of arms, especially tanks and planes, the Iraqi regime, which also had been receiving sophisticated aircraft from France, moved to further improve its ties with the United States. In an interview in early October 1984, Iraqi Foreign Minister Tariq Aziz noted that "a very agreeable atmosphere" now existed in US-Iraqi relations and he hinted that full diplomatic relations would be restored after the US Presidential elections.[138] It was perhaps for this reason that on his visit to Moscow two weeks later, the discussion which he had with Gromyko was described as having taken place in a "frank and friendly atmosphere."[139] At the end of November the United States and Iraq announced the restoration of full diplomatic relations, a development which the Prime Minister of Iran, Hussain Mousavi, stated would increase anti-US sentiment in Iran.[140] Yet, less than a week later Iran agreed to replace the two Iranian judges who had physically abused their Swedish colleague at the US-Iran claims tribunal,[141] an action which enabled Iran to keep at least one line of negotiation open with the United States, while also resuming the process of regaining its credit-worthiness in the Western world.

Meanwhile, as Moscow remained frustrated by the continuation of the Iran-Iraq War and its inability to secure major gains for its influence in the Gulf, Egypt continued its process of reentry into the Arab world, a development that rekindled Moscow's concerns about a revival of the Camp David peace process. In late September 1984, Jordan reestablished full diplomatic relations with Egypt and followed this up by permitting the Palestine National Council to convene in Amman in November. It appeared as if the "Jordanian option," a central feature of the Reagan Plan, had revived, and Moscow must have become even more concerned when Arafat and Hussain joined in a formal agreement, in February 1985, on an approach toward peace with Israel.

At this point, with Moscow's position both in the Gulf and in the Middle East as a whole again in decline, the USSR suffered the loss of yet another leader, the third in less than 2 1/2 years, when Konstantin Chernenko died. Chernenko's death provides the possibility to draw some conclusions about Soviet policy toward the Gulf in the period from the outbreak of the Iran-Iraq War in September 1980 to his death in March 1985.

CONCLUSIONS

In viewing the course of Soviet policy toward the Gulf in the period since the outbreak of the Iran-Iraq War, several conclusions can be drawn. In the first place, Soviet policy has been primarily reactive in nature as Moscow has sought to overcome the problems to its Gulf and general Middle East position that were caused by the outbreak and continuation of the war. Second, Soviet influence in the key states of the Gulf, Iraq, Iran, Saudi Arabia, and Kuwait, remains quite limited as Moscow, in large part because of the war, has proven unable to exploit either the crisis in American policy caused by the fall of the Shah or the US debacle in Lebanon to increase significantly Soviet influence in the Gulf.

The problems which Moscow faced as a result of the Iran-Iraq War included the strengthening of the political/military position of the United States in the Gulf, as the regional states felt an increased need to rely on American protection against Iran. In addition a very severe split opened up in the Arab world as two of Moscow's closest Arab allies, Syria and Libya, backed Iran; while the Centrist Arab states backed Iraq—and, in doing so gravitated to the pro-Western grouping of Arab states led by Egypt, a development that held the possibility of the expansion of the Camp David process.

Moscow's central strategy during this period, besides trying to end the war as soon as possible, an action it proved unable to accomplish, was to try to undermine the strengthened US position in the Gulf. The tactics involved the calling for the neutralization of the Gulf, made by Brezhnev in India in December 1980; the continuing attempt to woo Kuwait so as to prevent the GCC from gravitating toward Egypt; the modeling of the Soviet Middle East plan of 1982 on the Fez plan in order to lessen Arab support for the Reagan plan; and the effort to exploit such events as the Israeli strike against Iraq's nuclear reactor in 1981, the Israeli invasion of Lebanon in 1982, and the US debacle in Lebanon in 1984 to portray the United States and Israel as the main enemies of the Arab world and thereby divert attention from the Soviet invasion and continuing occupation of Afghanistan, which was another barrier to Soviet influence in the Gulf.

Nonetheless, these tactics did not prove to be particularly successful. While Kuwait endorsed some of the principles of Brezhnev's plan for the neutralization of the Gulf, the plan received little support elsewhere; and even Kuwait, following the escalation of the Gulf war in the spring of 1984, began to move toward the United States. In the case of Iraq, Moscow's off-again, on-again arms supply policy during the war had the effect of moving Iraq closer to France, whose Super Etendard jets and Exocet missiles enabled the Iraqis to wage a war of attrition against Iranian oil exports. At the same time, Iraq gradually moved toward a better relationship with the United States.

In the case of Iran, Moscow met increased frustration. Despite Iran's break with the United States, Moscow found it very difficult to make any inroads in the Islamic fundamentalist regime of the Ayatollah Khomeini.

The Soviet invasion of Afghanistan, the activities of the Tudeh party, which included efforts to infiltrate the Revolutionary Guard (Pasdaran) and the Iranian military, and Soviet involvement with Iran's ethnic minorities, combined with memories of the Soviet occupation of Northern Iran, and renewed Soviet arms sales to Iraq, to prevent Moscow from exploiting the Iranian-American conflict to increase its influence in Iran.

Moscow was similarly unable to make much headway with the other major Gulf state, Saudi Arabia. Despite US-Saudi tensions over Camp David, the Soviet invasion of Afghanistan and the outbreak of the Iran-Iraq War reinforced Saudi dependence on Washington; and the sale of US AWACS to Saudi Arabia in 1981, and President Reagan's willingness to buck congressional opposition in 1984 to sell Stinger antiaircraft missiles to the Saudis, consolidated US-Saudi ties.

To be sure, during the greater part of the period under study, old and sick leaders (Brezhnev, died November 1982, Andropov, died February 1984, and Chernenko, died March 1985) headed the Soviet Union. It therefore remains to be seen what the impact of Moscow's new leader, the young and apparently vigorous Mikhail Gorbachev will be. So long as the Iran-Iraq War continues, and Iran threatens Iraqi territory, the Gulf Cooperation Council states will be in a partial position of military dependence on the United States, a factor which serves to limit Soviet influence there. Similarly the supply of arms has not brought Moscow much influence in Iraq; and unless Gorbachev wishes to permanently alienate Iran, it is unlikely that the USSR would provide Saddam Hussain, or his successor, with the kind of weapons that would enable Iraq to score a decisive victory in the War. Finally, given the consolidation of the Khomeini regime and the severe weakening of the Tudeh party, there seems little, short of an outright invasion of Iran, that would serve to increase significantly Soviet influence in Iran so long as the Islamic fundamentalists remain in power.

At the same time, the costs of such an invasion, in terns of US-Soviet relations, Moscow's standing in the rest of the Middle East, and Soviet casualties, let alone the possible infection of Soviet Muslims, which would be the inevitable consequence of any invasion and prolonged occupation of Iran, would appear to make such an invasion unlikely, at least in the short run.

In sum, the Iran-Iraq War has proven to be a major obstacle for Soviet policy in the Gulf and it is to be expected that the new Soviet leadership will increase its efforts to bring an end to the war. The results of the Soviet endeavors, however, will depend more on the willingness of both sides, and especially Iran, to come to the negotiating table. Given the low-level of Soviet influence in Iran, it is unlikely that the Soviets will be any more successful under Gorbachev in ending the war, than they were under Brezhnev, Andropov or Chernenko, unless there is a major change in the thinking of the Iranian leadership.

ENDNOTES

1. For recent studies of Soviet policy in the Middle East, see Robert O. Freedman, *Soviet Policy Toward the Middle East Since 1970*, 3d ed. (New York: Praeger, 1982); Jon D. Glassman, *Arms for the Arabs: The Soviet Union and War in the Middle East* (Baltimore: Johns Hopkins, 1975); Galia Golan, *Yom Kippur and After: The Soviet Union and the Middle East Crisis* (London: Cambridge University Press, 1977); Yaacov Ro'i, *From Encroachment to Involvement: A Documentary Study of Soviet Policy in the Middle East* (Jerusalem: Israel Universities Press, 1974); and Adeed Dawisha and Karen Dawisha, eds., *The Soviet Union in the Middle East: Policies and Perspectives* (New York: Holmes & Meier, 1982). See also Yaacov Ro'i, ed., *The Limits to Power* (London: Croom Helm, 1979). For an Arab viewpoint, see Mohammed Heikal, *The Sphinx and the Commissar* (New York: Harper and Row, 1978). For a Soviet view, see E. M. Primakov, *Anatomiia Blizhnevostochnogo Konflikta* (Moscow: Mysl', 1978).
2. For studies of military aid, see Glassman, *Ibid.*, and George Lenczowski, *Soviet Advances in the Middle East* (Washington: American Enterprise Institute, 1972). See also Amnon Sella, *Soviet Political and Military Conduct in the Middle East* (New York: St. Martin's, 1981) and Bruce D. Porter, *The USSR in Third World Conflicts* (New York: Cambridge, 1984).
3. See Richard H. Shultz and Roy Godson, *Dezinformatsia: Active Measures in Soviet Strategy* (New York: Pergamon-Brassey's, 1984).
4. For a view of the role of Israel in Soviet Middle East strategy, see Freedman, *Soviet Policy Toward the Middle East Since 1970*, Chapter 8.
5. For studies of Soviet policy toward the Communist parties of the Arab world, see Robert O. Freedman, "The Soviet Union and the Communist Parties of the Arab World: An Uncertain Relationship," in Roger E. Kanet and Donna Bahry, eds., *Soviet Economic and Political Relations with the Developing World* (New York: Praeger, 1975): 100-134; John K. Cooley, "The Shifting Sands of Arab Communism," *Problems of Communism* 24 (March-April 1975): 22-42; and Arnold Hottinger, "Arab Communism at a Low Ebb," *Problems of Communism* 30 (July/August 1981): 17-32.
6. Translated in *Foreign Broadcast Information Service* (hereafter, *FBIS*) Middle East Iran Supplement No. 070, 24 March 1980: 7.
7. These events are discussed in detail in Freedman, *Soviet Policy Toward the Middle East Since 1970*.
8. *Ibid.*
9. Cited in the report by Dusko Doder, *The Washington Post*, 18 January 1980.
10. Cited in Reuters report, *The New York Times*, 5 February 1980.
11. For an analysis of the Saudi reaction to the invasion of Afghanistan, see Jacob Goldberg, "Saudi Arabia's Attitude toward the USSR, 1977-1980: Between Saudi Pragmatism and Islamic Conservatism," in Yaacov Ro'i, ed., *The USSR and the Muslim World* (London: Allen and Unwin, 1984): 263-270.
12. On the origins of the Iran-Iraq War, see Stephen R. Grummon, *The Iran-Iraq War* (New York: Praeger, 1982) and (Shirin Tahir-Kheli and Shaheen Ayubi, eds., *The Iran-Iraq War: New Weapons, Old Conflicts* (New York: Praeger, 1982).
13. For perhaps the best analysis of the hotly debated question of Soviet oil and natural gas production capabilities, see Marshall I. Goldman, *The Enigma of Soviet Petroleum* (London: Allen and Unwin, 1980).
14. Baghdad's treatment of its Communists is discussed in Robert O. Freedman, "Soviet Policy toward Ba'athist Iraq," in Robert H. Donaldson, ed., *The Soviet Union in the Third World* (Boulder, Colorado: Westview Press, 1981).

15. There were credible reports, however, that in the initial months of the war, Moscow's allies in East Europe along with North Korea, Libya and Syria were supplying Iran with arms, while Moscow was also allowing some arms to continue to flow to Iraq, albeit in small quantities.

16. The text of the declaration is found in *FBIS: USSR*, 11 December, 1980: D-7. It was also aimed at winning support for the USSR in Iran, which was the target of a US economic embargo because of the hostage crisis.

17. Cf. *Pravda*, 17 January, 1981 and Moscow Radio Persian language broadcast 17 January, 1981 (*FBIS: USSR*, 19 January, 1981: A2-A3).

18. For the text of Brezhnev's speech, see *Pravda*, 24 February, 1981 (translated in the *Current Digest of the Soviet Press* (hereafter *CDSP*), vol. 33, no. 8, 7-13.

19. For the comments of Iran's government spokesman, Bezhad Nabavi, on this incident, as broadcast on Radio Tehran Domestic Service, 30 December 1980, see *FBIS: South Asia*, 30 December 1980: I-5, 6.

20. Kuwait also was the only GCC state to buy arms from the USSR, although it was careful to balance its arms purchases from the USSR with arms from Western states including the United States.

21. This visit is discussed in Freedman, *Soviet Policy Toward the Middle East Since 1970*, 216-117.

22. For an interview with Sheik Sabah, see *The Middle East* (London), March 1981: 18. For an analysis of the domestic situation in Kuwait at the time of Sheik Sabah's visit to the USSR, see Helena Cobban, "Kuwait's Elections," *The Middle East* (April 1981): 14-15. Kuwait's foreign policy problems and strategy are discussed in Claudia Wright, "India and Pakistan Join in the Gulf Game," *The Middle East* (June 1981): 31-32. According to Wright, Sheik Sabah also went to Moscow to get a non-aggression treaty negotiated between the PDRY and Oman so as to lessen Omani dependence on the United States. On this point see also *Al-Hadaf* (Kuwait), 7 May 1981 (translated in *FBIS: Middle East and Africa*, 13 May 1981: C-5).

23. *Pravda*, 26 April 1981.

24. *Ibid*.

25. Cf. *Pravda*, 10, 11 and 16 June 1981.

26. Cf. *Pravda*, 16 June 1981.

27. Cf. report by Nathaniel Harrison, *Christian Science Monitor*, 2 April 1981.

28. Cf. Andrei Stepanov, "Taking Up A Point," (Soviet Neutrality in the Iran-Iraq War), *New Times*, no. 17 (1981): 31.

29. Cf. report by Michael J. Berlin, *The Washington Post*, 19 June, 1981.

30. Cited in report by Edward Cody, *The Washington Post*, 29 June, 1981.

31. By May 1981, Iran had begun to go on the offensive. See Grummon: 27.

32. Aziz Mohammed's speech was also printed in *Pravda*, 3 March 1981.

33. Cited in report by Bernard Gwertzman, *The New York Times*, 20 March 1981.

34. Cf. report by Don Oberdorfer, *The Washington Post*, 11 April 1981.

35. *Ibid*. Permission for the sale of the planes had been refused previously.

36. In early November, the *London Daily Telegraph* reported the shipment of 650 tanks from Poland (*Baltimore Sun*, 12 November 1981).

37. For a discussion of Soviet attitudes toward some of the Iranian leaders, see Robert O. Freedman, "Soviet Policy Toward the Middle East Since the Invasion of Afghanistan," *Journal of International Affairs* 34 (Fall/Winter, 1980): 290-291; 295-297.

38. Moscow Radio, in Persian, 1 September 1981 (*FBIS: USSR*, 3 September 1981: H-1).

39. Cited in AP report, *The New York Times*, 7 November 7 1981.

40. Cited in report in *The Washington Post*, 16 February 1981.

41. Tehran Domestic Service, 20 October 1981 (*FBIS: USSR*, 22 October 1981: H-7).

42. Cited in Reuters report, *The New York Times*, November 23, 1981.

43. Cf. report by Dusko Doder, *The Washington Post*, 16 February 1982, and *Izvestia*, 11 February 1982, which discusses the rise in Soviet-Iranian trade and Iranian oil sales to the USSR.

44. Bovin, a senior correspondent for *Izvestia*, delivered his criticism in *Izvestia's* weekend supplement, *Nedeliya*, 3-9 September, 1979. (For the background to Bovin's article, see Freedman *Soviet Policy Toward the Middle East Since 1970*, p. 365).

45. *Pravda*, 9 March 1982.

46. For Boldryev's background, see Moscow Radio, Persian Language Broadcast to Iran, 2 June 1982 in *FBIS: USSR*, 3 June 1982: H-7/H-8.

47. Cf. Freedman, *Soviet Policy Toward the Middle East Since 1970*, 386, 388-389.

48. Cf. report by Youssef Ibrahim, *Wall Street Journal*, 13 September 1982.

49. For an analysis of Soviet-Iranian relations at this time, see Karen Dawisha, "The USSR in the Middle East: Superpower in Eclipse," *Foreign Affairs* 61 (Winter 1982/83): 447-448.

50. *Pravda*, 12 April 1981.

51. *Literaturnaya Gazeta*, 27 May 1981 (translated in *CDSP*, vol. 33, no. 21: 11).

52. Ruben Andreasyan, "Disagreement in OPEC," *New Times*, no. 35 (1981): 13.

53. *Pravda*, 26 August 1981. Moscow was also unhappy that Saudi Arabia had "overbuilt" its airports—so they could be used by the United States—and by Reagan's famous comment "we will not allow Saudi Arabia to be another Iran."

54. Cited in *FBIS: USSR*, 2 November 1981: H-2. Radio Peace and Progress is the most outspoken of the "official" Soviet radio broadcasting services.

55. For a discussion of Soviet policy during the Israel invasion of Lebanon, see Robert O. Freedman, "The Soviet Union and the Middle East in 1982," in Colin Legum, Haim Shaked and Daniel Dishon eds., *Middle East Contemporary Survey 1981-1982* (New York: Holmes and Meier, 1984): 40-49.

56. Barry Rubin discusses the Reagan plan in "The United States and the Middle East," in *Middle East Contemporary Survey 1981-82*, 30-33.

57. Cf. *Izvestia*, 10 September 1982.

58. For the text of the Fez Plan see, *The Middle East Journal* vol. 37 (Winter 1983): 71.

59. *Pravda*, 16 September 1982. The Soviet plan is discussed in Freedman, "The Soviet Union and the Middle East in 1982."

60. Cf. Freedman, "The Soviet Union and the Middle East in 1982."

61. *Pravda*, 4 December 1982.

62. For a background analysis of the visit see Robert Rand, Radio Liberty Report No. RL 498/82, 10 December 1982.

63. Cf. report in *The Washington Post*, 12 December 1982.

64. Cf. report in *Christian Science Monitor*, 21 December 1982.

65. UPI report, *The Washington Post*, 5 December 1982.

66. Cf. report by David Ottaway, *The Washington Post*, 30 December 1982 and comments by Yasser Arafat as recorded in *The Washington Post*, 18 January 1983.

67. Cf. report by Edward Walsh, *The Washington Post*, 5 January 1983 and *The New York Times* report, 8 January 1983.

68. Cf. Robert Rand, Radio Liberty Report No. RL 31/83, 13 January 1983.

69. See the reports by Drew Middleton, *The New York Times*, 17 November 17 1982 and Robert J. McCartney, *The Washington Post*, 17 November 1982.

70. Rand, Radio Liberty Report No. 31/83.

71. The defection to England of a Soviet diplomat stationed in Iran, Vladimir Kuzichkin, who may have carried with him reports of Tudeh operations in Iran, could also have precipitated Kianuri's arrest. For a discussion of the arrest of Kianuri and other Tudeh leaders, and Tudeh efforts to infiltrate Iran's military, see Zalmay Khalilzad, "Islamic Iran: Soviet Dilemma," *Problems of Communism* 33 (January/February 1984): 1-20.

72. This episode would appear to at least in part refute the argument of Dennis Ross that Soviet coercive diplomacy is usually successful. See Dennis Ross, "The Soviet Union and the Persian Gulf," in Dan Caldwell, ed., *Soviet International Behavior and US Policy Options* (Lexington, Massachusetts: Lexington Books, 1985): 159-186.

73. *The Washington Post*, 5 May 1983.

74. AFP report, *The Washington Post*, May 5, 1983. The Soviet diplomats who were expelled included two minister counselors, four first secretaries and three military attaches.

75. For a description of the anti-Soviet atmosphere in Iran at this time, see the report by Shreen T. Hunter, *Christian Science Monitor*, 27 July 1983.

76. Cited in report in *Christian Science Monitor*, 26 May 1983.

77. *Pravda*, 17 June 1983.

78. Cf. report in *The New York Times*, 10 October 1983.

79. Reuters report, *The Washington Post*, 12 October 1983. Iranian threats to close the Gulf had been issued, off and on, since 1980, but were stepped up when Iraq announced it had acquired the Super-Etendard aircraft.

80. Cf. interview by Eric Rouleau, *Le Monde*, 8 January 1983 (translated in *Manchester Guardian Weekly*, 23 January 1983).

81. This was done by making public an 25 August 1982 conversation between Saddam Hussain and US Congressman Stephen Solarz (cf. *The Washington Post*, 3 January 1983).

82. Cited in *The New York Times*, 19 May 1983.

83. Cf. Reuters report, *The Washington Post*, 21 December 1983.

84. *Pravda*, 22 November 1983.

85. These events are discussed in Robert O. Freedman, "The Soviet Union, Syria and the Crisis in Lebanon: A Preliminary Analysis," in David H. Partington, ed., *The Middle East Annual - 1983* (Boston: G. K. Hall, 1984): 103-157.

86. *Ibid*.

87. *Pravda*, 10 December 1983.

88. Tass, 20 January 1984 (*FBIS: USSR*, 23 January 1984: H-5).

89. Moscow TV service 8 February 1984 (*FBIS: USSR*, 9 February 1984: H-6).

90. Baghdad INA in Arabic, 14 March 1984 (*FBIS: ME*, 15 March 1984: A-2).

91. Translated in *FBIS: USSR*, 7 March 1984: H-4.

92. *Kraznaya Zvezda*, 8 March 1984.

93. *Kraznaya Zvezda*, 22 March 1984.

94. *Pravda*, 20 March 1984. According to a report by David Ottaway in the 21 July 1984 issue of the *The Washington Post*, the agreement involved $2 billion in Soviet credits.

95. *Pravda*, 26 April 1984; see also report by Dusko Doder, *The Washington Post*, 28 April 1984.

96. *Pravda*, 26 April 1984.

97. Cited in *FBIS: ME*, 26 April 1984: i.

98. Cf. *Izvestia*, 23 May 1984.

99. For a Saudi evaluation of Saudi-US relations at this time, see the Reuters interview with Prince Bandar Bin Sultan, Saudi ambassador to the United States, *The Washington Post*, 11 April 1984.

100. For a description of the Saudi-French arms deal, see the article by Paul Lanier, *The New York Times*, 17 January 1984.

101. See report by Bernard Gwertzman, *The New York Times*, 18 May 1984.

102. Cf. report by Don Oberdorfer, *The Washington Post*, 22 May 1984.

103. Cited in report by David Ignatius, *Wall Street Journal*, 30 May 1984.

104. *Ibid*.

105. See report by Judith Miller, *The New York Times*, 4 August 1984.

106. *Kuna*, 14 May 1984 (*FBIS: USSR*, 16 May 1984: H-1). For a Soviet view of Kuwait at this time, see V. Yuryev, "Kuwait Facing the Future," *International Affairs* (Moscow), March 1984, pp. 141-147.

107. See report by Jonathan Randal, *The Washington Post*, 5 June 1984.

108. See report by John Goshko and Rick Allison, *The Washington Post*, 20 June 1984.

109. Cited in report by Bernard Gwertzman, *The New York Times*, 20 June 1984.

110. Cited in report by David Ottaway, *The Washington Post*, 19 June 1984.

111. Cited in report by Bernard Gwertzman, *The New York Times*, 20 June 1984.

112. See *Kuna*, 9 July 1984 (*FBIS: USSR*, 10 July 1984: H-2).

113. See *Kraznaya Zvezda*, 15 July 1984 (*FBIS: USSR*, 17 July 1984: H-3) and *Kuna*, 15 July 1984 (*FBIS: USSR*, 16 July 1984: H-3).

114. The agreement was signed in mid-August (*Kuna*, 15 August 1984 (*FBIS: USSR*, 16 August 1984, H-1). Although the Kuwaitis did not reveal the type of weapons systems they purchased from the USSR, it is possible that they were promised the SAM-8, which in some ways is similar to the Stinger in that it engages aircraft at relatively close range.

115. See *Kuna*, 18 July 1984 (*FBIS: USSR*, 19 July 1984: H-1).

116. See report by David Ottaway, *The Washington Post*, 1 December 1984.

117. *Ibid*.

118. See reports by David Ottaway, *The Washington Post*, 30 November 1984 and Judith Miller, *The New York Times*, 30 November 1984.

119. Translated in *FBIS: USSR*, 5 December 1984: H-1.

120. *Pravda*, 31 December 1983.

121. V. Komarov, "Highways and Byways," *New Times*, no. 2 (1984): 18-21.

122. Cf. report by Gerald Sieb, *Wall Street Journal*, 23 January 1984.

123. Iranian news agency report, cited in *The Washington Post*, 24 February 1984.

124. *Pravda*, 7 June 1984.

125. Cited in *FBIS: ME*, 12 June 1984, p. i.

126. See report by Jack Anderson, *The Washington Post*, 4 August 1984.

127. Radio Moscow, in Persian, to Iran, 12 April 1984 (*FBIS: USSR*, 18 April 1984: H-4).

128. Radio Moscow, in Persian, to Iran, 19 June 1984 (Igor Sheftunov commentary) (*FBIS: USSR*, 22 June 1984: H-7).

129. Cited in AP report, *The New York Times*, 22 July 1984.

130. Cited in report by Robert Duby, *Baltimore Sun*, 3 August 1984.

131. Cf. *Izvestia*, 24 September 1984.

132. Dmitry Volsky, "Horizontal Escalation," *New Times*, no. 45 (1984): 11.

133. Despite the claim, however, it appears on the basis of the limited evidence available that Libya was responsible.

134. See the report in the *The New York Times*, 10 August 1984.

135. See the report by William Pruzik, *The Washington Post*, 3 October 1984.

136. Cited in report by Elaine Sciolino, *The New York Times*, 4 October 1984.

137. *Ibid*.

138. Cited in report by Don Oberdorfer, *The Washington Post*, 7 October 1984. As part of the growing US-Iraqi relationship, the US Information Office was reopened in Baghdad for the first time since the Iraqi revolution of 1958 (*The Washington Post*, 24 October 1984) and the United States increased its agricultural exports to Iraq.

139. *Tass*, 19 October 1984 (*FBIS: USSR*, 22 October 1984: H-1).

140. Cited in report by Don Oberdorfer, *The Washington Post*, 29 November 1984.

141. Cited in report in *The Washington Post*, 5 December 1984.

80

TYPES
OF
INSTABILITY

CHAPTER 4

THE SOVIET NAVAL PRESENCE IN THE INDIAN OCEAN AND WESTERN SECURITY

by

Richard B. Remnek

Ever since the Soviet Union established a naval presence in the Indian Ocean in the late 1960s, the roles and missions of the Soviet navy in this region have been persistently misperceived. The Soviet Indian Ocean squadron has been portrayed as both a threat to Western security, particularly the oil tanker traffic from the Persian Gulf, and as a primary defense against a US ballistic missile submarine threat to the Soviet homeland. These aggressive and defensive roles ascribed to the Soviet navy in the Indian Ocean often have been used to place Soviet military intentions in the region in either a malignant or benevolent light. In this chapter, I shall first argue that these widely held conceptions of the Soviet Indian Ocean squadron's missions are mistaken and then consider the less well-publicized but nonetheless important ways in which the Soviet naval presence in the Indian Ocean affects Western security interests there. The general purpose here is to improve understanding of how the Soviet naval presence touches on Western security in the region. The first issue to consider is the so-called Soviet naval threat to Persian Gulf oil.

DOES THE SOVIET NAVY THREATEN WESTERN ACCESS TO PERSIAN GULF OIL?

If it were simply a question of extrapolating intentions from capabilities, then, indeed, such a threat would be serious; for even the most antiquated warships the Soviets deploy in the Indian Ocean can disable an oil tanker. Once Soviet mission priorities are taken into account, however, a Soviet naval interdiction campaign against oil tanker traffic seems highly improbable. In a major war in the theater, more likely, Soviet naval forces would challenge Western naval forces and military installations, particularly those critical ones on Diego Garcia. If a major war were to break out elsewhere, Western warships would probably be withdrawn from the Indian Ocean during the prehostilities crisis phase. The Soviets might follow suit. If, for some reason, the Soviets decided to keep their naval forces in the region even after Western forces had pulled out, they would probably still be targeted against Western military installations (e.g., Diego Garcia, Oman, Reunion, etc.) to prevent their possible employment for staging strategic bomber operations against the USSR should a coalition war escalate into an all-out global war at a later stage. Since a few P-3 antisubmarine warfare (ASW) planes armed with harpoon missiles could probably disable the six or seven surface combatants the Soviets generally leave on station in the Indian Ocean, only one or two attack submarines might survive to torpedo targets of opportunity.[1] But it would be highly unlikely that there would be many oil tankers remaining at sea for the submarines to attack. During a crisis leading to major hostilities, oil tankers would likely put into protected harbors and remain there until the Soviets had been swept from the seas.

Nor would the Soviets be able to mine effectively the Strait of Hormuz. Though the Soviets usually keep one or two small surface warships or auxiliaries on patrol in the Gulf of Hormuz,[2] they undoubtedly do not carry mines. The Soviets do not need the negative publicity that would come from public exposure that their Strait of Hormuz patrol vessels carried mines in peacetime. Their sensitivity to such publicity is reflected by the absence of Soviet submarines in or near Persian Gulf waters. Furthermore, if the Soviets tried to use surface ships, submarines or bombers to mine the Strait of Hormuz in wartime, they would not get very far before detection and destruction by improving regional and Western armed forces. The Soviets would certainly not be able to mine enough to interdict effectively traffic through the fairly wide and deep straits. And barring a Soviet invasion of the Gulf, whatever mines were laid could be cleared within a matter of weeks, if not days.

However, there is one way that the Strait of Hormuz patrol may play an instrumental role in a possible Soviet strategy for interdicting Western oil supplies in wartime. The information collected by the patrol about oil tanker traffic gives Moscow a better idea of worldwide Persian Gulf oil distribution patterns—data that could be helpful in war planning.

To say that the Soviet navy does not pose a direct threat to Persian Gulf oil traffic does not mean that Western oil supplies would be safe in war. They would not be. The most vulnerable points in the oil lifeline to the West are the oil pumping stations and terminals. These would likely be attacked by saboteurs, and the damage might be so extensive that neither repairs nor replacement could be made expeditiously in wartime conditions. From the Soviet perspective, the most efficient and potentially effective way of interdicting Gulf oil would be through sabotage by specially-trained proxy or "Spetznaz" units, not through wasting their naval assets on impractical missions.

DOES THE SOVIET INDIAN OCEAN SQUADRON SEARCH FOR US SSBNS?

Having disposed of the supposed Soviet naval threat to Persian Gulf oil, let us now consider the notion that the Soviet Indian Ocean squadron performs a strategic defensive mission against US ballistic missile submarines (SSBNs) operating in the Arabian Sea. Ever since Geoffrey Jukes pointed out 14 years ago the potential advantages of Polaris and Poseidon missile submarines using the northern Arabian Sea to fire at targets in the USSR and Western China,[3] many observers have assumed that the United States does use the Indian Ocean for SSBN patrols and that the Soviet navy entered these waters in the late 1960s to counter this alleged threat. Some recent proponents of this view have noted that the Soviets designate many of the surface combatants they deploy to the area as antisubmarine ships, both large and small.[4] In addition, the Soviets have replaced many of the older surface combatants with more modern ones featuring better ASW capabilities. Also, the Soviets have used Il-38 Mays, designated as ASW planes, to patrol these waters. From the fact that Soviet ships and planes routinely deployed to the Indian Ocean possess ASW capabilities, many observers have concluded that the Soviet Indian Ocean squadron hunts US SSBNs. This conclusion, however, does not consider other evidence pertinent to the issue.

To evaluate this thesis, we need to examine both Soviet words and actions. The Soviets, in fact, have written a great deal and for a long time about a US strategic threat in the Indian Ocean, but they tend to be coy. They refer to Pentagon plans for deploying SSBNs to the Indian Ocean, to construction of facilities on Diego Garcia preparatory to strategic submarine deployments, and to Western reports of US ballistic missile-carrying submarines operating in the Indian Ocean. They used references to a US SSBN threat as part of a larger propaganda campaign aimed particularly, but not exclusively, at Third World audiences, mainly to cast US military activities in the region in a negative light, as well as to rationalize their own naval presence as a purely reactive measure dictated by the need to protect the Soviet homeland. Interestingly, articles published in their professional naval journal, *Morskoi Sbornik*, were silent on the issue of US SSBNs in the Indian Ocean. An article on the Indian Ocean published in the January 1985 issue of that journal referred not to an SSBN threat, but to USAF B-52s operating out of Diego Garcia as a strategic threat to the USSR from a southern azimuth.[5] In recent months, however, Soviet articles appearing in both foreign policy and military journals have stated without qualification that US SSBNs patrol Indian Ocean waters.[6] Why this change of line has occurred only recently and what it portends for future Soviet naval operations in the Indian Ocean are questions for which answers are not readily apparent. It is nevertheless worth noting that the Soviet claim that US SSBNs patrol the Indian Ocean occurred almost two decades after the Soviet navy entered these waters to stay. This gap raises strong doubts that there was ever a connection between the Soviet Navy and a putative US SSBN threat in the Indian Ocean.

Moreover, when we look closely at the composition and pattern of operations of the Soviet Indian Ocean squadron, it becomes clear that the squadron does not perform any strategic defensive mission. Despite the improved ASW capabilities of the ships the Soviets routinely deploy to the Indian Ocean, the Soviet navy, according to the Office of Naval Intelligence, possesses very limited open ocean ASW search capabilities.[7] Although there are some indications that the Soviets may be on the verge of a breakthrough in ASW technology,[8] if they do acquire an effective ASW capability, it will be many years before they will be able to employ it.

To be sure, the Soviets have exercised their existing ASW capabilities, but in waters closer to Soviet naval bases. The locations of these exercises suggest that they may have been designed to counter Western hunter-killer attack submarines. In Soviet naval doctrine, protection of Soviet SSBNs against formidable Western attack submarines is a mission of highest priority, ranked one step above strategic defense missions.[9]

The possibility cannot be excluded, however, that Soviet ASW exercises reflect a general approach towards countering Western submarines irrespective of designation. If so, comparing how the Soviets perform ASW exercises with the composition and modus operandi of the Soviet Indian Ocean squadron should help to confirm or invalidate the view that the squadron performs an anti-SSBN mission. In conducting ASW exercises, the Soviets have employed a combination of air, surface, and submarine forces equipped with ASW sensors, antisubmarine missiles, and torpedoes.[10] Many of the primary weapons platforms used in such ASW exercises—*Kara*-class cruisers equipped with SS-N-14 ASW missile launchers, *Kiev*-class carriers carrying KA-25 *Hormone* ASW helicopters, and *Victor*-class SSNs capable of firing antisubmarine missiles—have deployed to the Indian Ocean in the 1980s, but *not* at the same time. The 1979 *Minsk* and 1983 *Novorossisk* aircraft carrier deployments in the Indian Ocean occurred during transits to the Pacific Fleet base of Vladivostok.[11] They were not part of the contingents deployed to the Indian Ocean on a semi-annual rotational basis. The Victor SSNs were deployed on a more or less continuous basis in the Indian Ocean in the early 1980s, but were withdrawn from the area by 1982, just as *Kara*-class cruiser deployments began to lengthen.[12] This timing suggests the Soviets deployed the Victors to counter the US naval buildup in the Indian Ocean following the 1979 fall of the Shah. When the United States reduced its naval strength in the region in the early 1980s, the Soviet navy followed suit and reduced its combatant strength commensurately. In 1980, the year US naval power in the Indian Ocean peaked at four carrier battle groups, Soviet naval strength in the area averaged a little over 13 combatants, including four submarines. That number dropped to roughly 8 1/2 the next two years, dropped to a low of five combatants in 1983, and bounced back to roughly 6 1/2 combatants in 1984 and early 1985.

The combatant contingent of the Soviet Indian Ocean squadron in recent years looks very much like it did throughout most of the 1970s. It is a general purpose force consisting of a major surface combatant (i.e., cruiser or destroyer), one or two minor surface combatants (i.e., frigates or minesweepers), one or two amphibious warfare ships and one or two attack submarines. The main change is that the Soviet Indian Ocean squadron has undergone modernization.[13] *Kara*-class cruisers, which first went to sea in the early 1970s, have replaced 1960-vintage *Kyndas*; 1970 vintage *Krivak*-class frigates have replaced 1960-vintage *Petyas*, many of which have now been transferred to foreign navies; 1950-vintage *Foxtrot*-class attack submarines still deploy but on a less routine basis than in the past. Their presence has been eclipsed by *Charlie*-class, cruise-missile equipped nuclear-powered submarines (SSGNs), which became operational in the late 1960s. The reduced *Foxtrot*-class submarine strength in the Indian Ocean (from nearly two to less than one on average since the early 1980s) may reflect the growing export of these versatile submarines.

The improving ASW capabilities that have accompanied this modernization still are not sufficient to conduct effective open ocean ASW operations. At best, the Soviet Indian Ocean squadron, particularly when supported by Il-38 May ASW planes, can provide some protection against Western "hunter-killer" submarines. Indeed, the fact that the Soviets use Il-38 May ASW planes for ocean surveillance instead of the far longer-range Tu-142 Bear F ASW planes is another indication that the Soviets do not hunt for US SSBNs in the Indian Ocean. The Il-38 Mays have only a 1,000 nm combat radius (with a three-hour on-station loiter time).[14] Staging as they often do from Aden, Il-38 Mays could provide surveillance coverage of roughly the Western half of the Arabian Sea—obviously insufficient to hunt any SSBNs in the broad depths of the Indian Ocean.[15] Tu-142 Bear F patrols would give the Soviets far wider coverage. But to the best of our knowledge, the Soviets have not used them over the Indian Ocean and not because they cannot.[16] They have, after all, employed Tu-95 Bear D long-range maritime reconnaissance planes on Indian Ocean patrols by staging them from Soviet airfields and overflying states along the northern Indian Ocean littoral,[17] and there is no apparent reason that they could not use the Bear Fs in a similar manner, at least for area familiarization purposes.

The pattern of Soviet naval operations in the Indian Ocean also invalidates an anti-SSBN mission there. Soviet naval units generally spend two-thirds of their deployment time in the Indian Ocean at anchor or in port.[18] When they do navigate, it is usually among anchorages around Socotra Island (PDRY), in the Gulf of Aden and Red Sea, in slow transit along the long route to and from their Vladivostok home port, or to local ports; Ethiopia's Dahlac Island and Aden are used most often and mainly for operational visits; ports in Mozambique and the Seychelles have also been frequented in recent years. During crisis periods, of course, Soviet ships have sallied forth against Western warships. In the major exercises that have been held in the Indian Ocean (e.g., 1970, 1975 and 1983), the Soviets simulated antisurface warfare attacks.[19] In short, none of the peacetime or exercise activities of the Soviet navy in the Indian Ocean have any strategic defensive orientation.

This does not mean they have not reacted to a possible strategic offensive threat to Soviet territory from the Indian Ocean area. They have, but *not* with naval forces. What they have done instead is to enhance their capabilities to track missiles targeted against Soviet territory from a southern direction. They have recently begun construction of six new large phased array radars that can track more ballistic missiles with greater accuracy than the existing HENHOUSE network.[20] One of these radar stations is being built near Astrakhan and will fill an existing gap in the HENHOUSE radar coverage of the Indian Ocean.

It is doubtful that this construction is closely connected with the recent Soviet change in writings about US ballistic missile submarines in the Indian Ocean, however. It seems rather to be part of a general program designed to upgrade Soviet warning and tracking capabilities against ballistic missiles fired at the USSR from *any* direction. All that can be safely asserted is that in improving their radar network, the Soviets chose not to ignore a possible missile threat from a southern azimuth. Improvements in Soviet capabilities on land to detect and counter US ballistic missiles or other strategic offensive weapons (e.g., B-52s, sea or air-launched long-range cruise missiles) will probably remain the sole effective means the Soviets have to counter a possible strategic missile threat from the Indian Ocean until their naval ASW capabilities improve dramatically.

HOW DOES THE SOVIET INDIAN OCEAN SQUADRON REALLY AFFECT WESTERN SECURITY?

The argument above has dealt with two widely held and often repeated myths about the Soviet Indian Ocean squadron. If, as I have argued here, the Soviet Indian Ocean squadron is neither a serious threat to Persian Gulf oil traffic nor a plausible counter to any possible US SSBNs in the region, then how does it affect Western security?

Soviet Naval Diplomacy

To answer this question, we must first recognize that the principal mission of the Soviet Indian Ocean squadron is a politico-military one: to defend Soviet state interests and promote Soviet foreign policy in the region. The Soviet Indian Ocean squadron has become a part of Moscow's diplomacy of force in the Third World.[21] Soviet naval diplomacy has entailed both cooperative and coercive aspects.[22] Noncoercive forms of that diplomacy include: diplomatic port visits, humanitarian relief efforts (e.g., disaster relief in Mauritius following the 1974 cyclone); harbor clearing of Bangladesh's Chittagong Harbor following the December 1971 Indo-Pakistan War; and mine-clearing of the Suez Canal in 1974, after the October 1973 War, and of the lower Red Sea in 1984, following the mining of the Red Sea, allegedly by a Libyan vessel. Coercive forms of naval diplomacy have included: intelligence collection directed at Western naval forces and installations (e.g., Diego Garcia, Reunion Island); monitoring Western economic activities (e.g., the Soviet "Strait of Hormuz" patrol); crisis surge deployments (e.g., during the 1971 Indo-Pakistan War; following the October 1973 Middle East War; during the 1977-78 Ogaden War;[23] during the 1980 US hostage crisis in Iran; etc.); naval support for local forces (e.g. the 1973 sealift of South Yemeni troops to the Dhofar border area); and logistic and fire support for Ethiopia forces operating against Eritrean insurgents. Many of these politico-military missions that the Soviet Indian Ocean squadron has performed have affected Western security interests adversely. But sometimes the Soviet navy has been used in ways that either complement or support Western security. Below we shall consider how and with what effect the Soviet navy has affected, negatively and positively, Western security in the region. The discussion will consider Soviet Indian Ocean naval diplomacy in order of decreasing operational complexity. Superpower naval confrontations will be considered first. We shall next consider one major Indian Ocean crisis where the Soviet navy acted alone—the Ogaden War. Since that war has been considered a landmark in the demise of detente, we shall give the Ogaden War and the Soviet policy that led to it special attention. We shall then examine noncrisis related uses of the Soviet navy to promote Soviet foreign policy goals in the region. Finally, we shall consider what impact current limitations on naval capabilities have had upon the practice of Soviet naval diplomacy in the Indian Ocean.

Superpower Naval Confrontation

Certainly the most widely publicized displays of Soviet coercive naval diplomacy have been the crisis surge deployments against Western warships. During the December 1971 Indo-Pakistan War, the Soviets surged additional naval forces into the Indian Ocean to counter British and American task forces.[24] When the USS *Hancock* carrier group steamed toward the Arabian Sea during the closing phase of the 1973 October war, a group of Soviet warships followed suit. And during the April 1980 aborted US hostage rescue mission, when four US carrier battle groups were stationed in the northern Arabian Sea, the Soviets surged more than 30 ships into the area. In each of these crises, the Soviet response has been similar: the general purpose forces the Soviets routinely maintain in the area have been augmented by matching Western carrier groups with anticarrier groups.[25] Soviet naval units have been tasked as "tattle-tales" to track and monitor Western naval activities, and Soviet reconnaissance planes have often surveilled Western warships.[26] Moscow will be able to respond more rapidly to future Indian Ocean crises by augmenting its Indian Ocean squadron with units from the 20-25 Soviet ships on station in the South China Sea.[27] A Soviet naval presence there means that they can respond to

Indian Ocean crises far more rapidly than was possible when all surge deployments originated in Vladivostok.[28]

It's worth noting, however, that in no Third World crisis has rapid surge capability alone seemed to be important. Being first upon the scene has not had a perceptible impact on the course or outcome of a Third World conflict.[29] Nor has it ever limited the other superpower's military options.

How Effective Has the Soviet Navy Been in Superpower Confrontations?

How effective Soviet naval forces are against Western groups is difficult to determine. If the question were simply one of relative capabilities, Western carrier forces (i.e., US and French) would have the edge. But when it comes to war at sea, the outcome of engagements is likely to be scenario-dependent. The Soviets might be able to so position their forces during a crisis as to be able to inflict considerable damage to US naval forces in the event of hostilities. In fact, they did so during the October 1973 Middle East War when US warships came within effective striking range of Soviet ship-launched missiles. Since that crisis, however, the US Navy has demonstrated its ability to elude Soviet "tattle-tales" on at least two occasions—during the 1980 aborted Iranian hostage rescue mission and the joint US Air Force/Navy air strike on Libya six years later.[30] What this suggests is that at least during crucial moments in a crisis, the United States has the ability to render Soviet naval forces ineffective. To a certain extent, the Soviet ability to constrain US naval power seems less impressive today than it appeared to have been in the recent past.

Historically, however, the Soviet naval presence during superpower crisis confrontations in the Indian Ocean and other Third World venues has served as a restraining factor. The Soviet insertion of credible forces, capable of inflicting damage on their opponent, gives the opponent ample reason to pause. Even if Soviet forces were to be destroyed, their destruction may require an answering blow, leading perhaps to an escalation of the conflict. This possibility creates a "hostage" effect that further adds to the political weight of Soviet naval forces deployed in crises. The Soviets recognize the political value of coercive naval diplomacy. As Admiral Gorshkov wrote in 1979: "In many cases, naval demonstrations have made it possible to achieve political goals without resorting to an armed struggle merely by exerting pressure through one's own potential power and by threatening to initiate military hostilities."[31]

The "Rules of the Game" of Superpower Naval Diplomacy

This does not mean that the Soviet navy has neutralized US military power in Third World crises. A study of 26 cases of Soviet naval diplomacy from the June 1967 War through the 1976 Angolan Civil War has shown that the latitude for action during Third World crises, most of which have not involved the vital interests of the superpowers, seems to have been a function of which superpower was defending the *status quo ante*—with respect to such principles as freedom of the seas, the sovereignty of established states, and the territorial integrity of states.[32] The status quo is certainly not an immutable principle, nor is it self-enforcing. After all, if there is no policeman, there may be no law.

The point, however, is that when employing its military forces for political purposes in the Third World, Moscow has demonstrated its respect for this principle wherever the United States could have been expected to uphold it with a show of force. This condition was not present when the Soviets overthrew an established government while invading Afghanistan. In that situation, Soviet interests and their ability to bring local military forces to bear were so preponderant that a US military response was out of the question; the riposte instead was to invoke linkage. The major improvement in US capabilities to project power into the area since the Soviet invasion of Afghanistan probably has checked Moscow's ability to preempt a US military response in future crises. This offers scant ground for optimism, however.

The Danger of Miscalculating Over Iran

The potential for miscalculation of the other superpower's intentions now is greater mainly because the vital interests of both superpowers have been affected by the recent events in Iran, whose territory embraces both the security of the USSR's southern borderlands and Western access to Persian Gulf oil. The Soviets might be inclined to regard any US military action as a threat to their security. Had the aborted 1980 hostage rescue mission succeeded, one wonders how they might have reacted. Conceivably, they might have misread US limited intentions during the hostage rescue mission and initiated military actions designed to preempt a (mis)perceived US threat to Soviet territory.[33] Historically, the Soviets—and the Tsars before them—have been concerned that Iranian territory could be used to mount attacks on them. This concern found concrete expression in the 1921 treaty with Iran which gave the Soviets the right to send troops into Iran if a third party intervened militarily or if Iranian territory were to be used as a base for an attack on Soviet soil. Although subsequent Iranian governments have renounced the treaty, Moscow has continued to insist on its validity. They invoked it when they moved into northern Iran in 1941 to protect their wartime supply lines to the West. And they invoked it again to warn the United States against intervention during the last months of the Shah's regime in 1978.

Continued instability along the northern tier of the Gulf will undoubtedly create opportunities for superpower military involvement.

92

Since Iran affects the vital interests of both superpowers but in different ways, the potential that miscalculation of the other superpower's intention could lead to hostilities here may be greater than in any other region of the world.

Afghanistan's Role in a Theater War

Should such a superpower military conflict take place, the Soviet military presence in Afghanistan would enhance Soviet theater warfare capabilities. By staging fighter aircraft from airfields in Afghanistan, such as the one the Soviets are building near Kandahar, the Soviets could extend the range of fighter protection to the shores of the Arabian Sea for *Backfire* bombers, attacking US naval forces and perhaps fixed military installations in the region as well.[34] Moreover, the routine use of Afghan airfields by Soviet fighter aircraft in the Afghan war means that strategic warning of a Soviet naval air attack could be reduced.

How much the extended range of fighter escort for Backfires and reduced strategic warning that Soviet use of Afghan airfields affords would affect the outcome of a superpower conflict is difficult to determine. At the minimum, it would mean that US carriers might have to be stationed farther away from land at the early stage of the conflict. This would make the task of projecting US naval air power ashore more difficult, though whether this would also decisively affect the outcome of a superpower conflict in the region is uncertain.

Nonsuperpower Crises: The Ogaden War

The Soviet navy in the Indian Ocean also affects Western security in ways that do not involve naval confrontations with Western forces. There have been, in fact, some Indian Ocean crises that have involved Soviet but not Western naval forces. Perhaps the most prominent case was the 1977-78 Ogaden War, when the Soviets augmented their Indian Ocean squadron by approximately 50 percent—after they had been expelled in November 1977 from Berbera, their principal support base in the Indian Ocean until then.[35] Soviet LSTs lifted supplies from Aden to Ethiopia, and other warships protected sea and air lines of communication to Ethiopia. In addition, 1950-vintage *Riga*-class frigates featuring shallow drafts and 100 mm guns were deployed to the area for the first time, presumably to provide fire support if needed against Eritrean guerrillas threatening to overrun Ethiopian positions along the coast.[36] According to a BBC report,[37] Soviet ships fired shots against shore targets in early 1978; if this report is accurate, it would have been the first time that the Soviet navy fired a shot in anger in Third World waters.

Soviet naval support for Ethiopia during and after the Ogaden War was not matched by a corresponding US naval response, mainly for two reasons: Soviet actions in support of a victim of aggression (Ethiopia)

93

were limited to restoration of Ethiopia's territorial integrity—the *status quo ante*; and the Carter Administration saw no need for, or utility in, making a show of strength. It was widely assumed that a US carrier deployment would have been interpreted as a sign of support for Somalia—the aggressor state.[38]

Insofar as the Soviet naval augmentation during the Ogaden War upheld the principle of territorial integrity and hence preserved international order, it conformed with Western security interests. But Washington also regarded the Soviet naval buildup, whose timing coincided with the intervention of Cuban combat troops on a large-scale, as evidence of Moscow's lack of restraint in a Third World conflict.[39] The Soviet-Cuban intervention in the Horn added to the doubts, first raised by Soviet/Cuban intervention a few years earlier in the Angolan Civil War, as to whether Moscow's seemingly unrestrained activism in the Third World was at all compatible with detente, one of whose "Basic Principles" spoke of the superpowers' special responsibility "to do everything in their power so that conflicts will not arise which would serve to increase international tensions."[40] In retrospect, the Ogaden War became a landmark in the unravelling of detente.

Whether or not the Soviet/Cuban buildup did, in fact, reflect a lack of restraint on Moscow's and Havana's parts remains unclear, however.[41] There are many factors underlying the Soviet/Cuban military intervention, and some of them raise doubts about how unrestrained their reponse was after all. Even though the intervention was not required by the battlefield situation in the Ogaden, where the front had already stabilized, it may have been needed nonetheless to alter Ethiopia's rapidly deteriorating control of Eritrea. Rather, the Soviet-Cuban intervention was prompted by other factors, some of which raise doubts about how unrestrained the military buildup was after all. The Soviets and their allies undoubtedly expected that large-scale Cuban participation and Soviet direction of the Ethiopian/Cuban forces in the Ogaden would bring victory sooner. And, a quick victory would enable the Ethiopian forces to be diverted sooner to Eritrea, where insurgent forces threatened to overrun the major towns. In addition, Soviet-Cuban intervention enabled them to gain greater control of the fighting so as to insure that it remained limited to the eviction of Somali regulars from the Ogaden and the restoration of the territorial status quo. Some Ethiopian generals had earlier expressed interest in invading northern Somalia—a less demanding operation from a military perspective. It would, however, have internationalized the conflict and created a pretext for US involvement on Somalia's side. This also suggests that the Soviet-Cuban intervention may have been inspired, in part, by Moscow's desire to prevent the conflict from turning into a superpower military confrontation. If so, it indicates that Moscow's (and Havana's) actions reflected a greater sense of prudence and restraint than may have been perceived at the time.

Where Moscow Really Lacked Restraint

Where the Soviets displayed a clear lack of restraint was not so much during the Ogaden War itself, but rather in their arms transfer policy in the region which led to the conflict. After all, had they not given Somalia the wherewithal to invade the Ogaden, the Ogaden War—the largest ever between Black African states—would have resembled the Polisario conflict in level of intensity. Moscow's decision to develop impoverished Somalia's armed forces into one of the largest and best-equipped in Sub-Saharan Africa was due exclusively to the Soviet Indian Ocean squadron's needs for shore-based support.[42] In the half-decade prior to the Ogaden War, Soviet arms were in effect bartered for naval access privileges, as Berbera became the Soviet navy's principal support base in the Indian Ocean.[43] Moreover, when the danger arose that growing instability in Ethiopia following the 1974 revolution would tempt Somalia to exercise its military option to achieve its irredentist goals in the Ogaden, Moscow did not curtail its arms supply to Somalia. Arms deliveries to Somalia increased in 1976, a year of Eritrean guerrilla successes against Ethiopian forces and mounting instability elsewhere in Ethiopia. The Soviets responded to the growing danger of Somali attack by formally dissociating themselves from possible Somali military adventurism. In the 1974 friendship treaty they signed with Somalia, the Soviets inserted a clause that stated that Soviet military assistance was for "strengthening the defense capability of the Somali Democratic Republic."[44] The defense clauses of almost all other Soviet friendship treaties with Third World states are couched in general terms that do not specify a given state as the beneficiary of military assistance. In retrospect, it seems that the Soviets sought a pledge from Somalia not to use Soviet-supplied weapons for aggressive purposes. They, in fact, invoked this clause during the Ogaden War to disavow any responsibility for Somalia's aggression.[45]

Moscow's willingness to provide Somalia with weapons which started a major war seems inconsistent with the 1972 US-Soviet Basic Principles Agreement which calls upon the superpowers "to do everything within their power so that conflicts will not arise which would serve to increase international tensions." The needs of the Soviet Indian Ocean squadron for shore-based support in the 1970s worked to distort Soviet policy in the region and thereby contributed to the unravelling of detente.

Noncrisis Forms of Soviet Naval Diplomacy

In addition to its highly publicized employment in Third World crises, the Soviet Indian Ocean squadron has affected Western security in other, less visible ways. Probably the squadron's most important noncrisis mission has been as a tangible expression of Moscow's support for pro-Soviet regimes. The Soviet Indian Ocean squadron provides Moscow with an independent military presence that enhances its ability to be a factor in regional affairs. Admiral Gorshkov himself characterized Soviet naval deployments to the Third World as "a great aid to Soviet diplomacy in strengthening the presence of the Soviet Union in the international arena and in strengthening friendship and cooperation between our state [i.e., the USSR] and many countries of the world."[46]

The Soviets have used their naval presence to strengthen ties to Indian Ocean states in numerous ways. The least demanding and most frequent employment is making port calls. Because the Indian Ocean contains more countries than any other area of Soviet naval operations, it is not surprising that the Soviets pay more diplomatic visits in this region than in any other area. The vast majority of these visits simply are a general expression of existing friendly relations between the USSR and the host government. But some visits appear to have been a direct Soviet show of support to bolster the authority of the local government. In April 1970, for example, the Soviets prolonged a routine official visit to Mogadiscio amidst false rumors about an Ethiopian attack against northern Somalia. (The rumors may have been designed to draw Somalia's Soviet-equipped and trained regular army forces away from the capital so as to enable a coup to take place.)[47] More recently, the Soviets prolonged visits to the Seychelles on two occasions, in November 1981 and October 1982, following coup attempts that failed.[48] In 1982, a *Kara*-class cruiser visited Massawa, Ethiopia, at a time of heightened Eritrean and Tigrean insurgency.

In some cases, the Soviets have used port visits to try to reassure host regimes about Soviet naval capabilities. A missile-firing demonstration by a *Kynda*-class cruiser took place in Mogadiscio during Marshal Grechko's February 1972 visit,[49] when important military cooperation agreements were signed. This occurred just after the *Enterprise* carrier group left Indian Ocean waters following the December 1971 Indo-Pakistan War. A more recent case came during the spring 1979 visit of the *Minsk* to Aden, when her Ka-25 *Hormone* helicopters and Yak-36 *Forger* vertical take-off aircraft flew demonstration sorties, and the accompanying amphibious landing ship, *Ivan Rogov*, flooded her well-deck and launched air-cushioned vehicles and conventional landing craft.[50] This demonstration occurred soon after the crisis in the Yemens, in which the US Navy sent the *Constellation* carrier group toward the Arabian Sea. In both cases, the Soviets seem to have tried to show that they were capable of fulfilling security commitments to friendly regimes.

Soviet warships also have played an active role in protecting the assets of a friend. In 1973 Soviet tank landing ships (LSTs) moved troops and heavy equipment from Aden to the eastern region of South Yemen in support of the Popular Front for the Liberation of Oman (PFLO) insurgency in the Dhofar region of Oman.[51] As noted earlier, the Soviets used extensively their naval forces during and after the Ogaden War to provide logistic and other support for Ethiopia, reportedly including fire support to an Ethiopian garrison surrounded by Eritrean guerrillas at Massawa in early 1978.

All these examples of naval diplomacy show that the Soviet naval presence in the Indian Ocean has given concrete expression to Soviet commitments to the security of friendly regimes. Many of these regimes, moreover, have actively supported insurgencies aimed at subverting pro-Western regimes, for example, People's Democratic Republic of Yemen (PDRY) support for the PFLO; Somalia's backing of both the "West Somali Liberation Front" against Ethiopia and the "Somali Coast Liberation Front" in the mid-1970s against the former French territory of the Afars and Issas, as Djibouti was known prior to independence in 1977; and finally Ethiopia's support of the Somali Democratic Salvation Front in the 1980s. In one case, the 1973 sealift in the PDRY, Soviet ships in fact provided logistic support for a guerrilla insurgency. The Soviet Indian Ocean squadron has thus helped to strengthen Moscow's ties with regimes which were supporting, often with Moscow's encouragement and assistance, "national liberation movements" seeking to subvert pro-Western regimes. To the extent that the stability of the latter enhances the West's security, the Soviet navy in the Indian Ocean has been instrumental in Moscow's efforts to undermine Western security in the area.

How effective the Soviet navy has been as an instrument of Moscow's diplomacy in the Indian Ocean cannot be determined with any degree of precision. The question may be somewhat easier to consider if we contemplate how the Indian Ocean area may have evolved politically if the Soviet navy had not established a continuous presence there in the late 1960s. Would the number of recipients of Soviet bloc weapons among Indian Ocean littoral states have increased as it did?[52] Would all of the seven Indian Ocean littoral nations that signed friendship treaties with the Soviet Union since 1971 have been willing to do so had Soviet naval power not been present in the area?[53] While the evidence that could answer these questions does not exist, it nevertheless seems reasonable to assume that without establishing a local naval presence to give visible expression to Moscow's ability and willingness to fulfill whatever security commitments are implicit in the military aid, agreements and treaties signed by Moscow with Indian Ocean nations, the latter certainly would have been more reluctant to enter into security relationships with the USSR.

Has Moscow's Limited Power Projection Capabilities Constrained its Naval Diplomacy?

Whatever success Moscow's naval diplomacy has enjoyed in the Indian Ocean may be partly due to the fact that the Soviets have not undertaken any operation that was beyond their capabilities, and, as the Soviets themselves acknowledge,[54] their power projection capabilities remain limited. The most glaring deficiency is the lack of modern aircraft carriers capable of launching sophisticated, long-range aircraft. They are building large, nuclear-powered carriers, but even after they enter service, it will probably take a long time for the Soviets to master complicated carrier flight operations—an art the US Navy pioneered and perfected over many decades. Judging from recent reports, Soviet naval aviators have a long way to go before acquiring the skills of their US counterparts.[55] Until such time as the former perfect their skills in flying aircraft far more formidable than *Forgers*, the Soviets will not have the capability to achieve air superiority in distant areas such as the Indian Ocean.

For the near- and mid-term future, this means that the Soviets will not be able to project power ashore in hostile environments against adversaries possessing modern aircraft and surface-to-air missiles. As a result of this constraint, they have had to chose their adversaries with care. They have, of course, assisted successful Ethiopian amphibious operations against Eritrean guerrillas, but only because the latter do not possess adequate defensive weapons. However, the Soviets appear to have shied away from tangling with South Africa's armed forces, even in defense of Mozambique or Angola. And indeed, the Soviets would probably fare poorly in an armed clash with South Africa, whose capabilities to take on Soviet naval forces were displayed in 1981, when its submarines and patrol aircraft tracked for six days the movement of Soviet naval units around the Cape of Good Hope.[56]

The lack of large, modern aircraft carriers also means that the Soviets cannot adequately protect their own long sea and air lines of communication to distant areas such as the Indian Ocean. During crises, they often station along air transit routes surface combatants equipped with surface-to-air missiles. The protection provided by their ships for the unarmed Soviet transport and reconnaissance aircraft used in crises is very limited and would be ineffective against a concerted air interdiction campaign initiated by a nation possessing modern aircraft capable of performing interdiction missions over international waters. Presently, probably no Indian Ocean nation possesses such a capability, but some may acquire it as their air defense capabilities improve (e.g., Pakistan).[57]

Thus far, Soviet military activities in the Indian Ocean area do not appear to have been constrained by this deficiency. Their rights to use international air space and navigate freely on the high seas have never been challenged, regardless of whether the objectives of their military operations infringed Western security interests (e.g., the 1973 sealift in support of PFLO insurgency on Oman). This permissive international legal regime has not only benefited the practice of Soviet coercive naval diplomacy, but it has also served to protect other Soviet state interests in the region as well. These interests include the security of the USSR's southern sea route which passes through the Red Sea and Indian Ocean. This is the shortest sea route that is open year round between the USSR's European and Pacific coast ports. The Soviets also use their cargo ships to support their expanding trade with Indian Ocean littoral nations. In addition, their fishing fleet operates extensively in the Western Indian Ocean. Finally, the Soviets have recovered their space capsules in Indian Ocean waters, and have routinely deployed space-event support ships for this and other space-related purposes. It has been estimated that on any given day, between 100 and 200 Soviet merchant ships, fishing trawlers and oceanographic research vessels may be found in the Indian Ocean.[58]

These maritime activities constitute important "state interests" for the Soviet navy to protect. They also give the Soviets a strong incentive to respect the principle of freedom of navigation on the high seas from which they are a major beneficiary. On occasion, they have demonstrated their support for this principle, for example, by their mine-clearing operations of the Red Sea and Bab el Mandeb, mentioned above.

Can Moscow Be Counted Upon to Respect Other Nations' International Rights?

Despite their stake in this principle, however, one should not expect the Soviets to respect necessarily other countries' rights to freedom of navigation in international waters, particularly if the nations involved do not possess the capability to enforce their rights or are not able to gain assistance from countries that are capable of doing so.

The Ogaden War can serve as an example. As noted earlier, the US Navy maintained a low profile during the crisis, mainly because the US Government did not want to do anything that would make it appear that the United States was identifying with the aggressor nation—Somalia.[59] The Soviets' latitude for action in defense of the victim of aggression—Ethiopia—was broad. In such a situation, with the United States effectively on the sidelines, it is conceivable that the Soviet navy did more than just provide logistic and fire support for, and protect sea lines of communication with, Ethiopia. According to Somali sources,[60] Soviet ships interfered in international waters with an Egyptian vessel carrying

99

supplies to Somalia. They reportedly did not prevent the vessel from continuing on to Somalia, but only stopped it to inquire about its cargo. If this report is accurate, it suggests that the Soviets might have been trying to intimidate the Egyptians in order to curtail the flow of war materiel to Somalia. If true, this incident also indicates that the Soviets do not regard as immutable the principle of freedom of navigation on the high seas. If they assess the risk to be low, as may have happened here, that their violation of another nation's navigation rights would precipitate an international incident, the Soviets may opt to contravene international law.

This lends further support for the view that a US naval presence could have played a useful role as a policeman—to ensure that Soviet military activities were limited to the restoration of the status quo. The implication for US policy regarding the employment of military power in the Third World seems clear. Even when the situation places major constraints on US activities, as it did in the Ogaden War, a naval presence may nevertheless play an important role in encouraging other nations' respect for international law. If the United States does not play a role as "world policeman," it should not expect other international actors to obey internationally recognized principles of law, for these principles are not self-enforcing.

SUMMARY

To recapitulate briefly, I have argued in this paper that the Soviet Navy does affect Western security interests in the Indian Ocean basin, but in ways that are not commonly understood. The popular notions of the Soviet navy in the Indian Ocean as either a threat to Persian Gulf oil traffic or a defender of the Soviet homeland against a US SSBN threat are groundless myths, designed to malign or rationalize Soviet intentions. This public debate over the Soviet Indian Ocean squadron has obscured the real connection between the squadron and Western security, which is rooted in its politico-military mission as an instrument of Moscow's diplomacy of force in the Third World. In peacetime and crises alike, the Soviet navy has promoted, to an incalculable degree, Soviet foreign policy goals, which have included, in part, the subversion of pro-Western regimes, some of whom now (e.g., Oman) are critically important to US strategy in the region. Whatever success the Soviets have enjoyed in the practice of naval diplomacy is due in part to their prudence in not undertaking operations beyond the limitations of their naval capabilities. Largely dictated by the absence of modern, high performance aircraft carriers, these limitations have forced the Soviets to avoid confrontations with adversaries possessing modern aircraft or surface-to-air missiles. Moscow's limited ability to defend long sea and air lines of communication to the Indian Ocean has not been a major handicap, however, because of the protection afforded by international law to its military and civilian assets. Moscow may not have always respected other nations' rights to enjoy the same maritime privileges that have benefited its own civilian and military activities.

IMPLICATIONS FOR US POLICY

This assessment points to the continuing need for a major US naval presence in the Indian Ocean. This presence is needed not so much to counter any putative Soviet naval "threat" in the Indian Ocean, for the capabilities of the Soviet Indian Ocean squadron itself (i.e., excluding *Backfire* bombers) are modest. Hence, the squadron can be neutralized with far less of a force than the US Navy currently stations in the region. Rather the case for a highly visible US naval presence in the Indian Ocean presented here rests on its use to ensure Soviet respect for international law. For in the absence of a limiting US show of naval force designed to confine Soviet actions to strategically defensive ends, there is no guarantee that the Soviets will respect another nation's international rights as suggested by the reported Ogaden War incident involving the Egyptian vessel.

To be sure, much has changed since then. The US Navy now maintains a continuous carrier presence in the Indian Ocean, supplemented two-thirds of the year by amphibious ships carrying a contingent of 1,800 Marines on board. It would be comforting to believe that the US naval buildup in the Indian Ocean has helped to deter the Soviets from undertaking any further actions infringing other nations' sovereignty and international rights. But there are scant empirical grounds for optimism here. Crisis situations inviting a Soviet military response have simply not materialized in the Indian Ocean during this decade. And the reasons for this are unclear. To a large extent, therefore, the US commitment to the security of the region has yet to be tested.

The US Government may find itself in another situation, similar to the Ogaden War, where our options to employ military power are politically constrained and the Soviets have considerable latitude for action. Were the United States likewise to stand aside in such an event, it might encourage the Soviets to abuse once again another nation's international rights. Should such an infringement take place, the political fallout would be far greater now with a high US military profile established in the region. The United States might then be regarded as a helpless giant, and the value of the US commitment to the region's security would be questioned. Our persistent efforts to overcome the misgivings of our

101

friends in the region about our reliability and staying power would suffer a setback with incalculable negative repercussions for Western security interests there.

However, the very fact that there was, as described above, a politically feasible military option (even though it was not exercised) for a limiting show of force during the Ogaden War suggests that diplomatically skillful employment of military forces in complicated crises situations is both possible and desirable. At a minimum, this will require a concerted effort by military planners to develop refined concepts for the employment of military power in situations where US military options are severely constrained. The need to fashion military responses finely tuned to meet specific political requirements in an area of great unpredictability stands as an important challenge for US decision makers. The overall credibility of our military posture in the region will be judged by our ability to meet this challenge.

ENDNOTES

1. The Soviets normally maintain one or two attack submarines in the Indian Ocean. I am assuming here that the Soviets would not reinforce their submarine strength in the Indian Ocean in a major war starting outside this theater. In such a scenario, the Soviets would undoubtedly need their attack submarines for higher priority missions elsewhere (e.g., protecting SSBNs in the sanctuary areas of the Norwegian/Barents Seas and Sea of Okhotsk). See *Understanding Soviet Naval Developments*, 5th ed. (Washington: US Government Printing Office, 1985): 24; and P. Lewis Young, "Soviet Naval Activity in the Indian Ocean, 1980-1985," *Asian Defense Journal* (November 1985): 55, which contains data on Soviet naval deployments in the Indian Ocean, supplied by the Australian Department of Defense.

2. See Charles C. Petersen, "Trends in Soviet Naval Operations," in *Soviet Naval Diplomacy*, ed. Bradford Dismukes and James M. McConnell (New York: Pergamon Press, 1979), 54.

3. Geoffrey Jukes, *The Indian Ocean in Soviet Naval Policy*, Adelphi Paper No. 87 (London: International Institute for Strategic Studies, 1972).

4. See, for example, P. Lewis Young, 53.

5. Captain (First Rank) M. Ovanesov, "K voprosu o voenno-politicheskoi obstanovke v Indiiskom okeane" ("On the Question of the Military-Political Situation in the Indian Ocean"), *Morskoi Sbornik*, no. 1, 1985, 25.

6. See Colonel F. Nikolaev, "Indiiskii Okean: zona mira ili 'tret'ia strategicheskaia zona' SShA? ("Indian Ocean: Zone of Peace or 'Third Strategic Zone' of the USA"), *Zarubezhnoe voennoe obozrenie*, no. 7, 1985, 5; and I. Lebedev, "Indiiskii okean - zona mira ili konfrontatsii?" ("Indian Ocean - Zone of Peace or Confrontation?"), *Mirovaia Ekonomika i Mezhdunarodnye Otnosheniia*, no. 8, 1985, 91.

7. See *Understanding Soviet Naval Developments*, 5th ed., 15, 31.

8. For indications of a possible Soviet breakthrough in ASW technology, see "Spotting Soviet Strategic Advances," *Wall Street Journal*, 5 September 1984; and "Soviets Said Able to Target US Subs From Space by Radar," *Washington Times*, 16 August 1984, 5A.

9. See *Statement of Rear Admiral John T. Butts, US Navy, Director of Naval Intelligence, before the Seapower and Strategic and Critical Minerals Subcommittees of the House Armed Services Committee on the Naval Threat* (24 February 1983), 16.

10. For a detailed description of Soviet ASW, see Milan Vego, "Soviet Anti-Submarine Warfare Doctrine," *RUSI* (June 1983): 46-53.

11. See *Strategic Survey 1979* (London: IISS, 1980), 20-24 and *Statement of Rear Admiral John T. Butts, US Navy, Director of Naval Intelligence, before the Seapower and Strategic and Critical Minerals Subcommittees of the House Armed Services Committee on the Naval Threat* (24 February 1983): 11.

12. The information contained in this paragraph on Soviet naval deployments in the Indian Ocean in the 1980s is drawn from data supplied by the Australian Department of Defense published in P. Lewis Young, 55.

13. See *Ibid* and *Understanding Soviet Naval Developments*, 5th ed., 24.

14. See the map on p. 59 in Petersen.

15. See *Statement of Rear Admiral John T. Butts, US Navy, Director of Naval Intelligence, before the Seapower and Strategic and Critical Minerals Subcommittee of the House Armed Services Committee on the Naval Threat* (24 February 1983), 13.

16. Bear Fs have made routine deployments to Vietnam in recent years. By overflying international waters, Bear Fs could surveil the eastern Indian Ocean, but that would still leave large gaps in Soviet coverage. *Ibid*, 14.

17. See Petersen, 54-59.

18. See *Strategic Survey 1979*, 23; and Petersen; and "Soviet Activities in the Indian Ocean," *Background Brief* (London: Foreign and Commonwealth Office, March 1983).

19. See *Understanding Soviet Naval Developments*, 5th ed., 30-31.

20. See Department of Defense, *Soviet Military Power 1986* (Washington: US Government Printing Office, 1986): 43-45.

21. For a comprehensive discussion of ths subject, see Bradford Dismukes and James M. McConnell, eds., *Soviet Naval Diplomacy* (New York: Pergamon Press, 1979), where most of the examples listed in this paragraph are described at length.

22. Cooperative diplomacy refers to the application of military power to support another nation's behavior or policies. Coercive diplomacy refers to the application of military power to threaten or impose violent sanctions in order to influence another nation's behavior. Since intelligence collection can enhance the credibility of the threat, it is included as a form of coercive diplomacy.

23. For further detail, see Kenneth G. Weiss, "The Soviet Involvement in the Ogaden War," *Professional Paper* No. 269 (Alexandria: Center for Naval Analysis, 1979).

24. For further detail, see Dismukes and McConnell, 183-92.

25. Since early 1970s, Soviet general purpose forces in the Indian Ocean have usually averaged 18 to 20 ships, including 1-2 submarines, 1-2 major surface combatants, several minor surface combatants, 1-2 amphibious warfare vessels and 11 or more auxiliary vessels. See *Understanding Soviet Naval Developments*, 5th ed., 24; and P. Lewis Young, 55.

26. An anticarrier group has usually included one major surface warship equipped with surface-to-air missiles, a second surface combatant equipped with surface-to-surface missiles, a cruise-missile-firing submarine and an attack submarine. With a US carrier group continuously present in the Indian Ocean in the 1980s, an anticarrier group has become an integral part of the Soviet Indian Ocean squadron. For a description of Soviet ACW and ASW groups, see Petersen, 49-51.

27. To support these naval forces, the Soviets have developed at Vietnam's Cam Ranh Bay an elaborate support complex which includes an electronic intelligence complex. In addition, they have operated out of Vietnamese airfields Tu-95 Bear D long-range maritime reconnaissance and Tu-142 Bear F long-range ASW planes. Department of Defense, *Soviet Military Power 1985* (Washington: US Government Printing Office, 1985): 118.

28. These fixed and airborne assets enable the Soviets to monitor US military operations and communications between East Asia and Diego Garcia. This information could be used to enhance Soviet effectiveness in a superpower confrontation in the Indian Ocean. See *Understanding Soviet Naval Developments*, 5th ed., 25.

29. For further elaboration of this observation, see Dismukes and McConnell, Ch. 8.

30. See Fred Hiatt, "US Attack on Libya: A Raid That Went Right," *The Washington Post*, 20 April 1986, A24.

31. See S. G. Gorshkov, *Morskaia moshch' gosudarstva 2e izd. (Sea Power of the State*, 2d ed.) (Moscow: Voenizdat, 1979): 360.

32. For a full discussion of this thesis, see James M. McConnell, "The 'Rules of the Game': A Theory on the Practice of Superpower Naval Diplomacy," in Dismukes and McConnell, Ch. 7.

33. Certainly, the Soviet intervention in Afghanistan serves as a recent precedent of a Soviet move to preempt an undesirable anticipated outcome—the collapse of a Marxist regime and ensuing "Islamic revolutionary" chaos.

34. Besides submarines, the *Backfire* bomber is probably the most formidable weapon system the Soviets possess for naval warfare. The *Backfire* bomber can carry AS-4 Kitchen missiles with a range of 150-250 n.m. See *Understanding Soviet Naval Developments*, 5th ed., Appendix D.

35. See *Strategic Survey 1979*, 23.

36. Soviet ships continued to provide support for Ethiopian forces after the expulsion of the Somali army from the Ogaden in 1978. In December 1979, for example, they evacuated Ethiopian forces at Marsa Takla after an unsuccessful offensive to take Nakfa from the Eritrean People's Liberation Front. *Sunday Times* (London), 8 June 1980, 9.

37. See *The Manchester Guardian*, 29 January 1978.

38. Kenneth Weiss of the Center for Naval Analyses has suggested that a US carrier task force deployment during the crisis could have played a positive role without linking the United States to Somalia's aggression. Had a US carrier group so deployed and paid port calls at Djibouti and Mombasa, Kenya—states which, along with Ethiopia, were subject to Somalia's irredentist claims—the Unites States could have both identified with the principle of territorial integrity and inserted a capability into the region to ensure that the Soviets, Cubans and Ethiopians kept their word—to limit their February 1978 military offensive to the eviction of Somali armed forces from the Ogaden.

39. The US Government referred to this buildup when suspending the bilateral Indian Ocean naval arms limitations talks after the fourth round in February 1978. See *The New York Times*, 22 February 1978, 2.

40. *Basic Principles of Relations Between the United States of America and the Union of Soviet Socialist Republic*, signed in Moscow, 29 May 1972; reproduced in *SALT: The Moscow Agreements and Beyond*, ed. by Mason Willrich and John B. Rhinelander (New York: The Free Press, 1974): 310-11.

41. For further elaboration, see the author's "Soviet Policy in the Horn of Africa: The Decision to Intervene," in *The Soviet Union in the Third World: Successes and Failures*, ed. by Robert H. Donaldson (Boulder, CO: Westview Press, 1981): 140-41.

42. This point is developed at length in the author's "The Soviet- Somali 'Arms for Access' Relationship," *Soviet Union* 10, pt. 1 (1983): 59-81.

43. The Soviets built at Berbera one of the most elaborate support infrastructures they have ever built in the non-Communist Third World. The facilities there included a pier, a floating drydock, expanded POL storage tanks, an ordnance storage and maintenance facility capable of handling a wide variety of tactical air- and sea-launched missiles as well as torpedoes and other conventional munitions. At the time of their expulsion, the Soviets were also completing construction there of a large airfield, capable of supporting any plane in the Soviet inventory. These facilities are described in US Congress, Senate, Committee on Armed Services, *Disapprove Construction Projects on the Island of Diego Garcia, Hearings*, 94th Cong., 1st sess., 10 June 1975; and US Congress, Senate, *Soviet Military Capability in Berbera, Somalia*, Report of Senator Bartlett to the Committee on Armed Services (Washington: US Government Printing Office, 1975).

44. The Russian text appears in *Izvestia*, 30 October 1974, p. 4; and a summary of the Somali text in *October Star* (Mogadiscio), 29 October 1974.

45. See *Moscow Radio* in English to Africa, 15 November 1977, in *Foreign Broadcast Information Service: Soviet Union Daily Report*, 16 November 1977, H2.

46. As quoted in *Statement of RADM Sumner Shapiro, US Navy, Director of Naval Intelligence before the Subcommittee on Seapower and Strategic and Critical Materials of the House Armed Services Committee on the Soviet Naval Threat*, 26 February 1981, 11.

47. See Bradford Dismukes, "Soviet Employments of Naval Power for Political Purposes, 1965-75," in *Soviet Naval Influence*, ed. by Michael McGwire and John McDonnell (New York: Praeger Publishers, 1977): 487.

48. See *Financial Times* (London), 11 October 1982.

49. For further descriptions of this visit and its significance, see the author's "The Soviet-Somali 'Arms for Access' Relationship," 68-72.

50. See *Strategic Survey 1979*, 22.

51. See Dismukes and McConnell, 137.

52. If you compare the periods 1964 through 1973 and 1979 through 1983, the earliest and latest periods for which US Government information on arms deliveries is publicly available, you will find that the number of recipients among nations bordering on the Indian Ocean or its tributaries (i.e., the Red Sea and Persian Gulf) increased from 9 (1964-73) to 14 (1979-83). Based on data contained in US Arms Control and Disarmament Agency, *World Military Expenditures and Arms Trade, 1963-73* (Washington: US Government Printing Office, 1975), 67-71; and US Arms Control and Disarmament Agency, *World Military Expenditures and Arms Transfers 1985* (Washington: US Government Printing Office, 1985), 131-34.

53. These nations are Iraq (1971), India (1971), Somalia (1974), Mozambique (1978), Ethiopia (1978), the PDRY (1978), and the Yemen Arab Republic (1984).

54. See, for example, Admiral Amelko's interview in Tass, Russian Service, 11 August 1982, in which he notes that the Soviet naval presence in the Indian Ocean is both qualitatively and quantitatively inferior to the US naval presence there. See also V. Kosovan, "Indiiskii okean: dva podkhoda," ("Indian Ocean: Two Approaches"), *Sovetskaia Rossia,* 4 May 1984, 3, which states that the Soviet warships deployed in the Indian Ocean on a continuous basis are not equipped with the means for conducting operations against the shore.

55. While deployed in the Indian Ocean in December 1982, the *Minsk* launched *Forger* VSTOL aircraft in reaction to US carrier operations, for the first time trying to intercept US carrier planes. US Navy pilots reported that the *Forger* interceptor operation was not very polished. Reported in *Statement of Rear Admiral John T. Butts, US Navy, Director of Naval Intelligence Before the Seapower and Strategic and Critical Materials Subcommittee of the House Armed Services Committee on the Naval Threat*, 24 February 1983, 8.

56. See *Defense Journal*, 5 October 1981.

57. The Israeli Air Force probably is capable of performing deep air interdiction missions over water. There is also one scenario—a Red Sea blockade—in which the Israelis might employ their aircraft on deep strike and interdiction missions to break the blockade. In the unlikely event that the Soviets would become involved directly or indirectly in a Red Sea blockade, they might find their sea and air assets targeted by Israeli warplanes. The very fact that Israeli Air Force deep strike capabilities are well proven (e.g., in operations against targets in Iraq and Tunisia) provides a powerful incentive for the Soviets not to participate in such a blockade.

58. For an excellent discussion of the economic importance of the Indian Ocean to the USSR, see LTCDR James T. Westwood, USN, "The Soviet Union and the Southern Sea Route," *Naval War College Review* 35 (January/February 1982): 54-67.

59. A small 4-ship US Navy force headed by the guided-missile cruiser, *Fox*, entered the Indian Ocean in late February 1978, as the successful Soviet/Cuban/Ethiopian offensive to evict the Somalis from the Ogaden was winding down. See *The New York Times*, 22 February 1978, 2.

60. Interview with Somalia government officials, conducted in Mogadiscio, Somalia, March 1984.

CHAPTER 5

IDEOLOGICAL CHALLENGES TO AMERICAN INVOLVEMENT IN THE PERSIAN GULF

by

Jerrold D. Green

For scholars and policy analysts the political role of ideology is frequently misunderstood. This is particularly the case both in the Middle East and in the Islamic world more broadly defined. At times the political role of ideology is underestimated and at times it is exaggerated. This conceptual weakness becomes painfully evident when we consider events preceding and comprising the Iranian Revolution. Initially, most observers of Iran, as well as many Iranians themselves, attributed little potential to Islam as a means to mobilize against the Pahlavi dynasty. As if to compensate, after the fall of the Shah, Islam was endowed with greater power and unity than it deserved as observers on the sideline, and some Islamic activists themselves, breathlessly awaited a global confrontation between Islam and secular political orders. It never developed. In the Middle East field, uncertainty about what is the precise political role of ideology remains.

Although it may seem arcane, it can be asserted that a partial solution to this problem may lie in a more systematic and objective approach to the analysis of the relationship between ideology and politics. This seems a fairly obvious solution, but the field of Middle East politics has more than its share of journalists and historians who want to be political scientists, political scientists who want to be journalists, and so forth. This excessive "blurring of genres" involves serious analytical costs, and it produces healthy differences of opinion. For example, in the area of Islam in Soviet Central Asia we find a serious disagreement between those who are awaiting a major challenge to Moscow on the basis of Islamic political consciousness and those who feel that social mobilization and adaptation are likely to obviate such conflict.[1] A similar debate seems to be emerging in analyses of Lebanon in which we find one analyst of the Shi'a arguing that their goal is the "eradication of Western Civilization."[2] This catchy perspective is later qualified to refer to de-Westernization, but its hysterical tone is hardly accidental. The difficulty is that ideology not only provides an analytical challenge, but also serves as an impediment to such analysis. In the latter case we are talking, of course, about the ideology of the analysts themselves. Ideologized investigation is self-defeating and analytically bankrupt. Systematic analysis is likely to prove far more productive than invective. In policy terms, the potential for understanding the Islamic world is no less or no greater than the prospects of understanding other parts of the globe. And every instance of Islamic-based anti-Americanism is premised on readily understood and identifiable political or economic differences, not on religious ones.

This last statement may sound counterintuitive and thus bears explication. Islam, as all ideologies, serves as a lens for evaluation of an adherent's spiritual, moral, economic, political, and cultural universe. Yet few issues are purely religious. And when Muslims turn back to Islam or Poles to Catholicism, it is usually as a means to right some perceived wrong in their lives. Irish Catholics and Protestants vehemently argue that their conflict is not one of religion; Lebanese make the same claims. This is fundamentally correct although, perhaps, hard to understand. Yet a content people rarely turn to religion. As I have written elsewhere:

(We often fail) to recognize the fundamental role of religion as the source of strength and sustenance for adherents of innumerable faiths over countless centuries in all corners of the world. Such commitments are especially salient aspects of the modernization process, with religion serving as a particularly effective refuge from the more dehumanizing and anomic aspects of dramatic and rapid social change.[3]

The consequence of such a politicization of religion, and the obverse, can be a particularly salient attribute of Middle East politics where:

> . . . in light of the absence of conventional participatory mechanisms, formalized religious organizations can, and in the view of some religious leaders, should serve as vehicles for improving the quality of life for their adherents. Those disturbed by such religio-political movement must ask themselves: Are religions any more troubled than the societies that house them?[4]

By linking ideological postures with more easily understood social and political problems, we position ourselves both to understand this complex relationship in an academic sense *and* to provide another dimension for the policy maker to understand and even anticipate the implications of ideological politics in the Middle East and the Islamic world.

ISLAM AND POLITICS

Institutional Islam is an essential part of the political life of Saudi Arabia, Sudan, Pakistan, and the Islamic Republic of Iran. Popular Islam, that is Islam which can at times be used as a means to challenge political elites, is important in all of these states as well as Egypt, Iraq, and Syria. Indeed, oppositional popular Islam is a significant political fact of life in virtually every Islamic state, be it those with Islamic majorities (Indonesia) or minorities (the Philippines). Distinguishing Islam from the top where it is used to enhance elite legitimacy, from Islam below, where it is used to challengi elites, is essential to understanding the political roles of Islam in all Islamic societies.

In those states which consider themselves formally Islamic, political elites use Islam to emphasize their personal control as well as to centralize their own power. Islam provides a solution to a political problem, it fulfills an important political role rather than a narrower theological one. In Iran Islam was enlisted to overthrow the Shah, in the Sudan as a means to mobilize and unify the north in its civil war with the south, in Pakistan to distinguish Zia al-Haq from his westernized predecessor whom he had executed, and in Saudi Arabia to support family rule and political parochialism. In these states the language of politics is Islamic yet the content of politics differs but little from politics elsewhere.

Although we may assume that political elites in all these countries are firmly committed to Islam, we may also assume that they are no less committed to their own personal political hegemony. That is, Islam will not be allowed to stand in the way of their pursuit of the national interest

109

as they see it (presumably they render this synonymous with their own political survival). Three out of the four states enumerated above are pro-American (Iran excepted) and, indeed, the political elite of Numieri's Sudan, Saudi Arabia, and Pakistan in part staked their political survival on close ties with the United States. Nonetheless, given the opportunity, the necessity, or the incentive they could shift their political allegiances accordingly. It is important to recognize however, that the United States could do the same thing if petroleum ceased to be important (Saudi Arabia) or the Soviets were to withdraw from Afghanistan (Pakistan). America can be as unreliable as anyone else.

The foreign policies of these states belie somewhat their claims to be guided by Islam in a strict or formal sense. Iran has sought support in its war with Iraq from Libya and Syria. Yet, the Iranians hold the Libyans responsible for the death of the Lebanese Shi'a leader Imam Musa al-Sadr (Khomeini even refused to receive Qadaffi's emissary, Colonel Jalloud, who visited Tehran after the success of the Iranian Revolution), while Syria is committed to maintaining a political order free of Islamic influences. Assad's destruction of Hama and slaughter of a significant portion of its population reflects an opposition to Islamic groups—an orientation certain not to be supported by Ayatollah Khomeini who is committed to the propagation of Islam not its extermination. The Islamic state of Saudi Arabia vigorously supports Iraq against Iran despite the fact that Saddam Hussain's commitment to keeping Islam at bay is hardly in accord with the Saudis' Islamic orientation. Thus, simple formulas for understanding the relationship between Islam and politics are of limited value.

Although the content of seemingly Islamic politics is not necessarily Islamic per se, the form and language of politics in these societies is. This Islamization of politics is crucial, as no state boasting a significant Muslim population can or will fully trust the United States because of American support for Israel and its lack of interest in resolution of the Palestine problem. However, this fundamental Islamic-based distrust of the United States, a feeling that it is not a reliable partner, is mitigated by the fact that for many states it is "the only game in town." American willingness to jettison the Shah of Iran hardly makes the United States the object of great confidence, particularly in the sheikhdoms of the Gulf. On the other hand, the Soviet invasion of Afghanistan, its expulsion from Egypt, and its support for such radical states as Libya and Syria makes it clear that for some, the United States can serve as an infinitely more attractive source of politico-military support.

GREAT POWER RIVALRY AND ISLAM

The American traveller in the Middle East will frequently be asked why the United States is so anti-Islamic. This seemingly naive question raises a variety of important questions. Although the United States is unquestionably pro-Israel, this simple fact of life hardly makes it anti-Islamic. Indeed, America's relations with states in the region are influenced by Islam only when the politics of Islamic states turn anti-American. Is Khomeini anti-Islamic when he buys airplane tires from Israel? The point is that many Muslims and those Westerners who take extreme varieties of rhetoric too seriously make essentially the same argument. Despite the crude ideology of the Reagan Administration, the President is primarily concerned with communism and anti-Americanism. Islam plays a small role, if any, in its foreign policy formulation. The United States neither feels positively about Islam in states with which it has close relations (Saudi Arabia or Pakistan), nor anti-Islamic in states with which it has tensions (Iran). Certainly there are those who extrapolate from terrorist attacks on American personnel and installations in Lebanon to Islam and all Muslims. Yet such histrionics are for the most part confined to the more sensationalist corners of the media or those scholars trying to catch Washington's eye.

Most Middle Eastern leaders are more sophisticated about American support for Israel than their speeches would indicate. Indeed, it can be argued that in creating the Palestine issue, Arab political elites created a Frankenstein monster which they cannot nudge back into its cage. This is not to argue that the Palestine issue is unimportant, for it remains the core of the Arab-Israeli conflict. Yet, in terms of regional politics, perfunctory support by Arab elites for the Palestinians as well as the historical relationship between elite linkage of support for the Palestine question and elite legitimacy has created a situation in which most leaders in the region cannot turn their backs on the problem as much as they might like to. Yet the chasm between rhetoric and action is as wide as ever. For example, Hafiz al-Assad cheerfully and successfully undermines the PLO in the name of Palestinian nationalism, Anwar Sadat turned his back on the Palestinians in order to help them, and so on. Although Arab masses are not fooled by such antics, they still feel a strong and genuine commitment to the Palestinians. On this issue there is little hope for an improvement of attitudes towards the United States throughout the region.

Nonsupport for the Palestinian people is only one of many issues in the region. And in terms of great power rivalry the United States potentially occupies a far stronger position than do the Soviets. Why this has not been exploited by the United States is unclear. A strong case in favor of the Soviet Union being the most anti-Islamic state in the world can easily be made. First, one merely has to point to the Soviet Union itself where a significant Muslim population is actively prohibited from religious freedom and expression. The Soviet Army is a hot-bed of ethnic conflict, and the ethos of the Soviet Union as a whole is one which is avowedly and unambiguously antireligious and thus anti-Islamic. The second point is that the Soviet Union has invaded and occupied Afghanistan. Its brutal occupation is geared to subduing the Islamic mujahidin and it has gone so far as to "export" Afghan children to Moscow for indoctrination and de-Islamization. Third, the Soviet Union supports those states in the Middle East which are most threatening and most opposed to Islam. Libya, Iraq, Syria, and the People's Democratic Republic of Yemen are at the top of any orthodox Muslim's "hit list." These countries, particularly the latter three, are the most opposed to the propagation of Islam and the type of Islamization which seeks a seamless web between Islam and all other aspects of human endeavor. Political elites throughout the Islamic *ummah* [community] are well aware of the Soviet Union's position on Islam, the masses are also aware of it although less well-informed. Proper emphasis on these issues certainly could help to rehabilitate America's Islamic credentials which are far stronger than is generally recognized. On the other hand, the Soviet Union's ability to function reasonably effectively in the Islamic world highlights the fundamental point of this paper—as a political force ideological Islam is far less significant to most elites than is the pursuit of their national interest.

VIEWING POLITICS THROUGH AN ISLAMIC PRISM

Separating American Middle East policy from its Israeli one is only part of the task confronting American policy makers. For it is important to recognize the manner in which these policies are understood. As is argued above, there is little that is narrowly Islamic in a doctrinal sense about Islamic politics. As Ali Dessouki correctly notes;

> Islamic movements have to be seen in relation to the specific processes of social change taking place in their societies, in particular to issues of the changing position of classes and groups, political participation, identity crisis, the stability of regimes and distributive justice.[5]

Thus, Islam is not automatically antithetical to American culture, values, or policies. Rather, political elites and counterelites who are opposed to such policies may *embed their opposition in an Islamic idiom*. Unpopular American policies will promote Islamic-based opposition, acceptable policies will not. And as Dessouki so aptly points out,

Muslims are concerned with the same types of political, economic, and social issues as are people everywhere.

It bears repetition that the Iranian Revolution was not "about" Islam but instead reflected popular dissatisfaction over the absence of political participation, economic inequity, a lack of justice, cultural alienation, and the fundamental unpopularity of the Shah. The assassination of Anwar Sadat by Islamic fundamentalists was a reflection of his aloofness from Egyptian society and his apparent lack of concern for his own people which was made to appear even worse because of his close ties with the United States. The attacks by Lebanese Shi'a on American personnel and installations reflect a Shi'a perspective that the United States had become a participant in the Lebanese imbroglio. It appeared to the Shi'a that the United States sanctioned the Israeli invasion and was in Beirut to support the Phalangists against them. Thus, by their lights, an American military contingent was a fair target. Had the United States been more concerned about the manner in which the Shah ruled Iran, Sadat ruled Egypt, or was even aware of Shi'a concerns in Lebanon, the Islamic-coated opposition to the United States might never have happened. For if Islam is so intrinsically anti-American, how do we explain close American ties with the Sudan, Pakistan, and Saudi Arabia? Why is it that the American Embassy in Islamabad was burned to the ground yet the United States is suddenly so valued in Pakistan?

The problem is not one of ideology but of political differences. "Great Satans" and "Evil Empires" will never really change. On the other hand, their critics can pick and choose which aspects of their political relationships should be emphasized and which should be downplayed. For many Muslims Islam provides a solution to problems but it is not the problem itself. Islam is a means to an end which is not necessarily spiritual in character.

LESSONS FOR AMERICAN POLICY IN THE PERSIAN GULF

One of America's major interests in the Persian Gulf is the free and unimpeded access to petroleum for herself and, more importantly, for the Western alliance and Japan. With this goal in mind the United States maintained a single-minded commitment to the Shah of Iran and why his downfall was so disastrous for American interests. As the policeman of the Gulf, the Shah allowed America to avoid stationing troops in the region—a type of involvement that the Vietnam experience made politically too costly for any American president. With the fall of the Shah and the Soviet invasion of Afghanistan, President Carter promulgated his doctrine in 1980 which was meant to deter the Soviet Union from taking advantage of the power vacuum in the region.

President Reagan further articulated the Carter Doctrine by stating definitively that the United States would never allow the government of Saudi Arabia to fall, and that the United States would use force, if necessary, to keep the Straits of Hormuz open.[6]

The main challenge to American policy makers today is the operationalization of these doctrines. The Rapid Deployment Force, now called US Central Command (USCENTCOM), has functioned as a symbolic military force in order to demonstrate American commitment to maintaining access to the Gulf. It is a useful, although hardly a convincing, paper tiger. Yet the Carter Doctrine and USCENTCOM do not address the most likely type of regional instability. *For the factors most likely to undermine security in the Gulf are political rather than military*. Furthermore, *their origins are likely to be indigenous.* Although the Soviet Union could, has, and will continue to try to exploit such instability, challenges to prevailing elites throughout the Gulf area cannot be ameliorated by American troops. There are rarely military solutions to political problems. The scars of Vietnam and Beirut are still fresh so that the political costs of deploying American troops to prop up the Saudi royal family, for instance, would make such an endeavor as unlikely as it would be ineffective. One possible remedy to this dilemma lay in the creation of an *Arab*, Jordanian Rapid Deployment Force. Initiated in secret, the moment the scheme became public knowledge on Capitol Hill pro-Israel forces began vigorously to oppose it. This impelled President Reagan to take the unorthodox step of pleading with a United Jewish Appeal dinner audience, on the eve of the upcoming election, to support his plan for arms sales to Jordan! He failed.

The literature on the Persian Gulf, which is remarkably undistinguished, is often devoted to various military scenarios in which the Carter Doctrine dilemma can be resolved. In fact, the problem defies resolution as we can neither commit large numbers of troops nor can we "buy" local potentates to do the job for us. Even though the Shah policed the Gulf for us, it is questionable how effective he would have been if ever genuinely challenged. For example, the performance of his military in Oman was less than stellar. Yet the problem is different than those who have jumped on the Gulf bandwagon tend to portray it. That is, since we would find it exceedingly difficult to deal with major military problems in the region, we should be asking what problems are likely to arise and how we can anticipate and hopefully nullify them. To repeat an earlier assertion, these problems are likely to have political rather than military origins.

EXPORTING THE IRANIAN REVOLUTION AND DOMESTIC DISCONTENT

The Iranian Revolution, despite the grandiose proclamations of Ayatollah Khomeini, can only be transplanted into fertile soil. The fertility is likely to be a direct reflection of political, economic, and social conditions in any country. To date, the revolution has not significantly taken root outside of Iran. Even the Shi'a of Iraq have not flocked to Khomeini's banner despite Saddam Hussain's well known antipathy towards Islam. Thus, fears that an Iran-style revolution will sweep the Gulf seem somewhat exaggerated at the present time. On the other hand, significant numbers of Gulf residents could conceivably seek an acceptable alternative to the political status quo in their countries if conditions deteriorate sufficiently. Given the oil glut and the economic cutbacks in a number of Gulf states this is certainly a possibility. Iran's potential role as a model is somewhat minimized due to its own domestic problems that are well-known throughout the Islamic ummah. One frequently hears admiration for the Khomeini who overthrew the Shah combined with doubts and reservations about the fashion in which he is ruling Iran.

Revolution, Islamic or otherwise, does not occur in a vacuum. Thus, the best deterrent to a Gulf-style recurrence of the Iranian experience lies in the hands of regional elites themselves—not the United States. There is an American policy imperative here as the United States should endeavor to promote political reform throughout the region. Yet there are limits to saving-Saudi-Arabia-from-herself policies. Given America's dismal record in Iran during the revolution, the United States should be sensitized to the manner in which it can be blamed for the failings of its friends. Such a monodimensional dependency theory gone wild is, unfortunately, a standard feature of Middle East politics where it is always easier to blame someone else for one's own problems. Yet the degree of American involvement in most Gulf states is of such magnitude that critics of this involvement, no matter how exaggerated their claims may be, will still strike a positive chord in appealing to the masses.

Unlike the vast majority of those writing on the Persian Gulf, James Bill has a sensitivity to this issue. As an Iranist he is aware of the risks of popular revolution and he correctly argues that:

> The United States must be wary of involvement in regional conflicts and resist the urge to respond to complex social and political problems with a policy of military intervention. Creative diplomacy should take precedence over military methods. The United States might attempt to work with the forces of constructive change rather than buttressing a weakening status quo. Specifically, America could

encourage the leaders of friendly, moderate states to develop more constructive policies towards their constituents. Force, corruption, and arbitrary decisionmaking need to give way to programs of reform that will build stability and legitimacy. . . . American diplomacy will require special skills and ingenuity to encourage the reform essential to the long-term stability of US friends in the Gulf without damaging our official relations with these governments.[7]

Easier said than done perhaps, but what other options does the United States have? In his analysis, Bill considers the growth of popular Islamic institutions throughout the Gulf region while paying special attention to growing Shi'a-Sunni conflict. Yet these are symptoms of broader unrest. Revolutions are not made, they happen, and thus they have to be anticipated. They are much harder to suppress once set in motion.

OUT OF SIGHT, OUT OF MIND?

One issue that tends to be overlooked is the responsibility of the Gulf leadership itself as a result of its ambivalent relationship with the United States. A major concern in all Gulf states is their collective inability to defend themselves against external threats. Thus, they are heavily reliant on the United States. At the same time, they are reluctant to be perceived as being too close to the United States and well remember the fate of Anwar Sadat and the Shah of Iran. Therefore, they unrealistically would like the United States to adopt what is termed a "just over the horizon" military posture. This mode of deterrence presupposes a close strategic relationship with the United States that no one will ever discuss or know about. But in case of a military threat, the United States will swing in on a rope, a la Errol Flynn, and then immediately swing out of the picture again. The United States is put in a confusing no-win situation in which it is blamed for a variety of political ills in the region but, at the same time, serves as the cornerstone of national defense. This absurdity cannot permanently obtain. And it is a reflection of the problems enumerated by Bill that regional elites have had little success in improving their popular legitimacy and relationship with their populaces. America is, in this case, too sensitive to the unrealistic expectations of regional elites and is essentially paying the cost of the Gulf leaderships' unwillingness to forge somewhat more viable and stable relations with their own people.

Saudi Arabia provides the best example of this self-defeating syndrome. The Saudi leadership, living in its own private *jahiliya* [state of ignorance], has decided that the best way to protect its rather fragile hegemony lies in closing its borders to the outside world. This Albania strategy is particularly fallacious when we realize how many foreigners, among them Americans, are resident in the country as well as the not insubstantial number of Saudis who have exposure to the West through education, training, and travel to places like Cairo and the West. It is noteworthy how little confidence the Saudis have in their own system. And why America is expected to share responsibility for the Saudi's unwillingness to modernize politically is inexplicable. The sham of the ruling elite's "Islamic legitimacy" is well known to Muslims everywhere. And a recent episode in which the former Minister of Electricity was exiled to the position of Saudi Ambassador to Bahrain for publishing a poem critical of the ruling family may presumably be understood as the tip of the iceberg. The problem in Saudi Arabia is not its close strategic and commercial relationship with the United States, for despite those who romanticize this relationship the Saudis are as anxious to sell oil as we are to buy it. Rather, the problem is the timidity and unrealism of the Saudi leadership itself. It is well known that Saudi Arabia is dependent upon American security guarantees. Yet, by its unwillingness to concede this point while at the same time avoiding political reforms, the Saudi government accentuates its fragility rather than minimizes it. Hypocrisy and an aversion to reality are attributes unlikely to enhance the ruling elite's public personna.

The above reluctance is a partial consequence of American support for Israel and its unwillingness to attempt resolution of the Palestine question. Political stability in Saudi Arabia is of direct concern to the United States as, with all its flaws, the Saudi elite is somewhat pliable and pragmatic. If replaced by a more extreme or ideological successor, America's situation in the region could become even more difficult. Thus, despite these problems, the United States should continue to encourage Saudi realism as well as political reform. The United States should not, however, allow itself to be blamed for domestic political problems, real or potential, which only the Saudi government can ameliorate.

THE PALESTINE PROBLEM AND THE GULF

As I indicated above, a standard concern of all Arab regimes is the nature and magnitude of American support for Israel. Furthermore, the United States is perceived to be notably unsympathetic to the Palestinians, and thus suffers in terms of credibility throughout the region. The implications of these "flaws" may not be as significant as we have been led to believe. It is well known that at best the Saudis are consensus "buyers," not leaders in the region. Their concerns with national security are clear, as is their inherent conservatism. These two factors help to explain much of Saudi Arabia's commitment to the Palestine cause. Although the religious significance of *Al Quds* [Jerusalem] should not be overlooked, it can certainly be argued that the

Palestine issue remains of great significance primarily due to the popular sympathy enjoyed by the Palestinians and because the Palestinians themselves are dispersed throughout the Arab world, particularly in the Gulf region where they frequently occupy positions of great responsibility. The Gulf leadership is acutely aware of the potentially disruptive role its expatriate Palestinian workers could play and the situation of these workers in the Gulf is one of continuing uncertainty.

No Gulf government will be overthrown due to inadequate or unsatisfactory support for the Palestinians. On the other hand, the main obstacle to Palestinian self-determination is seen as Israel and it is widely assumed that if it were not for the United States, Israel would cease to exist in its present form. Furthermore, the United States is credited with responsibility or at least overt support for many of Israel's more extreme actions so that whatever Israel does the United States shares the blame. The logic behind this is that a country of three million people cannot successfully defy one of 232 million. American claims to be unable to control Israel are usually rejected out of hand (in the Arab world). It is thought that American lack of influence on Israel results from a lack of desire. Most Arabs are unable to believe that America, given the will, could not force Israel to return the occupied West Bank for example. And given that Israel receives more American financial and military aid than any other state in the world, it is not difficult to appreciate Arab concerns about US-Israeli relations.

Although the situation is obviously not as simple as outlined above, this is how it is widely perceived in the Arab world. American support for Israel historically has complicated American influence in the region but has rarely eliminated it. But is there not something self-defeating about Arabs allowing American-Israeli relations to jeopardize American-Arab ones? Indeed, by allowing America's close ties with Israel to weaken Arab-American ties, the likely beneficiary is Israel herself. It would benefit both the United States and the Gulf leadership if American-Israeli relations could be separated from those between the United States and the Arab world. Given that American support for Israel is likely to continue on much the same course, and that the Gulf states are unlikely to increase their influence on the United States as well as their defense capabilities, this is the only prudent course to take. It bears repetition that only the regional elites in the Middle East will be able to accomplish this difficult yet not necessarily impossible task. By allowing their commitment to the Palestine problem to weaken their relations with the United States they are in fact weakening themselves. It cannot be emphasized too strongly however, that direct American-Palestinian negotiations would be the most effective course of action and would benefit not only America and the Arab states but also Israel.

CONCLUSIONS

The primary argument in this chapter has been that the United States should not allow seemingly antagonistic ideological positions to deter it from seeking continued involvement and influence both in the Arabian/Persian Gulf area and the Arab world more broadly defined. Just as is the case with the United States, underneath its fluctuating and at times counterproductive ideologizing the Arab world is populated by a collection of rational policies overseen by pragmatic and calculating elites. Ideology is important. It highlights the rules of the political game, provides a useful lexicon for understanding elite-mass relations, and allows us to see how political elites would like to be perceived and understood. On the other hand, we cannot allow such ideology to blind us to the political realities of the countries with which we are concerned. What elites say may not be what they mean. And policy makers should not allow the former to obscure the latter.

Another issue of concern in this chapter has been a definitional one. Whereas many analysts of the Persian Gulf are concerned with Gulf security, they equate this with military might. Yet, as I have argued, political security equals Gulf security. This should not be misunderstood to mean that the Carter/Reagan Doctrines should not be operationalized. What is meant instead is that notions of Soviet military threats, strategic consensus as it was termed, are both untenable and unrealistic. If we were to look at a regional instability ledger we would find one major instance of Soviet force projection—its invasion of Afghanistan. On the indigenous origins side of the ledger we would find the Iranian Revolution, the assassination of President Sadat, the Sudanese Civil War, the take-over of the Grand Mosque in Mecca, the disintegration of Lebanon, and the Iran-Iraq War. None of these is the result of Soviet designs. All can be interpreted as being the manifestations of domestic political, social, and economic dissatisfaction of varying magnitude. What is needed is a political "RDF" equipped to understand the forces that brought about these major events, to anticipate others, and, when in our interest, to prevent them.

ENDNOTES

1. See a recent article by Alexander Benningsen, "Mullahs, Mujahidin, and Soviet Muslims," in *Problems of Communism* 33 (November-December 1984): 28-44. Benningsen is of the school that anticipates severe Islamic-based unrest throughout Soviet Central Asia.

2. Daniel Pipes, "'Death to America' in Lebanon," *Middle East Insight* 4, no. 1 (March/April 1985): 3-9.

3. Jerrold D. Green, *Revolution in Iran: The Politics of Countermobilization* (New York: 1982): 150.

4. *Ibid.*

5. Ali E. Hillal Dessouki, ed., *Islamic Resurgence in the Arab World* (New York: 1982): 8.

6. US Congress, House. Subcommittee on Europe and the Middle East of the Committee on Foreign Affairs, *Developments in the Persian Gulf: 1984* (Washington: 1984): 8.

7. James Bill, "Resurgent Islam in the Persian Gulf," *Foreign Affairs* 63, no. 1 (Winter 1984): 127.

CHAPTER 6

THE SAUDI ECONOMY IN TRANSITION: PROSPECTS AND BOTTLENECKS

by

Riad Ajami

Saudi economic planners are facing their first major recession since the oil boom years. The international oil industry is undergoing a period of transition and flux. Many western economists predict that oil revenues will continue to drop until the late 1980s. The oil industry is the economic base of Saudi Arabia; disruptions in this industry could have very damaging effects for the country's political and economic stability. Moreover, this transition comes during a period when Saudi Arabia is moving into it's five year development plan. In the next five years, development emphasis will be on diversifying the economy, where, as previously, attention was directed to building the infrastructure.

SAUDI OIL REVENUES
IN BILLIONS OF DOLLARS

Source: *Washington Post*, November 26, 1984.

TABLE B

SAUDI ARABIA: ACTUAL PUBLIC SPENDING AND INCOME, 1982-85

SR *000 Million

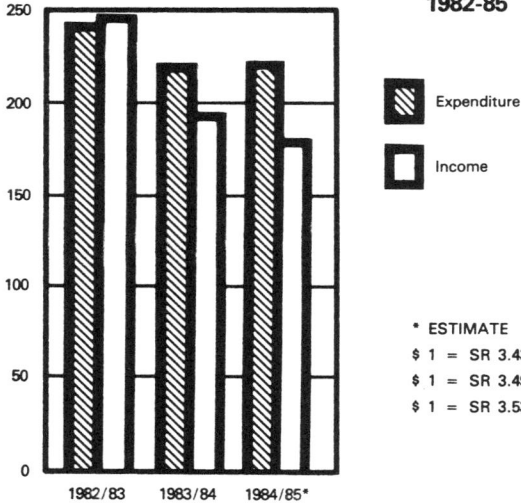

Expenditure

Income

* ESTIMATE
$ 1 = SR 3.4350 (1982);
$ 1 = SR 3.4950 (1983);
$ 1 = SR 3.5312 (1984)

Source: Ministry of Finance & National Economy, Riyadh.

122

CHANGES IN THE ECONOMY

Oil revenues, which make up the lion's share of Saudi income, have dropped $70 billion since 1981.[1] (See Table A). In order to contain fear and to prevent a flight of money from the country, it is generally believed that the Saudi government is withholding exact economic figures. Estimates, while not exact, still prove invaluable for illustrating trends. Government revenues continued to decline during fiscal year 1984-85, yet observers feel that the decline was slower than during the previous fiscal year. It is estimated that government expenditures during fiscal year 1984-85 had been held very close to that of fiscal year 1983-84. This being the case, the resulting deficit would be similar to that illustrated in Table B.[2]

In order to meet government expenditures, it has been necessary for officials to dip into their reserve holdings. Last fiscal year it is estimated that Saudi government revenues were reduced by $50 billion. The decline in revenues has changed government spending practices. Government officials declare that spending policies have been adapted gradually in order to avoid disrupting the basic functioning of the economy. Yet, the Saudi government has adapted a tighter fiscal stance that resulted in cutback of less essential projects and current outlays. In fiscal years 1982-83 and 1983-84, budgetary expenditures were reduced by 22 percent compared to a drop of approximately 60 percent in oil revenues.[3] While it was generally believed that oil prices would stabilize in 1986 or 1987-- near levels announced during January in Geneva—current price instability will defer the date for price recovery for some years. The demand for oil is eventually expected to stabilize, as well.

This stability will result from developments which to some extent, offset each other. On the one hand, a strong U.S. dollar has tended to increase oil prices for countries whose currencies have depreciated against the dollar. In recent years, countries like Japan and France have tended to restrain domestic demand for oil as prices rose in terms of their own currencies. As those currencies gradually strengthen relative to the dollar, the demand for oil in these, and other, countries could revive. Furthermore, the demand for oil would strengthen if the pace of economic recovery accelerates in Europe, and in newly industrialized countries like Brazil, India and Turkey.[4]

In view of predictions that oil revenues will stabilize, continued deficit spending is not acceptable to economic planners. Officials expect the stabilization of revenues at approximately $50 billion. The projected expenditures for fiscal year 1985-86 are $50 billion, thus an optimistic goal for fiscal year 1985-86 is a balanced budget.

FOURTH DEVELOPMENT PLAN

As of March 22, 1985, Saudi Arabia will have entered into its fourth five-year development plan. The three previous development plans directed political and economic attention toward building a modern infrastructure, and toward developing basic productive sectors, such as industry, agriculture and mining. Over the past 15 years the Saudi government has invested about $400 billion on these development plans. The result of this sizable investment was the creation of sprawling cities, a network of super highways and the construction of thousands of skyscrapers, public buildings, factories and farms. This emphasis on construction necessitated vast imports of labor from both developed and underdeveloped countries, in order to alleviate shortages of indigenous labor. One should remember that goals set in these development plans were easily attainable due to the huge influx of oil dollars during the boom years. The fourth development plan will provide more challenges to policy makers since there has been a sizable drop in government revenues.

The fourth development plan focuses on four important goals: First, to continue to reduce dependence on crude oil exports as the principle source of income by diversifying the economic base. One of the recent attempts to diversify the economy has been the development of a petrochemical industry. Petrochemicals are used in making building and construction materials, fabrics, soaps and pharmaceuticals, as well as numerous other materials consumed by industrial societies. Upon completion there will be a total of seven petrochemical plants and two fertilizer factories involved in production. It has been estimated that by 1986, Saudi Arabia could be marketing 5.3 million tons of petrochemical products, one million tons of fertilizer and 850,000 barrels per day of refined oil products. The Middle East will soon replace the United States as a principal supplier of both low density polythylene and linear low density polythylene. Yet, the United States will have a large role in marketing the Gulf output.

The proposal of a new and efficient producer in an already oversupplied market is causing panic among the petrochemical producers of the European Economic Community (EEC). The West European anxiety towards the Saudi new petrochemical industry stems from three factors: 1) Saudi plants are starting up at a time of oversupply. A price war could easily begin with even a small additional amount entering the market. 2) Saudi factories were built with the latest designs and preferred size. Almost all of the companies are 50-50 partners with US and Japanese corporations which will provide technology, management training and a share of the marketing. 3) The Saudis also have a tremendous edge in access to raw materials at low cost to supply these factories. In response to EEC complaints about these advantages, the Saudis quickly point out the obstacles for them in this industry. 1) There is a higher cost for building the necessary facilities in Saudi Arabia. 2) The distance from production facilities and the markets for the product is great. 3) Start-up outlays (for training employees and building housing for them) is much higher for the Saudis.[5] Whatever advantages or disadvantages Saudi Arabian companies have, the West Europeans will be required to make important political decisions in order to deal with this new competition. The EEC will either have to arrange or to coordinate the closure of outdated plants, or to introduce heavy import tariffs to try to preserve internal markets. When the first shipments of petrochemicals reached Western Europe, a 13.5 percent tariff was immediately instituted. The result was an angry threat by Saudi officials to reciprocate on EEC imports to Saudi Arabia. Western observers believe that this issue should be addressed only as part of a broad trade and cooperation agreement between the two regions. The Europeans want assurances from the Saudis that they do not plan to sell heavily in West European established markets. On the other hand, the Saudis want the range of EEC duties on petrochemicals brought in line with their own 4 percent tariff on EEC petrochemical imports. In view of the fact that Saudi Arabia could dump cheap petrochemicals on European markets if pushed too hard, it is doubtful that the EEC will opt for placing high import tariffs on Saudi imports.

In another attempt to diversify its economic base the government has committed itself to maintaining agricultural development. Before the effort to expand the agricultural sector, the Saudi government was importing over 49 percent of its food requirements. In 1984, Saudi Arabia became self-sufficient in wheat, poultry, eggs, and fresh dairy products. The most dramatic productive increase concerns wheat. Saudi Arabia, this year, will reach a position of exporting a wheat surplus to neighboring countries. The government's decision to attempt self-sufficiency in food is based on the desire to escape the pressures that major food exporting nations can impose upon importing countries. The incentives provided to farmers make agriculture a safe and profitable investment. Farmers are guaranteed that the government will buy their wheat for $1 thousand per ton (5 to 6 times the world market price). The package of incentives also encourages putting more land into production. Grants of land may be made by the Ministry of Agriculture and Water. Interest-free loans are available from the Saudi Arabian Agricultural Bank. Moreover, there are generous subsidies for fertilizers, pesticides and animal feed. Subsidies for farm machinery are available up to 50 percent.[6]

This farming policy has been sharply criticized because of such large subsidies. In 1984, government subsidies to wheat farmers amounted to about $1 billion and $386 million went to subsidize farm machinery, pumps and feed. Since 1980 the government has spent $2.3 billion in interest-free loans and service. Also, $12 billion was invested in developing water resources and $1 billion for grain storage facilities. In view of the high figures, a valid question can be raised about the ability of the government to maintain these subsidies with a decline in revenues. Another important question raised is whether Saudi Arabia's limited water supply will survive the extensive irrigation necessary to produce wheat in an arid climate. An estimated 75 percent of Saudi water resources is currently consumed by agriculture. The water tables of some regions have fallen significantly. Water and irrigation specialists also warn that long-term agricultural development will suffer if a moratorium on the exploitation of water resources is not instituted soon.

The final diversification project that will be discussed stems from the Peace Shield Program. The government of Saudi Arabia will turn the enormous expenditures necessary to update its defense program into investment dollars. The Peace Shield Program will link airborne warning and control system (AWACS) aircraft with the Royal Saudi Air Force headquarters in Riyadh and with a country-wide network of radar stations. In order to be awarded the defense contract, there was a stipulation. The complicated agreement called for bidders to ensure that 70 percent of the cost of goods and services associated with the Peace Shield Program be offset through establishment of high technology, manufacturing and service joint ventures within the Kingdom.[7] In economic terms, these joint venture projects would transform the new electronics industry by setting up industrial plants to make avionics and telecommunications equipment. The contract award was made to the Boeing-lead consortium totalling $1,181.95 million. The off-set program appears promising for diversification of the economy, but the system is not expected to be operational until at least 1989.

The second goal of the Fourth Development Plan is to develop the indigenous human resources of Saudi Arabia, while continuing transfer of high technology. Demographically, the native Saudi population is too small to meet the demand for labor. The need to import labor from other countries was expanded quickly during the oil boom years. The vast surplus of money allowed cheap expatriate labor to occupy the menial and undesirable positions. It eventually led to a leisure society where expatriates (Western and Third World) are working at all levels in the economy. It has been estimated that 67 percent of the total Saudi workforce is foreign. The dependence of the Saudi economy on these expatriate workers has been illustrated with the recent decline in government revenues. Filipinos and Pakistanis are being replaced by less expensive workers from Bangladesh and Sri Lanka. Moreover, expatriate workers have had to wait months for their pay and often have had their wages suddenly cut by one-third to one-half. The decline in funds has also affected Western workers in Saudi Arabia. There are fewer Americans or American companies involved with Saudi companies. The Saudis simply cannot afford the high wages and fees for Americans any longer.[8] Saudi officials have been working toward the creation of a more efficient and productive indigenous labor force by attempting to transform Saudi Arabians into technologically literate participants in the economy. The government has spent large sums of money to educate potential skilled workers in universities of the West. Yet, the population of Saudi Arabia is not large enough to meet labor needs. This problem is magnified by the social, religious, and legal restrictions that prevent approximately one-half of the population from entering the labor force—the women. While recognizing their long-term shortage of indigenous labor, restrictions have been placed on expatriate workers in order to control their influx into the country. Such restrictions include limitations on the number of years allowed for a worker's visa and restricting the ability of expatriate workers to bring dependents into the country.[9] Due to the number of years required for an increase of population to enter the labor force, it appears as if labor shortages and dependency on expatriate labor will remain a constant strain on the development of the economy for the foreseeable future.

The third goal of the development plan is to emphasize qualitative development. This has been defined as "continuous upgrading of the performance of the public utilities and service sectors." The huge Saudi bureaucracy is widely known for sluggish and wasteful performance. This new approach indicates a campaign to clean up and cut waste from an over-sized bureaucracy. Qualitative development "also means new research and development in environmental control and energy, particularly in the fields of solar energy, electrical power and desalinization." This clarification illustrates several programs which are not likely to be cut from the budget as "non-essential."[10]

Although implementing the above three goals, the government has committed itself to a fourth one which is strengthening the private sector and reducing the role of the government in the economy. Although creation of a share-owning society and privatizing large state-owned enterprises is a goal, the idea has not been widely accepted by the private sector. Shares of the National Industrialization Company (NIC), offered on a 50 percent, partly-paid basis, were reported to have been modestly undersubscribed. Investor interest seemed to have been hit by the government's unexpected decision not to take stock in the new company.

Saudi investors' confidence has taken a recent hammering from a combination of factors—notably the continuing fiscal squeeze (which has depressed non-oil sector expansion); the sharp rise in riyal interest rates throughout 1984; and the obstacles to free share dealing created by a regulatory system that came into effect at the end of the year. The regulatory system stipulates that only Saudi banks are allowed to handle orders for shares and only transfers processed by the banks are acceptable by comparing registers responsible for keeping track of ownership. The benefits of this new system are that banks can ensure the price quoted for each share is equitable and relates to the market price at large. Moreover, this creates a larger pool of business which helps to avoid regional price variations. Opponents of the regulatory system cite several drawbacks. The banks are having difficulty closing deals since they are not permitted to hold an inventory position on their own behalf. While certificates of equity ownership can give control over large volumes of shares, banks are not permitted to break the shares into smaller, more tradable bundles. The time consuming system for application to buy or sell shares compounds these problems. In view of the number of disincentives for share trading and the lack of public enthusiasm, the government's goal of privatizing the economy will be difficult, at best, to accomplish.

SAUDI TECHNOCRATS' PERCEPTIONS OF US ROLE IN THE REGION

All is not too well in Saudi-US encounters. The attitudes and feelings of Gulf technocrats can best be characterized as a love-hate relationship. Hemmed in between two more militarily powerful combatants in a Gulf war (with no end in sight) the Saudis and other Arabs in the Gulf are uneasy; worse yet, they are disillusioned and disconcerted about US policy toward the region.

The United States appears to them to be not always in tune with local sensibilities, needs and ways, and at times seems incoherent and inconsistent. Other times, its presence is overpowering and too close for comfort. They fear that a direct and clear US presence in their midst will only serve to demonstrate that the Arab states of the Gulf are not yet viable state systems capable of protecting themselves from external threats. Equally alarming to some are Western pronouncements belittling the importance of Arab oil to US energy needs.

The euphoria of Arab technocrats generated after their apparent triumph over oil during the 1970s have given way to a sober resignation that they inhabit a world that they do not fully make and control. In a world where deeds and myths of heroes abound, the combination of material wealth and lack of power are devastating feelings which could leave the best of men bewildered. The Arab technocrats are puzzled about a promise not fully realized and fulfilled. The closely held views and notions among many were that with the American umbrella comes security and the feeling that one's own immediate surroundings are tame and tranquil. Though beliefs in America's unlimited possibilities and power are partially of their making, the disappointments are shattering and disorienting.

Most of these young men spent their professionally formative years in America. Here they were exposed to American ways, management and quick fixes. They also had faith in American remedies and instant solutions. They returned to their societies armed with their degrees, know-how and a great deal of optimism, ushered in also by a great deal of wealth and a feeling that they had "the world over a barrel"—to use a metaphor. Their elders did not study in America—most did not study at all—however, they speak too of the might of empires and big powers. Both, nevertheless, resent America's perceived lack of interest in ordering the world and in presenting them with options and scenarios easier to live with and in tune with local sensibilities. They see armadas and aircraft carriers over the horizon from their shores and believe that big powers can and should do things discreetly and without direct involvement.

The undelivered expectations of far and distant powers are more painful when one is faced with the realization of one's own limitations. The Arabs of the Gulf see around them advisors and consultants, skilled and nonskilled workers manning their economy. Billions spent generously for the development of viable and contained economies and societies capable of protecting them appear to have brought little protection. The Gulf economies continue to be run by expatriates and to maintain the existing industrial and commercial infrastructure and systems, they will have to rely upon expatriates into the 21st century. Western systems and hardware solved many problems and made many things possible yet created further dependencies and need for more advisors and expertise. Advisors and technicians whose skills were to be relied upon for brief and initial periods maintain industrial and mechanical systems whose logic defies local cognition. The Arabs are discovering that wealth and money alone do not build viable economies and that borrowed ideas and foreign know-how, though useful over the short run, are not a substitute for indigenous capabilities.

For once it is becoming also clear that they cannot buy their way out of conflicts. Fifty billion dollars given away since the start of the Iran-Iraq war did not buy them peace, placate friends nor deter enemies. Moreover, they are becoming aware that their economic prosperity depends upon the markets and needs of others; the distant oil markets of the West finance economic development, the armadas of others keep a close eye upon regional threats, and their peace and tranquility is dependent upon larger actors and powers—international and regional— taming saboteurs' ambitions and submerging their machinations. And after years of substantial expenditures on armaments and defense, they remain partially dependent upon an American defense umbrella whose use is at times costly and problematic for both the United States and the Arabs.

A way out of this will have to be worked out in the long run; however, the immediate concern of the United States should focus on how to keep open the sea lanes of the Gulf and guarantee the free flow of oil shipments—albeit without embarrassing and costly American involvement. Keeping the sea lanes open is in the interest of our Arab friends in the region as well as the European and Japanese allies. The rulers of the Gulf Cooperation Council member states have recently restated at their annual meeting in Oman that any escalation of the Iran-Iraq war threatens the stability of the region and the freedom of navigation in its waters. Paradoxically, the fortunes of Iran and Iraq and their ability to continue to wage war are also dependent upon the unrestricted flow of petroleum. A return to a state of noninterference with oil traffic thus appears to be in the interest of all. How might this be accomplished? A call for a conference on the freedeom of navigation in the Gulf, under the auspices of the International Chamber of Commerce (or other organizations)—with US encouragement—is clearly a desirable idea which might go far toward resolving the conflict. It is a more useful course of action and a far less problematic option for the Arab Gulf and the United States.

Best of all, calling for such a gathering might not necessitate the sending of American "advisors" and fighting men to the Gulf in the near future. It would not embarrass our Arab friends and will help the United States preserve the semblance of "neutrality" proclaimed earlier.

Moreover, it will not alienate further the Iranians with whom we need not close any more doors given that country's proximity to the Soviet Union.

CONSEQUENCES FOR SAUDI ARABIA

Political stability in Saudi Arabia has been unusually high for a country undergoing rapid industrialization and modernization. Yet, stability is easily maintained during a period of unprecedented budgetary surplus. The recent swing of oil revenues and the resulting tightening of budgetary expenditures may create more than economic problems for policymakers.

Politically, government cutbacks emphasize those projects which are deemed the most vital. Invariably, there will be power struggles within government leadership as to who will control the pursestrings. Officially, many Saudi observers are expressing relief over the new economic situation. It has been hailed as an opportunity to slow a spoiled society down to normal expectations and work habits. Undoubtedly, each budget proposal will cause power struggles within the power centers of Saudi society. The balancing of each of these interest groups and reducing government expenditures will prove to be quite a feat.

Socially, within Saudi Arabia's highly homogenous culture there does exist an indigenous minority—the Shi'ite Moslems. Eighty-five percent of the population are Sunni Moslems, and follow the puritanical Wahhabi sect. The Wahhabis control the wealth and power centers within the country. After the King and his cabinet, the next powerful group is the Ulema. The Ulema is a grouping of about 10,000 Islamic religious leaders (Wahhabi) throughout the country. The Ulema has a 25-man council that wields great power and influence over daily life and customs. It enforces rigid public morality through the religious law for Moslems. This strict enforcement of Wahhabi religious rules over all Saudi citizens, even the 15 percent that are Shi'ites, has helped to increase the discord between the two groups. Shi'ites, at best, hold lower-middle level management positions and are the largest recipients of much of the government's welfare spending. Usually minority groups hold little, if any, political clout, thus the parts of the budget which most affect them are not considered essential to development. When the continuing decline in oil revenues require spending cuts, subsidies applied to welfare and basic foods will probably receive the least support from the power centers. The economic disparities between these groups are compounded by the growing inflation that usually accompanies subsidy cuts.

These internal problems make the country quite vulnerable to potential external threats. The religious and political challenge from Iran's expansionary, fundamentally Shi'ite Moslem revolution is enhanced by the existence of an oppressed Shi'ite minority that is concentrated along the east coast. The threat of fundamentalism is particularly dangerous for the House of Saud, of the strict Wahhabi sect, whose special need for religious legitimacy as keepers of Islam's holiest sites in Mecca and Medina make it extremely vulnerable to Iranian accusations of corrupt or impious royal rule.

Maintaining internal stability and security from external political threats will be a problem to be dealt with as changes in the economy occur. Many analysts expect Saudi officials to institute gradual reform, rather than drastic action, to get the country's spending program under control. Slowing the disbursements of funds will continue to be the key element in cutting levels of expenditure.

Another serious drawback for Saudi Arabia is the increasing dependence upon the fluctuating world market. The industrialization projects undertaken in the name of diversification are aimed for exportation of products. With minimal internal consumption, government expenditures will be directly tied to the demand and price of each international market for the goods produced. In view of these problems faced by Saudi officials, it should be interesting to see how they will be resolved.

ENDNOTES

1. David Ottaway, "Society Tries to Cope With a New Era." *The Washington Post*, 27 November 1984.

2. "Getting to Grips with Saudi Spending," *Middle East Economic Digest*, 8 March 1985, 25.

3. Yusef A. Nimatallah, "The Economic and Fiscal Strategy of Saudi Arabia," International Monetary Fund Report, 20 March 1985, 4.

4. *Middle East Economic Digest*, 8 March 1985, 26.

5. John Roberts. "Saudi Petrochemicals: The Potential for Conflict," *Middle East Economic Digest*, 4 January 1985, 23.

6. David Ottaway. "Saudi's Create 'Wheat Belt' in the Desert," *The Washington Post*, 25 November 1984.

7. Saudi Arabia: Offset Poised for Take-Off," *Middle East Economic Digest*, 1 February 1985, 21.

8. David Ottaway, "Well Oiled Economy Starting to Sputter," *The Washington Post*, 26 November 1984.

9. *Ibid.*

10. Nimatallah, "Economic and Fiscal Strategy."

US
POLITICAL-MILITARY
RESPONSE

CHAPTER 7

RAPID DEPLOYMENT AND THE REGIONAL MILITARY CHALLENGE: THE PERSIAN GULF EQUATION

by

Maxwell Orme Johnson

When President Carter committed the United States to the use of military force to protect its vital interests in the Persian Gulf (and Southwest Asia), his decision was not without precedent. At the same time, once this commitment was made, it set into motion a series of actions which over the past six years have resulted in the formulation of a military response to a regional politico-military challenge. Simply put, while the President rattled the military saber on January 23, 1980, the fashioning of a military instrument and the forging of a credible deterrent to counter the Soviet Union in the Gulf comprise a convoluted series of events which merit detailed analysis. This chapter is a partial attempt to review and assess that series of events and to provide insight into how credible our rapid deployment capability is in meeting that regional military challenge.

In order to appreciate where we now are in planning for the use of military force as an instrument of US policy in the Persian Gulf, it is first necessary to recapitulate briefly whence we came and the wickets encountered enroute. Following disengagement from Southeast Asia, US attention shifted first to NATO and gradually to other regions of the world, specifically the Third World/Lesser Developed Countries. In early 1977, the National Security Council conducted a strategic appraisal of US policy outside NATO. This appraisal resulted in the promulgation in August 1977 of Presidential Directive (PD) 18. PD 18 recognized the need for the United States to maintain a rapid "deployment force of light divisions with strategic mobility, independent of overseas bases and logistical support, which could be used in the Middle East, Persian Gulf, Korea or elsewhere." This was essentially the birth of the Rapid Deployment Force (RDF) and the source of the generic acronym, RDF, which has come to be misused interchangeably with RDJTF and even with USCENTCOM.

The initial Marine Corps reaction was that the proposed mission of the nascent RDF best fitted the capabilities of the USMC. The Army, however, proposed the establishment of a new "Unilateral Corps" of rapidly deployable Army forces, approximately 100 thousand in all. In any case, even with forces identified—regardless of the source or service—in 1977 the United States had only a limited capability to deploy its military power to regions outside of NATO.

Ultimately, the fall of the Shah, the Yemen crisis in 1979, the seizure of the US Embassy and hostages in Iran, and the Soviet invasion of Afghanistan all converged, precipitating a need for diplomatic and military action by the United States. Thus, by late 1979, the United States faced an entirely new politico-military equation in Southwest Asia (SWA).

On October 22, 1979, reacting to the cumulative impact of several of these destabilizing crises, the Secretary of Defense directed the Joint Chiefs of Staff to establish a CONUS-based Joint Task Force which would have operational planning, training, and exercise responsibility for rapid deployment forces worldwide, with initial focus on SWA. In response, on November 1, 1979, the JCS established the Rapid Deployment Joint Task Force (RDJTF) as a separate subordinate element of US Readiness Command at MacDill AFB, Florida.

The new command received a reservoir of forces for planning—forces which had been identified by the four Services as capable of rapid deployment. For the Marine Corps, these forces could be drawn from any of the three active Marine Amphibious Forces (MAF), all of which were considered rapidly deployable. The Army, identified the XVIII Airborne Corps and the 24th Infantry Division (Mechanized). The Navy identified carrier battle groups and associated supporting forces, while the Air Force contributed a number of tactical fighter wings. By March 1, 1980, the RDJTF Headquarters had been established and was fully operational.

On January 23, 1980, in direct response to the Soviet invasion of Afghanistan in late December, President Carter declared the Persian Gulf to be a region of vital US interest. While this was correctly interpreted as signaling a major shift in US strategy, it should be evident that the option of a military response as an instrument of US policy in SWA had already been on the drawing boards for a considerable period of time. In other words, the establishment of the RDJTF was not simply a knee-jerk reaction of the Pentagon in response to the promulgation of the Carter Doctrine. Simply put, the link between the invasion of Afghanistan, the Carter Doctrine and the RDJTF is tenuous at best.

Almost from the outset, there was considerable skepticism about the true capability of the RDJTF. Some may have been justified; some was not. The major focus of this criticism was on deficiencies in strategic mobility and logistic supportability—the means to move the RDJTF units to SWA in a timely manner and the means to sustain them there.

In an attempt to resolve some of these deficiencies, recognized even before the establishment of the RDJTF, the Secretary of Defense instituted the Maritime Prepositioning Ships (MPS) Program in late 1979 as part of the Five Year Defense Plan. However, as an interim measure, the Near Term Prepositioning Ships (NTPS) Program was established in February 1980. The NTPS Flotilla, later called simply the NTPF, was assembled to carry the equipment and supplies to SWA for the 12,500-man 7th Marine Amphibious Brigade (7th MAB). These ships, with the equipment and supplies embarked, were on station at Diego Garcia in the Indian Ocean by June 1980.

Our earliest SWA strategy, which has not changed significantly in the intervening six years, was labeled the Zagros Mountains strategy. It called for the 7th MAB to be airlifted to SWA by planes of the Military Airlift Command. The MAB would debark at an airfield contiguous to a benign port in the crisis area, or would follow a forcible entry amphibious operation to secure the port and airfield, where the Marines could then marry up with their equipment carried aboard the NTPF ships. The Marines would be followed by Army units capable of sustained combat operations ashore. These Army units would deploy to and take up defensive positions in the Zagros Mountains in Iran as a counter to the Soviet invasion of Iran. The MPS Program, which has become operational during the past year, eventually will be comprised of

Figure 1.

Area of Concern for US Rapid Deployment Forces in Southwest Asia

SOURCE: Adapted by Congressional Budget Office from U.S. Department of Defense Annual Report FY82.

13 ships carrying three MABs of equipment to support commitment of Marine forces on a global basis. There is, of course, still a serious shortfall of strategic airlift, as will be seen below.

The change in administration brought a reappraisal of the role and mission of the RDJTF. The major change that came from this reappraisal was the designation of the RDJTF as a unified command— the US Central Command (USCENTCOM). The objective of

138

USCENTCOM, in the words of President Reagan, is to develop "with our friends and allies a joint policy to deter the Soviets and their surrogates from further expansion and, if necessary, defend against it."

USCENTCOM Headquarters is authorized over 900 officers and men; it has operational planning responsibility for all of SWA, the Middle East (less Israel, Syria and Lebanon), and the Horn of Africa (Figure 1). While the basic force list has not changed significantly, there has been a perceptible shift in emphasis to allow for the logistical realities to become a major factor in strategic planning for SWA (Figure 2). Operational plans have been continually refined to better reflect US capabilities to intervene in either an intraregional conflict or in a conflict with the Soviets. In other words, the use of military force as an instrument of US policy in this region is now more closely tied to reality and to our actual capabilities. The principal objectives of US policy remain fixed: to deter Soviet expansion and to ensure Western access to Persian Gulf oil.

Figure 2
Combat Forces Available to USCENTCOM

Army	Air Force
1 Airborne Division	7 Tactical Fighter Wings[b]
1 Airmobile/Air Assault Division	2 Strategic Bomber Squadrons[c]
1 Mechanized Infantry Division	
1 Light Infantry Division	**Navy**
1 Air Cavalry Brigade	3 Carrier Battle Groups
	1 Surface Action Group
Marine Corps	5 Maritime Patrol Air Squadrons
1 ⅓ Marine Amhibious Forces[a]	

[a] A Marine Amphibious Force Typically Consists of a Reinforced Marine Division and a Marine Aircraft Wing (Containing Roughly Three Times as Many Tactical Fighter/Attack Aircraft as an Air Force TFW).

[b] Includes Support Forces, Does Not Include 3 ½ TFWs Available as Attrition Fillers.

[c] These Bombers and Associated Reconnaissance, Command and Control, and Refueling Aircraft Make Up the Air Force's Strategic Projection Force.

Source: Annual Report to Congress FY 1985.

THE REGIONAL CHALLENGE

The North-South dimension of this area is about the same as the distance between Tehran and London, Its land is half again as large as the United States. The air line of communication from the East Coast of the US to the Persian Gulf is at least 7,000 miles long/a 15 hour trip on an air-refueled, non-stop C-5 aircraft. The sea line of communication through the Suez Canal to the Persian Gulf is over 8,000 miles long, and the route around the Cape of Good Hope is 12,000 miles long, almost half the circumference of the Earth.

The Persian Gulf region is characterized by isolated surface lines of communication and limited terminals for air and sea movement. Although the road networks and, in some areas, railroads have replaced the traditional camel as the dominant surface mode of transportation, the entire area has just two-thirds of the paved road mileage found in the state of Florida. The many modern air terminals being built in this area, however, reemphasize the region's ancient role as a crossroads of commerce.

The terrain of the Persian Gulf region, although generally arid, is diverse. The rugged Zagros Mountains of Iran contrast with the arid plains of the Horn of Africa. The Nile River Valley, with its dense population and urban centers, differs vastly from the uninhabited Empty Quarter of the Arabian Peninsula. Climatic extremes range from intense cold in the region's mountains to 130 degree Fahrenheit temperatures on the desert floor. Sandstorms wreak havoc on man and machine and availability of water is a constant problem.

US CENTRAL COMMAND: MISSION AND ORGANIZATION

USCENTCOM's principal mission is deterrence; its strategy is based on helping friendly nations defend themselves. This is done by formulating appropriate military contingency plans, conducting combined exercises, administering security assistance training programs, encouraging regional cooperation, and providing political and economic support. If, in spite of US efforts, a friendly country is threatened by either the Soviet Union or a regional power, USCENTCOM is prepared—when tasked by the Joint Chiefs of Staff—to initially but rapidly provide a carefully tailored package of noncombatant forces consisting of AWACS, tankers, reconnaissance aircraft, logistical support and advisors, or any combination thereof. This clear signal of US earnest has a successful track record of deterring actual regional aggression during the past six years. However, USCENTCOM is also prepared to deploy combat forces when directed by the National Command Authority. In addition to duties directly related to deterrence, USCENTCOM has collateral duties in noncombatant evacuation and disaster relief and must be prepared to carry out any other activities assigned by the JCS.

The USCENTCOM Headquarters at MacDill Air Force Base is organized into six major staff directorates, as well as into special staff agencies, all of which respond to the Commander-in-Chief (USCINCCENT). Additionally, on December 31, 1983, USCENTCOM established a forward headquarters element (FHE) afloat, collocated with the Commander, Middle East Force in the Persian Gulf. The FHE afloat assists USCINCCENT in carrying out his responsibilities throughout the region. It also can act as the nucleus for the rapid transition to establishment of a regional command headquarters during an actual contingency.

The fighting and support forces of USCENTCOM are contributed by all four military Services. The Commander, US Army Forces Central Command (COMUSARCENT), is the Third Army Commander at Ft. McPherson, Georgia. Through COMUSARCENT, USCINCCENT exercises operational command of the American troops of the Multinational Force and Observers (MFO) on the Sinai Peninsula. Commander, US Central Command Air Forces (COMUSCENTAF), the 9th Air Force Commander at Shaw AFB, South Carolina, controls the ELF-ONE AWACS and tanker assets at Riyadh that support Saudi Arabian air defense. Commander, US Naval Forces Central Command (COMUSNAVCENT), at Pearl Harbor, Hawaii, is the Naval component commander responsible for the five surface combatants of the Mideast Force in the Persian Gulf. This force has been operating in the region since 1949 and is an ever present token of US earnest in the security of the Gulf.

As the Army component of USCENTCOM, the Third Army has overall responsibility for planning the ground operations of USCENTCOM's Army units. These units include the XVIII Airborne Corps, 24th Infantry Division (Mechanized), 6th Combat Brigade (AIRCAV), and the 7th Infantry Division (Light). The combat and support actions of units assigned for theater operations will be under the direct control of COMUSARCENT. The fighting units available for planning are heavy on mobility and firepower. These airborne, air assault, and mechanized units are capable of deploying to the Persian Gulf region rapidly with formidable combat power. Combat support and combat service support forces deploy at the same time to provide sustainment for the combat units.

USCENTAF units provide a wide range of capabilities for combat in the Persian Gulf region. Tactical Air Command planes provide battlefield air superiority and defense, close air support, electronic combat, aerial reconnaissance, interdiction bombing, and airborne command and control capability with F-4s, F-15s, F-16s, A-7s, A10s, F-111s, EC-130, and E-3A aircraft. In all, seven tactical fighter wings are allocated to USCENTAF for contingency planning. Strategic airlift is provided by Military Airlift Command C-5 and C-141 aircraft, as well as the Civil Reserve Air Fleet (CRAF). Intratheater airlift of forces is accomplished by C-130 tactical airlift squadrons; combat air rescue, also

141

provided by MAC, is accomplished with HC-130, HH-3 and HH-53 aircraft.

The Strategic Projection Force, provided by the Strategic Air Command, is also tasked to support USCENTCOM theater operations. This force includes B-52H bombers for conventional weapons delivery, as well as various support (aerial refueling) aircraft. The penetration ability and extended range of the B-52H gives USCENTCOM forces a significant capability for deep interdiction missions.

The US Navy or Naval forces available for planning include the Middle East Force Surface Action Group made up of cruisers, destroyers, and frigates, three aircraft carrier battle groups (CVBGs), which, in addition to the aircraft carriers, include surface and subsurface combatants, supply and support ships, and various types of aircraft, and three amphibious ready groups (ARGs), with a mix of helicopter platforms and assault ships. Finally, five squadrons of maritime patrol aircraft are available to support USCINCCENT contingency plans.

Marine forces designated for planning consist of Headquarters I Marine Amphibious Force (I MAF) at Camp Pendleton, California, plus the 12,500 men of the 7th MAB, at Twenty-Nine Palms, California. As discussed earlier, the 7th MAB is a mobility intense organization which has its principal items of equipment—less its helicopters and fixed wing aircraft—in storage aboard the MPS ships at Diego Garcia in the Indian Ocean. On order, the 7th MAB can be deployed by air to join its prepositioned equipment at a port in the USCENTCOM area of responsibility. The rapid mobility of the 7th MAB and ready availability of its prepositioned equipment can provide USCENTCOM a significant combat force in the Persian Gulf region in less than 10 days, with the remaining 40,000 men of I MAF arriving within 30 days.

The remaining force designated for USCENTCOM planning is the Special Operations Command Central. This command is made up of various specialized units, including Army Rangers and Special Forces, Air Force Special Operations Squadrons, and a Navy Special Warfare Group (SEALS). This component is a significant force multiplier because of its clandestine skills, particularly in organizing regional irregular forces against Soviet units.

USCENTCOM is a unique military command because if called upon to employ military forces, USCINCCENT must deploy not only the bulk of the combat units to do the job, but also the required support equipment, supplies and communications network. The 7,000 mile air route to the Persian Gulf region requires at least 15 flight hours by C-5 from the US East Coast. The 12,000 mile sea route around the Cape involves an average 31-day transit for current cargo ships. Sealift improvements such as MPS and SL-7s (discussed below) will brighten this picture in the near future, but the great distance between North American bases and the USCENTCOM area of responsibility continues to be a major obstacle.

To help cope with the distances, political sensitivities, and lack of military infrastructure in the area, USCENTCOM forces use an "over the horizon" projection concept. As a matter of national policy, they will be sent only after being invited, and they will leave immediately after completing their mission. It goes without saying that the United States has no territorial or colonial aspirations in the Persian Gulf region.

As originally stated by President Carter, and reaffirmed by President Reagan on September 1, 1982, our nation's security interests are inseparably tied to those of friendly governments in the Persian Gulf region. Thus, a tertiary objective of US policy is to support the existing friendly rulers in the region. With the establishment of USCENTCOM, all nations in this region now have only one US command to deal with for the full range of security issues. The security assistance program, which includes the foreign military sales program, continues to develop new indigenous capabilities in the region, particularly among the Gulf Cooperation Council members.

To develop USCENTCOM's ability to project and sustain forces, several combined training exercises have been conducted in the USCENTCOM area of responsibility. These exercises have focused on field training and communications. Field training exercises such as BRIGHT STAR sharpen skills in ground maneuver, air defense, amphibious assault, and special unit operations in concert with friendly forces. Communications exercises have given USCENTCOM the opportunity to develop the systems and procedures needed to coordinate effectively its limited forces over the vast expanse of the region.

Additionally, these exercises polish our expertise in joint/combined operational procedures and they test host nation response to a temporary US presence. The USCENTCOM exercise program for the next four years includes CONUS and overseas communications exercises; CONUS and overseas field training exercises in the GALLANT EAGLE, BRIGHT STAR, and SHADOW HAWK series; overseas unconventional warfare exercises; and other JCS and USCINCCENT exercises as appropriate.

STRATEGIC MOBILITY, LOGISTIC SUPPORT AND ACCESS CONSTRAINTS

USCENTCOM is the only unified command not headquartered in its area of responsibility, and consequently, it faces unique challenges. In addition to the traditional tasks of deploying and employing a fighting force, this command must overcome significant mobility and logistic support obstacles. The largest hurdles presently faced are strategic lift availability, sustainment of forces, provision of timely and accurate intelligence information to decision makers, and establishment of a reliable communications network.

The problem of strategic lift availability is not new. It has faced all US forces for some time. USCENTCOM, however, has a more critical need for increased lift due to limited access to bases in the region, the extraordinary distances involved in reaching its area of responsibility, and the time critical requirement for credible forces once the decision has been made to deploy. It should be noted that a sizable amount of USCENTCOM airlift is dependent upon the Civil Reserve Air Fleet (CRAF).

To help relieve our nation's airlift availability shortfall, three airlift enhancement programs have been instituted. These programs will continue to improve our airlift capacity in the future.

The C-141 conversion program has increased the length of the air frame approximately 23 feet. This modification allows the C-141 to carry 13 cargo pallets vice 10. Now that all aircraft have been converted, the cubic volume which can be lifted by the C-141 fleet has been increased by approximately 90 C-141 aircraft equivalents. An inflight refueling capability has also been added for greater range.

The C-5A service life extension program is underway, strengthening the aircraft wings. Each month one to two aircraft enter modification, and all 77 are scheduled to be completed by 1987. This improvement will extend the C-5 service life well into the 21st century.

Procurement of the KC-10 aircraft provides an inflight refueling system that significantly improves the overall capability of the SAC tanker fleet. The KC-10 can air-refuel Air Force, Navy, and Marine aircraft, and the upper deck is available for cargo and passengers. Twenty-one of these versatile tankers are currently operational and are used worldwide to support military activities.

These programs, plus the procurement of 50 C-5B and 39 additional KC-10 aircraft, will double this nation's cargo airlift capacity by 1989.

Procurement of the C-17 aircraft will significantly enhance our capabilities by providing the flexibility of initial strategic lift to airfields in the Persian Gulf region that today can only be served by C-130 aircraft. The C-17 can also carry outsized cargo, including the M-1 tank, a capability not possessed by the C-130. Yet even with these current airlift enhancement programs, USCENTCOM would have a significant airlift shortfall in the event of a *global* conflict.

Another strategic lift challenge facing USCENTCOM is sealift. Current sealift enhancement programs provide phased increases in movement capability. The purchase of eight SL-7 containerships capable of 33 knot speeds reduces transit times to the Persian Gulf region by 25 percent compared to current shipping. While awaiting reconfiguration as fast-loading roll-on/roll-off (RO-RO) ships, the SL-7s have been placed under the Commander, Military Sealift Command in a reduced operating status, but are available for use in a crisis. Once the SL-7s are all converted to RO/RO ships, the reduced loading, transit, and unloading times should enable USCENTCOM to better realize its sealift objective.

For ports with limited capabilities for cargo handling, a concept termed LOTS—"logistics over the shore"—is employed. This involves the unloading of Army and Air Force supplies from ships at anchor and transporting the cargo ashore by lighter craft. Much of the resupply of ARCENT and CENTAF units is planned through the LOTS concept.

Sustaining forces deployed to the Persian Gulf region presents another major challenge. Neither forces nor supplies are available in the region to the degree that they are in Western Europe or in Korea. Consequently, USCENTCOM relies on a concept termed "maritime prepositioning." In order to reduce long-haul air and sea lift requirements, supplies and equipment have been prepositioned aboard NTPF and MPS ships in the USCENTCOM area of responsibility, not just to support Marines, but also Army and Air Force. The airlift savings associated with this prepositioning are significant. For example, the total ammunition tonnage aboard the NTPF and MPS ships would require roughly 2,450 C-141 sorties if airlifted from the East Coast to the Persian Gulf region. Further, for every 60,000 short tons of supplies and equipment prepositioned within 1,000 air miles of the objective, about 100 C-141 sorties per day can be freed for an entire month for other essential duties. This will allow USCENTCOM to reduce force closure times greatly and simultaneously enhance sustainability.

In the area of intelligence, critical challenges exist in war planning and war fighting abilities. In fact, the key to a successful response by USCINCCENT to a regional contingency is an early decision by the National Command Authority based on intelligence warning indicators. Accordingly, once the NCA decision to commit USCINCCENT is made, a larger, more detailed data base of intelligence information is needed to plan effectively for combat operations in the area. A significant redirection of resources is required to provide sufficient collection and analysis of intelligence data. To support his war fighting needs in the Gulf region, USCINCCENT needs the capability to rapidly collect, process, and distribute information. The improvements required include enhanced all-weather and night collection sensors and the next generation of deployable equipment for processing and transmitting data to the user level.

Yet another challenge facing USCENTCOM is the development of a robust communications system with the capacity to support the deployed headquarters and the flexibility to accommodate a wide range of contingency options. The specific obstacles include a sometimes harsh environment covering a vast area, the lack of sufficient equipment assets, and reliance on the heavily tasked, Joint Communications Support Element (JCSE). Planners at USCENTCOM are striving hard to resolve these issues. Detailed information on additional equipment requirements has been provided to Pentagon planners, and Congress has provided some additional resources to help the JCSE meet its many commitments. Nonetheless, more is required to meet effectively the unique communications requirements of USCENTCOM.

The significance of the shortfalls in strategic mobility and logistic support can be best understood in the context of the limited access to regional military facilities available to USCINCCENT. Although over $500 million have been spent during the past five years on upgrading certain military facilities in Oman, Kenya, Somalia, and Egypt, USCINCCENT has no iron-clad guarantees that he will be able to use these facilities when there is a real crisis in the region. Even though there exist formal agreements concluded during early 1980, because of political sensitivities among Gulf leaders there is less contingency planning reliance on the availability of these facilities than there was two or three years ago. This development argues for an even more comprehensive maritime prepositioning program.

In summary, USCENTCOM has the capability to project military force in support of US policy in the Persian Gulf region and to build upon the US presence already in the area to deter Soviet aggression. USCENTCOM can respond quickly to direct the rapid introduction of Army, Air Force, Navy and Marine forces to execute contingency plans when needed. USCINCCENT remains ready to act at any time to deter the Soviets in the Persian Gulf region.

CONCLUSION

US strategy for the defense of the Persian Gulf against the Soviets has been variously characterized as a "trip wire deterrent" and as a "paper tiger." The Zagros Mountain Strategy has received more than a fair amount of criticism. One respected analyst of SWA regional security affairs has even suggested that a limited series of Soviet moves into the region would pose serious problems for the United States, implying that

USCINCCENT might not be able to execute his mission in an actual contingency against Soviet forces.

This is particularly true if the Iranians were to resist the introduction of US forces, even after a Soviet invasion of Iran. In my view, these criticisms miss the point. The creation of the RDJTF may well have followed Sun Tzu's dictum regarding the use of drums and banners to deceive the enemy as to one's military capabilities (or lack thereof). What is perhaps key to any serious study of the planned use of military force in the Persian Gulf region is that a focused planning process, undertaken by a well-staffed unified command, has produced a limited capability to project and employ US force in the region. While there are logistic support and strategic mobility constraints, USCINCCENT has an increasingly credible deterrent force with which to execute US policy in this volatile region.

CHAPTER 8

ASSISTANCE TO THE PERSIAN GULF REGION

by

Michael W. S. Ryan

Close US relations with countries in the area will play a crucial role in whatever military or political strategy the United States pursues in Southwest Asia. Strong security assistance relationships, therefore, are necessary to the achievement of US national political-military objectives in the region. Security Assistance, however, is one of the least understood foreign assistance programs.

US Foreign Military Sales currently fall into two major separate channels: cash sales and sales supported by US financing, whether credit or grant. Both types of sales cases are governed by the Arms Export and Control Act of 1976 (AECA), as amended by further acts of Congress, while financed sales are also governed by the Foreign Assistance Act of 1961 (FAA).

The basic security assistance components of the foreign military sales programs were authorized by the Foreign Assistance Act (FAA). Like the

AECA, the FAA is amended periodically in Authorization Acts. These components include Foreign Military Sales Credits (FMSCR) (currently offered at market rates and a floating concessional rate that is one half of the current Treasury rate but not less than 5 percent); the Military Assistance Program (MAP) (currently a grant program for economically distressed countries); and International Military Education and Training Program (IMET), which makes grants available to eligible countries for training foreign military students chiefly in the United States. Another program associated with security assistance, but not military in nature, is the Economic Support Fund (ESF), which is allocated by the State Department and administered by the Agency for International Development (AID).[1]

Discussion of the security assistance process is meaningless, though, without understanding the context of US objectives. Such a discussion is necessary because the pursuit of political-military objectives by the sale of defense articles and services sets the United States apart from other Western suppliers. The Soviet Union also uses military assistance to achieve political-military objectives that are often opposed to US interests. In contrast to the United States, the Soviet Union often increases arms supply in a region adding to the peril of moderate regional nations.

The Soviet Union, of course, views revolutionary change as a good in itself; and in regions where nations favor strong economic and military relations with the United States, the stability of those nations and those regions represent, from the Soviet view, the success of US objectives. To oppose these objectives, the Soviet Union has historically promoted greatly expanded military force structures, especially in volatile regions such as the Middle East. Large deliveries of Soviet weapon systems in a short period of time, with no cautions about end-use, have given countries a sense of false confidence that war could achieve their goals. A security assistance relationship with the United States, as I shall demonstrate presently, has a different character. Nations know the restraints under which they receive defense material from the United States. They are not given the same sense of false confidence, because defense articles are always delivered with full explanations concerning the limitations under which they may be employed. Also, the United States stresses deterrence and war avoidance during the prolonged dialogue attendant upon the security assistance relationship. In many instances, the United States, using diplomatic channels, simultaneously urges negotiations or other bilateral discussions between potential belligerents.

In the Middle East/Southwest Asia region, US objectives over the past four decades can be stated simply: 1) to assure the security of Israel and other regional friends; 2) to assure the flow of trade, especially oil; 3) to block or reverse Soviet inroads into the region; and 4) to enhance regional stability and thus reduce the carnage to which this volatile region has been so often subjected.

US security assistance is designed to support these objectives. Unfortunately, a rich mythology concerning US security assistance and arms sales in general, which is reflected in the press, in academia, and in widespread conventional wisdom, tends to obscure the nature of these programs as instruments of US foreign policy and national security policy.[2] This chapter discusses the evolution of security assistance, its structure in terms of the governmental agencies that guide and implement it and in terms of the actual program contents, its regional implications, and, finally, some questions that have been raised about its applicability to Southwest Asia. First, however, it is instructive to examine some of the major myths concerning security assistance and arms sales.

MYTHS HELD BY THE PUBLIC

Traditional US isolationism has apparently contributed to the general tendency to view security assistance to foreign governments as a potentially dangerous entanglement. In a 1982 poll, 78 percent of all those queried indicated that they felt that "giving military aid to other countries" involved the United States too much in the affairs of those countries.[3] The question distinguished between the provision of arms and equipment and the use of American troops—clearly, only the provision of arms and services was included in the question. One often hears that the provision of security assistance causes arms races, causes or contributes to local conflicts, or bolsters repressive regimes. If these suspicions were not bad enough, security assistance also suffers from the general view that, like all foreign aid, it is a "give-away program" that sends American dollars overseas and probably costs American jobs at home.

An additional set of myths is held among a large minority that is concerned that security assistance is related in a zero-sum fashion to economic development. This view holds that the United States should feed the world instead of arming it. A slightly more refined version of this view argues that the provision of arms to Third World countries overloads these countries with debt and thus detracts from much needed development. Ironically, the seemingly incompatible myths that the Pentagon promotes and directs arms sales; and that security assistance and arms sales, nevertheless, do not add to the US defense posture are held by many people (although 71 percent believe that US security assistance programs do help the national security of recipient nations).[4]

Americans in general pay scant attention to US security assistance programs. Special interest groups, however, pay close attention to particular aspects of the program and articulate their views forcefully and often skillfully, sometimes in public and more often on Capitol Hill. When the public hears debate about security assistance, it is generally in connection with highly controversial cases and is almost always narrowly focused. In this atmosphere of generally held myth punctuated by narrowly focused and highly political argument, American public opinion is often ill-served and vulnerable to the persuasion of the few forceful voices that advocate a particular view.

MYTHS HELD BY CONGRESS

Security assistance programs have the unfortunate fate to command a high degree of attention in Congress while receiving low priority. In general, Congress adopts the current mythology held by the public. Thus, an overt vote for security assistance is often viewed as unhealthy, especially around election time. Liberals feel that their credentials may be tarnished by a vote for military assistance; conservatives often do not want to be perceived as voting for foreign aid, i.e. "give-away" programs. The exceptions to this rule of unpopularity, currently, are Israel, which has long had a special status, and Egypt, which received a special status with Israel because of its participation in the Camp David process; and to a lesser degree those countries that have granted basing rights or access to facilities for the US Armed Forces.

Critics of security assistance programs on both the left and the right tend to expect too much from them. Liberals expect the administration to be able to reform foreign governments according to American ideals, while conservatives often expect the United States to receive precise *quid pro quos* in return for security assistance or the granting of arms sales, whether the *quids* be base rights, favorable votes in the United Nations, or some other military or political desiderata. These expectations are represented by the familiar themes: what has country "X" done for the United States lately and how has country "Y" moved toward the reforms deemed necessary by congressional debate and comment? In the Middle East/Southwest Asia region, the *quids* for security assistance and arms sales are well defined: 1) how has the country advanced the peace process with Israel; and, 2) how has the country contributed to regional military requirements of US forces, however these may be conceived. These are matters that will be addressed presently, but first let us examine how administrations tend to view these myths in light of the consistent goals of security assistance.

MYTHS: A CONTRARY VIEW

Those whose work deals with security assistance on a daily basis tend to have views contrary to the myths discussed above. Contrary to the myths held by the public all administrations in the postwar period have viewed security assistance as a national mission rather than as a dangerous entanglement. Philosophically, different presidents have viewed these programs as more or less essential to both foreign policy and national security policy. The requirements of the law and exigencies of the real world soon obliterate philosophical distinctions, however, by forcing an administration to make tactics conform to the facts of international politics and conflicts. All the presidents of the modern period have found security assistance a valuable tool in international relations, whether it was a tool that was initially recognized or not.

FMS AGREEMENTS FY1975-FY1985
CONSTANT FY1975 DOLLARS

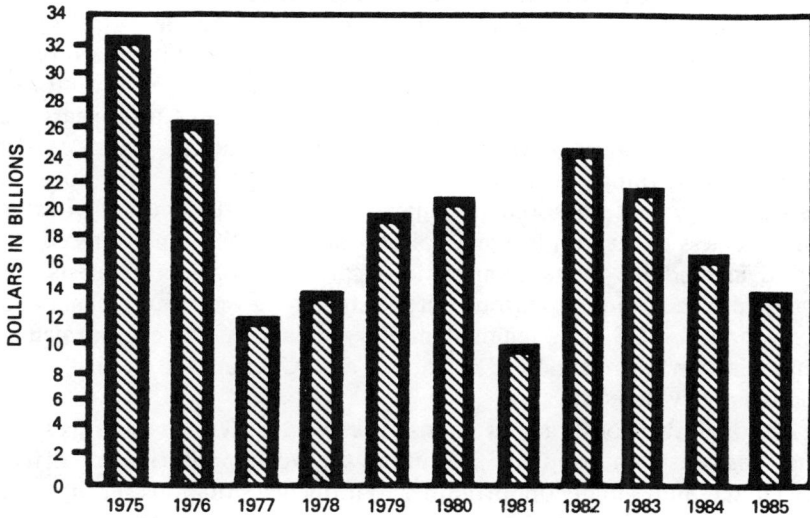

FISCAL YEAR

Figure 1

As a recent example, President Carter's and President Reagan's initially enunciated views of security assistance as a policy instrument show a sharp contrast. For Carter, arms sales were to be an "exceptional" foreign policy instrument, while, for Reagan, security

153

assistance was to be an "essential" foreign policy tool. The contrast in these views is not reflected in the US share of global sales or to the Third World as an isolated entity. If one averages the dollar values of arms sales during the Carter years (1977-80), the United States sold 29 percent of all the arms transferred to the Third World, while if one averages the Reagan years of 1981-84, the United States commanded only 25 percent of the same market and the current trend appears to be down.[5] The Carter and Reagan approaches, while differing in theory, turned out little different in volume of sales because security assistance is governed strictly by the Foreign Assistance and Arms Control Export Acts, which discourage governmental promotion of sales and tend to put the Executive Branch in a reactive posture, waiting for countries to request the sale of arms or defense services.

Dollar values are very bad indicators of the amount of arms sold. The United States knows what it spends or takes in, but calculations of other countries' sales in dollars are difficult and the results dubious. In addition, US arms seem quite expensive while Eastern Bloc arms seem relatively cheap. A dollar goes a lot further in the East than in the West and the United States sells full packages including spares and training, while the Eastern Bloc countries are much less forthcoming with these items. Furthermore, there are clear reasons why our arms sales are declining, among which are the effects of the recent world recession and the fact that many Third World armed forces filled up their inventories during the 1970s and early 1980s. On the other hand, the Carter years are high in part because of the sales that grew out of the Camp David process—something very few Americans, regardless of political persuasion, would question. But that is my point: the amount of arms sales has less to do with internal politics than with the conditions of the world around us. All administrations carefully consider requests for arms sales according to various criteria, including the requirements and restrictions of US law, regional military balances, US commitments, humanitarian and economic concerns, and US national security and foreign policy concerns.

Although the world market imposes its own restrictions on arms sales and thus resists philosophical definition, the world political scene offers the United States many opportunities to influence situations through the judicious use of security assistance. We will discuss the limits of influence as they apply to the Southwest Asia region later. In general, however, contrary to public and congressional mythology, the United States cannot "buy," or even "rent" countries through the provision of arms any more than it can with economic aid. Nations, even small or weak ones, obey national imperatives as interpreted by their leaders. These nations, particularly those with a colonial legacy, jealously preserve their sovereignty in the face of overt foreign pressure in even seemingly small matters and are more adamant when matters concern their own national interests. Foreign pressure brought to bear contrary to perceived national imperatives is almost always counterproductive, sometimes immediately, more often in the longer run. Strangely, the benefits the United States has obtained from countries have most often been freely given by those countries, growing out of a close relationship and mutual interest, not out of unilateral demands by the US. Such demands made by a superpower are always seen as heavy-handed by the smaller power. On the other hand, benefits freely given are not resented.

Despite the universality of the other public myth that security assistance is a "giveaway," security assistance programs, with few exceptions, put money directly into the American economy. The "Buy American" policy means that roughly 375,000 jobs are supported by security assistance programs. Sales financed by US funds are only part of the picture, averaging about $4.4 billion over the past five years, while sales deliveries during the same period averaged about $10.7 billion. The proceeds of both financed and unfinanced sales are spent in the United States with very few exceptions.

There is also another side to the constellation of myths concerning the negative effects of US security assistance on the economies of developing nations. The US Government does not add appreciably to Third World debt with its security assistance programs. Individual countries, notably Egypt and Israel, are the exceptions to this rule, but this problem has been alleviated for the future by the conversion of the programs of these two countries to all forgiven credits, a grant aid equivalent.

The "feed the world instead of arm it" sentiment, which sounds laudable, actually is rarely a choice. Famine does not generally occur in countries which have US security assistance programs. World food production is rising everywhere except in African drought regions and the Soviet Union. Where famine does occur, in fact, food relief programs have been responsive. They have been hampered only by a constellation of problems having little to do with the availability of food or funds. Much of the problem is a result of faulty distribution associated sometimes with inadequate transportation infrastructures, sometimes by local political problems, and often a combination of both. Eliminating all US security assistance funds by converting them into famine relief assistance will not help alleviate, much less solve, the world hunger problem. In fact, such a course might be counterproductive to the extent to which military infrastructure and communications would be hurt by the cutoff of US funding. Local militaries are often one of the key institutions for catastrophe relief. Also the US Government can often deal more effectively in humanitarian areas with governments with

155

which it has strong security assistance relationships, especially when the military is the major or crucial government institution responsible for disaster relief.

The United States must operate carefully within the parameters of its own interests and those of the recipients of security assistance. As a nation America has learned that it cannot run the world, but it can stay engaged to achieve as many of its interests as possible. By staying constantly engaged in every region where it has strategic interests, the United States helps achieve the possibility of gaining, eventually, those goals that have eluded it in the short or medium term and may preserve the benefits that it has already achieved.

Polls have shown that Executive Branch and congressional leaders consistently recognize the worth of these programs in achieving foreign policy and national security goals.[6] If one concentrates in the area of Southwest Asia and the adjacent lands of the Middle East, the subject of this chapter, one can discover the US security assistance programs and the relations that have grown out of them have had a stabilizing role in the region.

EXECUTIVE BRANCH ROLES AND FUNCTIONS

Because security assistance is a vital part of overall US foreign policy, the Department of State has overall authority over individual programs—what countries are eligible for security assistance and/or arms sales and how much (if any) US financing these countries receive. Because security assistance is largely a military program and part of the US national security policy, the Secretary of Defense plays a powerful role in determining the availability of equipment and levels of military technology releasable for sale to foreign countries. The Defense Department also implements the programs. The State Department generally places great weight on Department of Defense (DoD) recommendations. Overall policy, of course, is set by the appointed officials of the current administration.[7]

Within DOD, the focal point for security assistance is the Defense Security Assistance Agency (DSAA). The Director of DSAA, reporting directly to the Under Secretary of Defense for Policy, takes regional policy direction from the Assistant Secretary of Defense for International Security Affairs (ISA) and the Assistant Secretary of Defense for International Security Policy (ISP) for the regions under their purview. Policy for the Middle East/Southwest Asia region in DoD is set by the ASD/ISA. Matters with implications for US military strategy and defense also involve a consideration of the coordinated position of the Joint Chiefs of Staff.

Achieving and maintaining appropriate levels of support is crucial for the continuity of regional military programs. Addressing Congressional concerns is key for achieving these levels. Justifying the programs to Congress can be such a time-consuming and demanding challenge requiring extensive staffing that it may tend to dominate a great deal of the sparse high level attention devoted to security assistance. Financial support, however, is only part of the picture. Another crucial part of security assistance as a national defense program is cash sales, especially in the Persian Gulf region.

NATURE AND CONTENT OF PROGRAMS IN PERSIAN GULF

Cash sales form an important component of the worldwide FMS picture, but in the Persian Gulf region they assume an increased importance. If we consider the FY 1950 to FY 1984 period, Saudi Arabia alone accounted for approximately 22 percent of worldwide FMS agreements. The Kingdom dwarfs the other states on the Arabian peninsula as a purchaser of US defense articles and services, just as it dwarfs them in geographic size, wealth, and known oil reserves.

WORLDWIDE FMS AGREEMENTS
FY1982-1986 (EST)

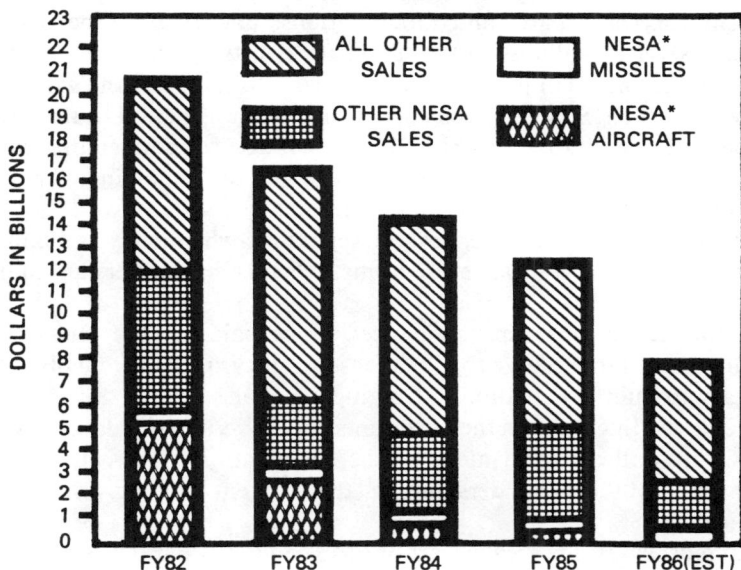

*NEAR EAST/SOUTH ASIA

Figure 2

157

For the sake of comparison, let us consider another large FMS customer, Israel. (Israel purchases US defense articles and services almost exclusively with US financing.) Israel, by contrast, during the same period accounted for about 6 percent of the world total FMS agreements. If one were to stop the analysis at this point, one would distort reality by implying that Saudi Arabia has been arming itself with American weapons at more than three times the rate of Israel. In this case, the dollar figures are misleading, as one can see by examining the contents of these purchases.

In the case of Israel, 65 percent of its FMS deliveries from the United States during the period FY 1950 to FY 1985 were for the purchase of weapon systems and ammunition; 8 percent was for support equipment; 20 percent went for spare parts and modifications; and, the remaining 7 percent went for support services such as construction and equipment repair. Israel, moreover, with its greater knowledge and skill at operating in the US defense market, signed an average of approximately $1.2 billion in commercial contracts directly with US companies over the last five years.

Saudi Arabia traditionally has had quite different defense requirements, involving much more work on infrastructure. Saudi Arabia spent about 14 percent during the same period for the delivery of weapon systems and ammunition, 7 percent for support equipment, 7 percent for spare parts and modifications, and fully 72 percent for support services—almost $13.6 billion for construction alone. To place these two countries in perspective, it is useful to note that the worldwide totals for US FMS sales agreements during the same period translate into 39 percent for weapon systems, 15 percent for support equipment 18 percent for spare parts and modifications, and the remaining 29 percent for support services including construction.

One must always consider several key points when analyzing military sales and security assistance programs, whether in the Persian Gulf or elsewhere.

- FMS agreements can be financed or be paid in cash, but each is equally important relative to US defense strategy since they involve close military-to-military relations. Commercial sales, while all licensed, confer less influence than the government-to-government sales of FMS.

- Citing dollar figures alone in the examination of so-called "arms transfers" obscures understanding the content of individual FMS relationships.

- In most cases, the greater part of FMS country programs is composed of various types of support services and equipment other than weapon systems and ammunition. The point here is not that these other articles and services are innocent from the point of lethality—they are the stuff which makes the combat component of the defense structure work—but the composition of US security assistance programs generally does not create arms races in the conventional sense of the phrase, i.e., accumulations of basic weapons platforms and vehicles like aircraft and tanks. In fact armed forces that rely on the United States as a security partner generally experience shrinking inventories relative to those that choose the USSR for their chief supplier. The US emphasis on military infrastructure, logistics, maintenance, and training grows out of US policy to promote self-sufficiency and independence.

- Congress is involved in both US financing of FMS agreements and with cash sales agreements by virtue of its role in the Foreign Assistance Act (FAA) and the Arms Export Control Act (AECA) and amendments, though there are different procedures for each.

THE ROLE OF CONGRESS

Congress plays a powerful role in US security assistance by providing funding, writing laws and attaching restrictive language to funding. Most terms and conditions of letters of offer and acceptance (LOA), the basic contract document of FMS agreements, come directly from language in the AECA. According to this act, the Executive Branch must notify Congress of all sales over $50 million and all sales of major defense equipment (MDE) over $14 million.[7] This notification (referred to as a 36b notification after the section of the law requiring it) is formally forwarded to the Congress 30 days before the LOA is offered in the case of a Persian Gulf country. (Most Third World nations are under the same regulation.) DSAA also forwards an informal classified notice 20 days before the formal notice. Thus, Congress has 50 days to consider a major sale.

The vast majority of cases go through the congressional notification process without comment. The Middle East/Persian Gulf region, however, is an area containing more than its share of controversy. We cited the four objectives held by all US presidents since World War II. One of these objectives, the security of Israel, has presented the Executive Branch with a seemingly intractable series of problems for security assistance relations with other nations in the region. Generally, both Houses of Congress have been extremely chary of the sales of lethal technology to Arab nations that have not signed a formal peace treaty with Israel. In recent times, "contributions to the Peace Process" serves as a measure to determine whether or not Arab nations may be sold additional military hardware.

The first test with Congress for the Reagan Administration's security assistance policy for the Persian Gulf came in 1981, when the president proposed to sell AWACS to Saudi Arabia. (Planning for the sale had begun under the Carter Administration.) Opposition to the sale centered on the presumed threats that the sophisticated surveillance aircraft would pose to Israel, but critics also made use of the argument that sensitive military technology could be compromised by the sale, an argument with some currency just after the overthrow of the Shah of Iran. I.M. Destler in an article devoted to the strategy employed to achieve congressional approval for the sale points to key paradoxes in the framing of strategic arguments for arms sales or security assistance to the Persian Gulf region:

> When it finally engaged substantively, the administration was cogent in rebutting the critics' strongest arguments— AWACS is not a serious threat to Israel; the threat to US technology was limited and manageable. It was less effective in making a positive strategic case, in part because such a case rested on hopes for close US-Saudi military cooperation that could not be explicitly stated.[8]

The first paradox cited by Destler seems to persist despite individual administration victories in Congress like the AWACS sale: what the administration sees as concurrently defending regional friends and US interests and objectives, Congress often sees as introducing additional threats to Israel. In this case, the Executive Branch is generally forced into negative argumentation to demonstrate that planned security assistance programs to Arab countries do not constitute a threat to Israel.

The second paradox, even more difficult than the first, also remains in full force: the Executive Branch proposes security assistance and arms sales to the Congress in a strategic context, but is hampered from making strategic arguments publicly because of regional sensitivity and/or because strategic cooperation is often viewed in this region as a step that countries should take only when the contingencies arise. They do not like to enter into joint arrangements or even commit to later joint cooperation beforehand out of fear of promoting the very threat that is planned against. The regional argument against a joint security pact takes the form that "we recognize the need for your help and would even welcome your direct involvement in certain circumstances, but those circumstances do not yet exist." References to such vague understandings, no matter how realistic, do not make for strong justifications for military programs in the eyes of many members of Congress. Moreover, the prolonged political debates that take place in the United States tend to strain relations with the country and make achievements in strategic cooperation even more remote.

PARADOX NUMBER 1: DEFENSE OF US INTERESTS IN THE GULF THREATENS ISRAEL

The first paradox figured prominently in the spring of 1985 when Congress first began hearing rumors of planned security assistance packages for Saudi Arabia and Jordan. Congress signalled the Executive Branch that it would oppose further major arms sales to these two countries because they were still in a technical state of war with Israel and, therefore, arms sold to them might be used against Israel in a future Arab-Israeli War. To this traditional argument was added an economic argument. Sales to the opponents of Israel, so this argument goes, cause Israel to increase its own defense expenditures, which in turn lays an extra burden either on the Israelis themselves or on the American taxpayers for increased military grant aid to Israel to offset the added threat. Responding to these political signals the administration announced on January 30th that it would suspend further 36b notifications of Middle East arms sales to Congress pending completion of an interagency policy review, which was soon dubbed the Middle East Arms Transfer Study (MEATS). This classified study was completed in late summer and its conclusions were briefed to various committees in both houses of Congress.[9]

The administration argued that US security assistance should be seen in its proper context as a complement to US national strategy to meet the challenges at lower levels of conflict—to prevent or contain minor conflicts to avoid escalation to a major conflict on a global scale. The Middle East/Southwest Asia was presented as a nexus of regional strategies, i.e., not only the locus of Southwest Asia military strategy and the diplomatic strategy to achieve peace between Israel and its neighbors, but also an important factor in NATO strategy because of the geographic proximity of those strategies and their associated sea and air lines of communications. Because of the interconnectedness of today's world, it could also be argued that any major contingency in the Middle East/Southwest Asia region would have unpredictable political and economic, if not military, consequences for NATO.

To address the paradox that defense of other regional friends threatens the security of Israel, the administration argued from history. No Arab nation primarily supplied by the United States had ever initiated a war with a neighbor. (Even non-Arab Iran under Khomeini did not turn its US-supplied arsenal to offensive use; it was attacked by Iraq, a nation primarily supplied by the Soviet Union with increasing European involvement.) Conversely, nations primarily supplied by the Soviet Union have contributed to instability. In fact, until the 1973 war, the Arab-Israeli wars were fought primarily without US arms. Significantly, the entrance of the United States into the security assistance arena after 1973 ushered in a period that has witnessed no major Arab-Israeli wars despite continuing tensions and air skirmishes between Syria and Israel and the Israeli invasions of Lebanon.

This general record is no accident, but rather comes from the way US security assistance programs are structured in contradistinction to the ways other nations treat arms sales. All US sales carry restrictions, written in US law, as part of the LOA. In general, the United States sells military equipment only for self-defense and prohibits third party access or retransfer without US approval.

More important than these legal restrictions is the very nature of US security assistance programs. The United States considers security assistance in the context of an overall political relationship. Sales are, therefore, primarily made on the basis of political-military objectives rather than on a purely economic basis. The only other country that closely resembles us in this aspect is the Soviet Union. Although it will sell simply to obtain hard currency, it does not have to sell against its political-military interests. Many other suppliers sell arms for economic reasons or because they need to sell to support their own defense industries. The United States develops a relationship to enhance its influence in the recipient nation. Influence is always difficult to define, but the key characteristics of the influence that US security assistance programs deliver have become fairly clear over the years.

The influence garnered from successful security assistance programs is instrumental not substantive, i.e., it does not in itself offer a substantive argument for another country to do or refrain from doing anything in the absence of additional arguments. It is an influence which allows other influences to function. In the first place, security assistance programs provide access—a foot in the door—to a country's leadership, since military programs of necessity tend to be of high priority and centralized in most countries. In most countries in the world, moreover, and certainly in the Middle East/Southwest Asia, the central leadership has a military background. Security assistance provides influence that functions incrementally over time. Other influences come to bear simultaneously. For a long time, for example, the economic relationship based on the oil industry was central in US-Saudi relations; it still is, though it has receded temporarily somewhat during the present oil glut. In other countries, other factors may be paramount, not the least of which is America's status as a superpower and the foremost economic force in the world. Security assistance programs provide the access that allows this influence to function in a practical fashion in many countries. Security assistance is not an influence that long survives threats to withhold or withdraw. It is not an influence that can convince leaders to do things that are not popular among their own political constituencies. The influence allows dialogue about mutual interests; it does not allow the United States to dictate. The United States can use its influence to urge restraint, especially when leaders realize they may lose the support they would need to prosecute a contemplated war. In short, it is a human influence built over years, not a sheer power influence.

Another characteristic of US security assistance that sets it apart from other nations is that American military assistance is tailored both to local threats and country capabilities to man, operate, and support the equipment the United States sells. Because of this approach, recipients of US arms generally develop smaller inventories than those countries that receive Soviet arms. The result of this policy is especially clear in the Middle East/Southwest Asia region. We have indicated that dollar figures are a poor measure of the impact of security assistance. The United States has been traditionally cautious about the transfers of large numbers of weapons to the Middle East. The Soviet Union, on the other hand, doubled the major equipment of frontline Arab states—chiefly Egypt and Iraq—from 1967 to 1973, a course of action that contributed to the events leading up to the 1973 war.

ARMS SALES TO MIDDLE EAST

1973-1980　　　　　　　　　　　　　**1981-1984**

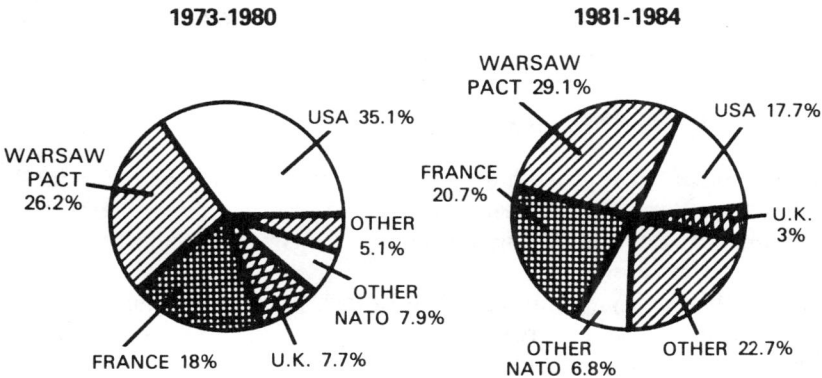

Figure 3

Prior to this period, the US involvement in the region had been relatively small. President Eisenhower even endorsed an arms embargo in 1957, the so-called Tripartite Agreement, which included Great Britain and France. Clearly this attempted embargo did not prevent an arms buildup in the region. After 1967 the United States began to supply Israel

163

in significant amounts to replace European support that had essentially disappeared because of the threat of Arab boycotts. Even during this crucial period, however, US sales of tanks to Israel were only 23 percent of Soviet tank sales to the Arab confrontation states; in artillery the US provided 6 percent of the Soviet total; in fighter aircraft 31 percent; in armored personnel carriers 50 percent; and surface to air launchers—9 percent.[10]

This trend, significant when seen in the context of Israel's security, is even more apparent when sales to the region in general are considered. In Richard Grimmet's most recent study for the Congressional Research Service on conventional arms transfers to the Third World, one can see the relative paucity of US arms sales to the Near East and South Asia when compared to the Soviet Union on an equipment basis.[11] Grimmet's study reveals that in the period 1977 to 1984 the ratio of Soviet tank and self-propelled gun deliveries to this region versus American-made deliveries was approximately 1.8 to 1; in artillery the ratio was 4.4 to 1; in supersonic combat aircraft, 3.9 to 1; in subsonic combat aircraft, 5 to 1; and in helicopters more than 51 to 1. US deliveries exceeded Soviet deliveries slightly in only one of the categories in Grimmet's study, noncombat aircraft, in which deliveries of US to Soviet produced systems was 1.04 to 1. It is fair to say that the numbers on the US side may have been higher if the Shah of Iran had not fallen to a regime hostile to the United States, but the actual record is undeniable and even with continued sales to Iran, US numbers would have been lower than those for the USSR. On the other side of the ledger, the Soviet Union, at first, held up deliveries to Iraq at the beginning of the Iran-Iraq War as it tried to garner favor with Iran, presumably considered the greater strategic prize. Failing in that endeavor, "the second greatest satan" resumed its supply relationship with Iraq. (The United States has consistently resisted supplying either side of this carnage and has urged others to refrain as well.)

In the final analysis, the Executive Branch has argued that US arms have never constituted a threat against Israel. In light of the record of US security assistance to Arab states and the powerful force these relationships have been in enhancing moderation and regional stability, it is highly unlikely that US arms in Arab hands would be used against Israel. The argument that one bullet used against the leader of a moderate state could change an Arab nation's willingness to use American weapons against Israel has no validity when one reflects on the nature and stability of the governments involved, as Egypt showed after the tragic assassination of Anwar Sadat.

Even the setback for America in non-Arab Iran, among other things, revealed that it is not easy or perhaps even possible to turn US arms to effective offensive use after a government turns radical. Iran mounted a successful defense, but did not mount a successful offensive until more than five years after the withdrawal of US security assistance. There are several reasons for this shortcoming. The United States stopped supporting Iranian weapon systems and largely prevented others from filling the gap. More importantly, the new Iranian government could not trust the professional armed forces that were tainted by association with the Americans. Today, the new Iranian armed forces are considerably changed. They are much less "modern" now than the old structure and certainly no longer American in any meaningful sense. There is a general rule that the Iranian case falls under. Because of the intense way the United States works with countries and the close military-to-military relationship that such a relationship inevitably entails, no radical regime would be able to trust its military leadership, many of whom would have been trained in the United States and are often sympathetic to the United States at the human, if not policy, level. If the resultant purges did not destroy American-provided military prowess, the inevitable US embargo of spare parts and resultant attrition to US systems would finish the job. The greatest Iranian success has been in the marshes of the mouth of the Shatt-al-Arab, a low technology operation.

On the other hand, as history has shown, arms provided by others in greater quantities to the region and without the restraints inherent in arms supplied by the United States would put other nations, and especially Israel, at greater risk. Some may argue that US arms are better than those supplied by others and thus Israel is safer if its neighbors receive only non-US weapons, no matter how great their numbers. The clear policy of the United States to preserve the Israeli qualitative advantage over its possible adversaries, however, makes this argument ring false as well. In fact other suppliers are often ready to introduce higher levels of technology into the region than US policy will allow for its own sales.

PARADOX NUMBER 2: US SECURITY ASSISTANCE TO THE GULF IS JUSTIFIED BY STRATEGIC CONCERNS, BUT NO DETAILED PUBLIC JUSTIFICATION IS MADE POSSIBLE ON THIS BASIS.

One of the principal features in US decisions about providing security assistance, whether it be for financing or arms sales, is that countries that provide the United States with bases or facilities access receive more favorable consideration. The history of the US global defense effort is the history of collective security pacts. The success of the NATO model colors all US thinking about security assistance both in the Executive

Branch and in Congress. Collective security pacts in the Southwest Asia region, however, have never taken root. The NATO model will never work in this region because these nations vigorously resist the formal structure and the open commitment that an alliance or security pact implies.

Regional states are hypersensitive about recognition of their sovereignty. The region, moreover, is beset by local tensions, local concerns, local rivalries, and fissiparous foreign and security policies. Furthermore, all moderate nations of the Gulf, to varying degrees, fear that overt identification with the United States in a defense role will prompt the Soviet Union to attempt to offset the US position either directly or, as is more likely, through others. The general attitude tends to be characterized by the notion that many countries would prefer to be close to the United States, but do not want that to engender superpower rivalry or radical agitation; they do want the United States to help them meet their local threats through security assistance and to have US forces prepared (but not prepositioned) to respond directly to threats that these nations could not handle alone, should such threats materialize. In the meantime, the moderate states of the Arabian Peninsula hope to rely on the Gulf Cooperation Council (GCC), a collective economic and security pact on the regional level, to coordinate response to local threats.

Bilateral relationships allow the United States to plan with countries to achieve security. From the US point of view this planning facilitates a number of mutually supportive objectives such as access to regional military leaders, greater likelihood of achieving interoperability with local forces, and the enhancement of deterrence both by the symbolism of US commitment to the defense of friends and by the actual defense capability the US helps them obtain.

When the United States achieves a level of cooperation that permits joint exercises, its readiness to meet contingencies is enhanced. Although no Persian Gulf nation would choose to build facilities with the massive capacity needed for major US operations, when the United States helps countries build viable military infrastructures, it not only increases the efficiency and viability of their own military forces, it enhances the capability of US forces to assist these countries in a contingency. This benefit is reflected in the 1986 Congressional Presentation Document for example, as it states about Saudi Arabia: "Saudi Arabia, equipped with systems interoperable with those used by US forces and trained by United States military advisors, would be in a position to facilitate deployment of US forces to the region in time of crisis were the kingdom to request such assistance."[12]

SECURITY ASSISTANCE: CONTRIBUTIONS TO OBJECTIVES AND STRATEGY

We began this chapter by referring to the four basic US objectives for the Middle East/Southwest Asia. We have also demonstrated how concern for the security of Israel affects all US security assistance programs in the Persian Gulf and adjacent areas, although these programs, in the traditional view of the Executive Branch, have no negative impact on Israeli security because of the intentions and concerns of the recipient states, because of the way in which these programs are structured, and because of the close relations with the United States they engender. The mythology surrounding security assistance tends to obscure the actual nature of these programs and how they relate to US objectives and regional strategy. We need to show how security assistance serves US objectives in the Persian Gulf region.

US regional objectives depend on higher order objectives, which are often lost in debate about the levels of technology, the nature of the threat, and implications of arms sales to Southwest Asian nations to the security of Israel. The prime US national security objective, which should never be lost sight of, is stated simply in the 1986 Annual Report to the Congress of the Secretary of Defense: "to preserve the United States as a free nation at peace, with its fundamental institutions and values intact."[13]

From this basic goal several other objectives flow, some of which have a direct bearing on how the US uses security assistance. For the sake of brevity these other objectives may be reduced to the following: to safeguard the United States, its allies, and friends from aggression and coercion; to achieve and maintain conventional deterrence or to ensure favorable results of conflicts should they arise; to ensure the free flow of trade, to obtain and preserve numerous close cooperative relationships to achieve/preserve stability, especially in areas of US strategic interests; to develop and preserve democracy and democratic values; and, to limit or balance Soviet military or political gains and, if possible, to roll them back.

In simple terms, the United States needs to ensure the flow of oil from the Persian Gulf region, to keep the Soviets out politically and militarily, and to help its moderate friends maintain their independence, not merely against the military threats but also against associated political coercion from radical neighbors and ultimately from the Soviet Union. Recalling the prime US national security objective, the United States needs to achieve these objectives in keeping with its own values by respecting the sovereignty of others. The United States should avoid a large or obtrusive presence that could be internally destabilizing to the nations that it assists. In keeping with its own values the United States needs to deter regional conflicts in a way that minimizes the carnage and abrogation of human rights and democratic values attendant upon war in this volatile area.

The Secretary of Defense's Annual Report to the Congress summarizes US defense strategy in terms that are in keeping with these principles.

—to deter aggression and coercion against the United States and its allies, friends, and vital interests.
—Should deterrence fail, to seek the earliest termination of the conflict on terms favorable to the United States, our allies, and our national security objectives, while seeking to limit the scope and intensity of the conflict.[14]

US security assistance is designed to meet the requirements of this general formulation of US strategy by working with the armed forces of regional friends on a bilateral or multilateral basis, seeking for them the defense posture that not only preserves their own sovereignty and political independence, but also safeguards US interests as a natural consequence.

Fortunately, US security assistance is framed to accommodate both US objectives and basic strategy, while being responsive to the desires of the nations the United States assists. Unfortunately, the myths that we discussed earlier tend to obscure this elegantly simple fact. In addition, the discussion of strategy in the popular sense usually amounts to a distracting discussion of tactics and the logistical aspects of moving the forces considered necessary to meet imagined contingencies. Real world contingencies, however, are seldom as imagined with the result that the only viable strategy is one that is flexible at its core. No mechanistic view of military operations is likely to add to an understanding of the requirements of the most likely military contingencies in the Persian Gulf, contingencies, in fact, which have occurred on a regular basis throughout the history of the region and thus are no mystery to the nations of the Gulf themselves.

The best strategy for the Persian Gulf area follows from providing local forces with the necessary military capabilities to deter aggressors. This course of action increases the likelihood that the local situation may be contained without the insertion of US forces. The actual composition of the US-provided program can only be determined after complete discussion with the country. Such a discussion grows either out of a prior relationship or out of a response to an immediate conflict situation. Unlike other countries, the US Government does not market arms as a matter of policy. This policy means that the United States helps only those who are prepared to help themselves in the first instance.

A discussion of a major arms buy or an extensive security assistance program can only grow out of a close political relationship. Thus the military relationship grows naturally out of shared objectives. It is ironic that the popular conception of military cooperation with countries outside of Europe assumes a simple quid pro quo relationship of military cooperation as a concession for US hardware, although the reality is often the reverse. Countries often offer the United States a measure of cooperation without a specific request from the United States. Most countries also want to have the same equipment as that in the US inventory, so a large measure of interoperability happens naturally. It is then up to the United States to make sure that interoperability and supportability remains in effect by informing countries of the availability of equipment upgrades when these become available to US forces.

Facilities access is perhaps the most difficult area because of domestic sensitivity to a foreign armed force's presence or even the suggestion that one is contemplated. In this area also, an active and successful security assistance program provides opportunities to discuss the conditions in which US forces could have access to local facilities and the mutual benefits of joint military exercises, which provide crucially important training for US and local forces in their mutual preparations for a collective response to a postulated contingency. Here again access and exercises grow out of a close relationship marked by compromise, dialogue, and US access to local military and political leadership. American emphasis on infrastructure building, training, and maintenance works toward providing self-sufficiency and independence, another facet of American security assistance that ensures that recipient countries intend to pull their own weight and not simply abdicate their defense to the United States—a course that history has shown to be disastrous. In short, close security assistance relationships in this area enhance already strong relationships and ensure that security assistance partners are better prepared to receive US help should they request it.

Individuals, not a lifeless mechanism, determine the success of a defense strategy. Only through close relationships can the United States hope to work with those individuals who make a difference in regional affairs. Hardware and tactics are nothing in comparison to human efforts and human resolve in determining the strength of mutually reinforcing strategies. Moreover, whether individual country programs have any relation to US strategic and regional objectives is determined by the discussions carried on within the framework of close political-military relations for which security assistance programs create the opportunity. Many times, such discussions take place within the framework of formal and periodic planning meetings, such as the long-standing Joint Military Commission with Jordan.

The political atmosphere within the Gulf region, as in the Middle East as a whole, dictates that US programs be based on a series of interlocking bilateral relations rather than on a multilateral basis. Thus the United States must always be sensitive to individual country needs and requirements. Insistent, public Congressional demands for particular results, no matter how well intended, tend to spoil the atmosphere and complicate US planning with the very countries that need US support and that the United States needs to achieve its objectives. Ever since Great Britain bowed out of "East of Suez," no other external power can do the job the United States does while respecting local sovereignty. The United States must stay engaged despite the difficulties or even the lack of immediate, palpable payoffs.

Finally, it is worth repeating the context in which any US strategy in this volatile region must function if it is to serve the broader objectives. The United States can help only those that can help themselves; it cannot defend those that will not defend themselves. No strategy is a good strategy that does not envision fighting alongside willing security partners. On the other hand, these nations must be allowed to defend themselves as far as is possible before any direct US involvement is contemplated. We must not let hypersensitivity about highly improbable threats to Israel obscure our traditional policy of maintaining many friends in the region to secure the full spectrum of our interests now and in the future. The loss of an opportunity to meet a legitimate defense requirement resulting in a regional friend turning to another to meet that need means the loss of a measure of interoperability and influence, now and in the future. Reliable US security assistance programs create the impression among friends and adversaries that the United States is a reliable security partner that intends to stand by its friends in a military crisis. Therefore, the United States must stay engaged in the region to help countries make the right defense choices; any other course abandons US interests in this region to chance or worse.

ENDNOTES

1. ESF, while not military assistance strictly speaking, is viewed as part of the security assistance effort. Because it is not tied to projects, like developmental aid, ESF is somewhat more flexible. In any case, there is a synergistic relationship between military and economic assistance to a country because both contribute to the security of a country—the one to build an economic infrastructure encouraging to the development of democratic institutions and the other to provide the defense shield necessary to defend that infrastructure and those institutions.

2. The identification of myths concerning security assistance is based, in part, on my experience with questions that surface during presentations before various audiences. Most of the inspiration, however, comes from conversations with Dr. Henry H. Gaffney and John T. Tyler.

3. Ernest Graves and Steven A. Hildreth, eds., *US Security Assistance: The Political Process* (Lexington: Lexington Books, 1985): 139.

4. *Ibid.*, 137.

5. Richard F. Grimmet, *Trends in Conventional Arms Transfers to the Third World by Major Supplier*, 1977-1984, Congressional Research Service of the Library of Congress, Unclassified Report No. 85-86 F, 1985, Table 2. Of course, it could be argued that the total volume of sales is larger during the 1981-84 period, but the sales trend for the United States is down as shown in Charts 1 and 2 of Grimmet's study.

6. Cf. Graves and Hildreth, 83-89. While all administrations have recognized the value of security assistance programs and have shown consistency in citing strategic rationales, the relative importance of these programs in overall foreign policy has waxed and waned.

7. See *Security Assistance Management Manual*, DoD 5105.38-M, Apr 1984.

8. I. M. Destler, "Reagan and Congress—Lessons of 1981," *The Washington Quarterly* 5 (Spring 1982): 9.

9. An unclassified version of the conclusions of the Middle East Arms Transfer Study was briefed to the Senate Foreign Relations Subcommittee on the Near East and South Asia on 27 September 1985. The references in this chapter are to the Defense Department's Briefing entitled: "Administration Study: Security Assistance for the Middle East—Persian Gulf."

10. *Ibid.*

11. Grimmet, Table 5.

12. US Department of State, *Congressional Presentation: Security Assistance Programs FY 86*, 166.

13. US Department of Defense, *Report of the Secretary of Defense Caspar W. Weinberger to the Congress*, 4 February 1985, 25.

14. *Ibid.*, 25.

CHAPTER 9

THE LIMITS OF ACCESS:
PROJECTING US FORCES TO THE PERSIAN GULF

by

Thomas L. McNaugher

The year 1979 was a traumatic one for US policy toward the oil rich Persian Gulf region. At its beginning, Iran's revolution utterly destroyed the foundations of US security policy in the area, which had relied heavily on the Shah, his forces, and his bases. At year's end, the Soviet invasion of Afghanistan brought Soviet forces closer to the Strait of Hormuz and raised serious concern for a similar military move into Iran. In January 1980, President Carter enunciated his doctrine and in March established the Rapid Deployment Joint Task Force (RDJTF — now US Central Command, or USCENTCOM). The United States also launched a series of diplomatic missions aimed at acquiring bases in the region to support the projection of US forces.

The search for bases has been only partly successful. Of the Gulf oil states, only Oman has granted USCENTCOM access to its bases, and this only under vaguely defined conditions that amount to giving Sultan Qabus control of the issue on a case-by-case basis.[1] Outside the Gulf proper, Egypt, Kenya, and Somalia have given USCENTCOM similar conditional access rights to both airfields and port facilities. And in 1982, Turkey, normally associated with NATO and strategically placed on the Soviet Union's southern flank, agreed to allow the United States to improve several air bases in its eastern territory for use in so-called NATO contingencies.[2] Although US military construction has proceeded in all of these countries, USCENTCOM's planners are understandably frustrated by the lack of certain access anywhere in the region save tiny Diego Garcia, some 2500 miles south of the Strait of Hormuz. And they are especially vexed by the lack of formal access, even on a conditional basis, to bases in the Gulf itself.

Members of Congress have also become frustrated by these uncertainties, and are angered when local rulers seek to extract maximum benefit from US construction projects without specifying conditions of access in return. The Gulf region seems neither as important (witness the oil glut) nor as vulnerable (witness the Soviet quagmire in Afghanistan) as it did in 1980, so patience is wearing thin. Funding for construction of facilities at Egypt's Ras Banas has been especially controversial on Capitol Hill, as President Mubarak has insisted on the use of Egyptian construction workers as forcefully as he has resisted putting the conditions for US access in writing. And during the FY 1985 budget hearings, construction funding for Omani bases was reduced because revetments and storage facilities on runways gave the look of permanence to the US presence in that country.[3] USCENTCOM's access to future funding for base construction is now as uncertain as its access to the bases themselves.

Of all the components the United States must assemble in order to project force to Southwest Asia, basing is the one over which it has the least control. How big a problem is this? Are there ways to lessen the uncertainties involved? In fact, although there is no way to eliminate the uncertainties that surround access, the situation may not be as bad as it seems.

HOW MUCH BASING DO WE NEED?

The need for basing is partly a function of the distances that must be covered in a particular area of operations. Naval aircraft and Marines conceivably could cover coastal areas with little or no basing, for example, but little more than that. It is also a function of the kind of forces that are projected into an area. Light forces need less support, hence less elaborate basing, than heavy forces. Military advisors or small special forces teams might even live off the land with supplies dropped in to them.

More importantly, however, the need for basing is a function of strategy, both grand and military. Grand strategy ranks interests and risks, and places military instrument in the context of the various forms of power by which US interests can be protected. It also determines whose forces—those of allies, the United States, or local states — are most appropriate. Military strategy chooses military objectives and determines how force can be used to achieve relevant political ends. There is no pressing need for access, for example, if we determine that local or allied forces can handle the military burdens of the region, or if we assume that America's nuclear arsenal is alone sufficient to deter Soviet or local military action. Beyond this, the need for basing access depends on what US forces are expected to do in specific cases.

Meeting Soviet Forces in the Gulf

What US forces alone can do in the Gulf region is deal with Soviet military power. This power is lodged principally in the numerous, mostly low-grade divisions the Soviets deploy along their border with Iran, the smaller number of combat-ready, albeit preoccupied units, currently in Afghanistan, and the hundreds of tactical aircraft that support these ground units. There has been considerable debate over Moscow's designs on Iran and Pakistan, not to mention how the United States should respond to Soviet military action around the Gulf. Few deny, however, that the responsibility for doing something falls squarely on the United States as the other superpower.

How much basing access plays in the US response is, however, a matter of debate. Escalatory strategies that envision the deployment of little more than a trip-wire force to the Gulf itself clearly demand less regional basing than strategies that call for a major conventional force engagement with Soviet troops. Some have criticized current planning, for example, precisely because it assumes the availability of bases. These critics would tailor strategy and force posture partly to avoid the planning and diplomatic headaches associated with the search for access.[4]

Putting aside questions about the strategic wisdom of escalatory strategies, however, few who favor such strategies seem to have thought through the logistics of inserting even a small force into, say, Iran. Suppose, for example, that all goes well: The Iranians welcome US help and US forces achieve their purpose. As the Soviet military machine grinds to a halt, Moscow calls for discussions of Iran's future. How is the US trip-wire force to be supplied as the talks proceed? At the very least, aircraft would have to drop supplies to these soldiers, suggesting at a minimum the need for transshipment points near the Gulf for transferring cargoes from strategic air and sea lift to C-130s. Are the C130s to fly without air cover? Indeed, is the force itself to be inserted beyond the range of US tactical air power? If not, then tactical aircraft will have to be based somewhere in the region. Finally, depending upon the size of the force and the duration of its stay in Iran, an overland resupply system may have to be constructed, producing a commensurate increase in the need for access to nearby bases. Ironically, escalatory strategies avoid the need for bases only when they fail, and the United States surrenders or launches a general war.

More ambitious strategies for dealing with the Soviets call for more elaborate basing schemes. The underlying problem is the sheer size of the region and the intratheater distances that must be covered to reach relevant military objectives. Putting aside the small number of B-52s available to USCENTCOM for conventional air interdiction, long-range tactical strike aircraft—notably Air Force F-111s and Navy A-6Es—have radii of less than 1000 miles even when refueled after takeoff. This makes it difficult to interdict Soviet forces advancing into northern Iran—the most common interdiction scenario—from carriers alone, since northern Iran lies well over 1000 miles from the Gulf of Oman. The need to enlarge the interdiction campaign by deploying strike aircraft of shorter range—A-7s, F-4s, and A-10s, for example—only makes the need for land bases more compelling.

This basing need not be close to the Gulf, wherein lie the rulers most skittish about access. Bases in eastern Turkey are well placed to handle the Iranian scenario, and the 1982 agreement has enabled the United States to begin improving several bases in this area. This does not alleviate the problem of access, however. Turkish fears of provoking the Soviet Union make them reluctant to discuss the circumstances under which the United States would have access to these bases; at the moment (and probably until a genuine crisis forces the issue) the Turks will only say that these are for NATO purposes, thus calming fears among Gulf oil states that eastern Turkey might be used to launch an attack on their oil fields.

The question remains as to the survivability of bases located so close to the Soviet border. Thus there are strong incentives to find alternatives or additional bases. Israel is an obvious and willing candidate. That only F-111s and A-6Es can make the run from Israel to northern Iran, however, limits Israel's potential contribution to US military action. This leaves the Gulf states, access to whose bases would offer the additional advantage of complicating Soviet air defenses by bringing US air strikes in from the south as well as from the west. At the very least, the United States might explore possibilities for access in these states as a means of diversifying its basing portfolio.

176

In contrast to the requirements for air interdiction, the insertion of ground forces in all but nominal amounts demands basing in the Gulf itself. Moreover, the insertion of even small forces into Iran would be virtually impossible without the acquiescence or active support of the Iranians themselves. The need for elaborate basing varies, to be sure, with how many troops are required and where they must be deployed. Generally, however, any long term stay in Iran is likely to require access to transshipment points on both sides of the Gulf. The issue is less whether bases will be required—they will—but how many and how elaborate a set of arrangements will they have to support.

Regional and Local Violence

Violence at the regional and local levels around the Gulf is more likely than Soviet military action in the region, but also likely to be of considerably lesser magnitude. Even the Iran-Iraq war has not seen violence on the scale that a major Soviet invasion of Iran would likely entail. Meanwhile, the most likely violence—terrorism—is small indeed, though it is hardly less worrisome for that. At the same time, there are plausible alternatives to the use of US military power. Finally, threats close to home are also threats local rulers are most interested in curbing, and hence those for which granting access to basing may be seen as appropriate and necessary.[5] While basing requirements can be identified for regional and local scenarios, they are not as elaborate as those demanded by Soviet action, nor are they likely to be as difficult to fill.

The Iran-Iraq War has provided the world with a vivid example of the potential scope of regional violence. Both countries have used some of the world's most sophisticated weapons, albeit not to their full potential. Both sides have deployed forces far larger than any of their neighbors around the Gulf could hope to deploy. If defending the oil-rich peninsular sheikhdoms is in the US interest—and this has certainly been the thrust of enunciated US policy—this would appear to be no easy task.

The obvious disparities in force levels between the sheikhdoms and their nearest neighbors are mitigated considerably, however, both by geographic buffers that surround the Peninsula and by natural political and military balances that focus military energy on others. If Iran were to defeat Iraq, for example, its forces would still presumably have to defend themselves against residual elements of Iraq's army and handle internal political threats. Iran might well find a substantial part of its force posture tied down and only a small portion free to attack Kuwait and Saudi Arabia. Much the same argument could be applied to Iraq. Thus, although a breach in the balance between Iran and Iraq would raise the most serious military threat imaginable to the peninsular states, it would not be as large as the overall force posture either of these countries deployed at the time.

It would still be larger than the forces either the peninsular states themselves or their regional friends could muster successfully, making this the most likely threat the United States itself might be called upon to handle. Still, the requirements for basing would hardly be as great as those associated with most Soviet scenarios. Air power could prove to be very effective against massed forces of either power, but since the action would occur near the northern end of the Gulf rather than still further north in Iran, it would be relatively easier to bring a variety of aircraft to bear. Proximity to the northern end of the Gulf would make the deployment of ground forces no more difficult, and perhaps a good deal easier, in this case in comparison to meeting Soviet forces in Iran.

Internal violence among US friends in the region is not only smaller in scale than the conventional force actions described above but indeed of an entirely different character. This violence ranges from insurgency— witness Oman's Dhofar rebellion from 1965 to 1975—to terrorist violence, to coup attempts, to internal subversion. Rulers in the area see these as the most likely and serious threats around. But they are not large. Hence meeting them is less a matter of force size than the subtlety of its application. Basing requirements may be minimal or nonexistent.

Moreover, both the small size and political delicacy of internal threats encourages local rulers to handle them either on their own or with regional friends whose presence in their countries poses fewer political risks than a US presence. Jordan and Pakistan are both deeply involved in the security of the peninsular oil states, and Pakistan in particular has several thousand troops of various types in Saudi Arabia and the other peninsular states.[6] The British and French have also been of some help to these states, with Britain, in particular, carrying a large share of the extended counterinsurgency campaign in the Dhofar.

Rulers in the Gulf sheikhdoms are more likely to turn to these allies than to the United States for help in an internal crisis. Conversely, they will not ask the United States for help unless they are willing to provide basing support. Given the relatively small size of such operations, basing and logistics needs for US forces will be smaller than those required for meeting the Soviet threat. Thus Soviet scenarios are the ones that drive US basing requirements.

PURSUING THE ALTERNATIVES

With only tiny Diego Garcia at its command, and conditional access at best to bases closer to relevant military objectives, USCENTCOM has been forced to pursue the logical alternatives to stationing troops and supplies in the Gulf region. In fact, much has been done since 1980, when the RDJTF was more wish than reality. Although little of this activity relieves USCENTCOM of its need for bases, it has substantially improved the command's ability to make good use of the bases it gets, even if access is granted on short notice.

With few places at which to store equipment and supplies on land, USCENTCOM has turned to seaborne prepositioning.[7] Equipment for a US Marine Corps brigade was quickly prepositioned on ships docked at Diego Garcia in 1981 to make the so-called Near-Term Prepositioned Force (NTPF). Since then steps have been taken to preposition the equipment for an entire Marine Amphibious Force and 30 days of supplies on board depot ships at various points around the world, creating the so-called Maritime Prepositioned Fleet (MPF). One brigade of the MPF has replaced the NTPF at Diego Garcia, and the rest will be deployed within 10 days maximum sailing time from the Gulf.[8] Meanwhile, 11 depot ships loaded with supplies and spare parts for "early arriving army and air force units" have also been placed at Diego Garcia.[9] Although the content of these ships is classified, simple calculations suggest that they contain sufficient supplies to handle about four weeks of conflict. Given that slow sealift can be expected to start delivering supplies to the Gulf region in about five weeks, seaborne prepositioning has done much to relieve the strategic supply problem.

The Defense Department has also purchased more strategic lift. The Navy has leased enough SL-7 fast sealift ships to move one of USCENTCOM's heavier divisions to the Gulf in two to three weeks, depending on whether they travel through the Suez Canal or take the longer route around the Cape of Good Hope. And after much wrangling in 1980-82, the Congress allocated money for more C-5Bs. In conjunction with other lift programs already underway in 1980, notably the C-141 "stretch" program, these purchases marginally improve the country's ability to fly rapid deployment units to the Gulf. Few would argue, however, that the nation does not need still more lift.

The United States has improved, through military construction, those bases to which USCENTCOM can hope for access. Perhaps the most notable example of this is in Turkey, where several billion dollars will be spent by the end of the current decade to prepare as many as ten bases in the eastern part of the country. The United States has constructed naval repair facilities in Kenya and Somalia, and airfields have been improved in Oman and Egypt. Bunkers have also been built at airfields, but at present they are not stocked. Indeed, whether USCENTCOM will be allowed to fill the bunkers is at the heart of the current debate in the Congress, where many legislators are reluctant to leave US stocks in the hands of local rulers unwilling to specify conditions of access.

Despite the lack of formal access agreements with Saudi Arabia, arms transfers have, in effect, prepared bases there for the entry of US forces. The Saudis, for example, have purchased more spare parts, repair equipment, and munitions for their F-15s than they actually need.[10] And their bases are generally much larger and better stocked with petroleum, oil, and lubricants (POL) than are required for Saudi needs alone. Things like shelters on runways, ammunition storage facilities, and hardened port facilities will be useful to the Saudis themselves, of course, but also to USCENTCOM, should it be granted access to Saudi territory. More could be done in this area, but the Saudis are headed in the right direction.

Much of this activity amounts to putting the pieces in place for the rapid projection of US forces to the Gulf region. Although the activity has been very low key, it has produced substantial results. But these steps only help USCENTCOM to hedge against obtaining bases very late, and to support operations once bases are obtained: they are not a substitute for basing, which is essential if the pieces of the puzzle are to be assembled. In this sense USCENTCOM's pursuit of the alternatives has made basing more, not less, important.

THE LOCAL COSTS OF BASING

Americans often blame the reluctance of regional states (including Turkey) to be more forthcoming with basing arrangements on an ostrich-like refusal to see the very real threats they may confront. These countries are not so much ignoring threats, however, as balancing them. In particular, they are balancing the benefits they obtain from closer military ties to the United States with the costs such ties incur. Given their location and the regional and local political dynamics rulers in these countries confront, their sense of costs and benefits is considerably different from that of US military planners.

Turkey is a special case. It lies north of the Gulf states and has long-standing historical ties to them, ties it has sought to enhance since the 1973 oil crisis. Yet Turkey tends to consider itself a European power, is a member of the Atlantic Alliance, and sees itself primarily as protecting NATO's southern flank. Of all the NATO states, Turkey alone shares a border with the Soviet Union.

The situation inevitably makes the Turks ambivalent about building more bases, especially in the context of general concern for the Gulf rather than for NATO's flank. Because the Gulf states tend to see such bases as a starting point for a US invasion of their oil fields, the Turks worry that allowing the construction of bases clearly connected with USCENTCOM will damage their growing links to the Gulf sheikhdoms,

Iraq, and Iran. Meanwhile, the Soviets cannot be expected to accept with equanimity several new and well-stocked bases just off their southern flank, whatever their supposed role. Hence in allowing construction to proceed the Turks risk some intimidation from Moscow.

The Arab Gulf states have their own reasons for avoiding firm access commitments, and Saudi Arabia serves as both a good case in point and also the single most important Arab state, so far as projecting US forces into the Gulf is concerned. Unquestionably, Saudi ambivalence on the basing issue—and on its friendship to the United States generally—stems in large part from the nature of US ties to Israel. Dealing with Israel's chief ally is an embarrassment to them domestically, a potential liability in inter-Arab politics, and, in the extreme, a source of personal danger. The Saudis also must hedge always against the possibility that, when fully enmeshed in the complexities and dangers of Middle Eastern politics (as for example in Lebanon in 1983), US policymakers will fall back on Israel as their "only stable ally" in the region, leaving Arab friends overextended diplomatically. Most of them assume that any "secret" passed to the United States will quickly find its way to Israeli intelligence.

None of these arguments can be easily dismissed. It would be wrong, however, to assume that problems in the US-Saudi relationship would disappear with a settlement of the Palestinian issue alone, assuming that were possible. Saudi Arabia is rich but weak, while the United States is strong and prone to speak in military terms. Only in the United States, the Saudis often note, was there a debate about the wisdom of seizing Saudi oil wells in the wake of the 1973 oil price hikes. This may be partly a Saudi diplomatic ploy, but it also bears witness to an understandable fear among small powers of large and powerful "friends."

Fundamental differences between Saudi and US politics also would plague the relationship between these two countries even in the absence of the Palestinian issue or strong US-Israeli ties. US politics are open and contentious; Saudi politics are secretive and consensual. US policies are neither very subtle nor predictable; the Saudis need both, especially from a power ultimately as important as the United States. The presence of vocal supporters of Israel in the US Congress may exacerbate these problems, but it hardly causes them.

Nor, finally, are the Saudis completely blind to the Soviet threat to the region. They simply see it differently from their US counterparts. To survive, the Saudis engage in a constant balancing act that can be successful only so long as they preserve their freedom of maneuver. Closer ties to the United States by themselves threaten to restrict Riyadh's flexibility. Soviet countermoves to a growing US presence around the Gulf would probably only compound Riyadh's problem. The situation creates incentives to keep the United States at a distance whatever the status of the Palestinian issue.

These impediments to more formal links between the United States and Saudi Arabia make it unlikely that the Saudis will soon change their stance on basing. Indeed, to the extent that many of the problems such links would raise in Saudi Arabia are domestic and regional in nature, a worsening domestic or regional security situation may make the Saudis less rather than more willing to discuss access, despite a growing sense of danger in Riyadh. Only a fundamental increase in Riyadh's fear of Soviet military action would seem likely to increase the Saudis' willingness to consider closer military ties to the United States. And even in this case the Saudis might well move slowly.

Nor is it advisable for the United States to push hard for access rights. Events over the past five years suggest that Saudi Arabia's concern for internal and regional threats is well founded. US pressure for bases is likely only to compound these problems, undermining the security of a major US friend in the region. Indeed, pressure for basing access, if successful, might only drag the United States into internal conflicts in Saudi Arabia that would be better left to local or regional gendarmes. In any case, the security of Saudi Arabia is no less a pressing concern for US military planners than the need to balance Soviet power in the region. Like the Saudis, the United States must seek to balance the dangers of doing nothing with the dangers of doing too much.

Too much can be made, in any case, of formal agreements. The Saudis may refuse to sign formal access documents, but few who deal with Riyadh would argue that Saudi bases will be wholly unavailable to US forces. Most would agree, moreover, that the presence of US arms in Saudi Arabia and the Saudis' tendency to overbuy and overbuild will make those bases quite useful if access is obtained. This situation is not appreciably different from that in countries like Oman and Egypt, which sign formal documents but refuse to discuss conditions of access.[11] Ultimately, US access to any bases save Diego Garcia will be subject to veto by local rulers. Conversely, access can be granted, with or without formal documents, if and when local rulers see it as in their interest to to do.

Consistent, low-key US diplomacy that is sensitive to the security problems Gulf rulers face can lower the costs these rulers attach to their relationship to the United States, making it easier to lay the groundwork for the projection of US forces to the Gulf. Clearly, maintaining a reasonable balance in US policy between ties to Israel and ties to the Gulf while working for a politically acceptable settlement of the Palestinian issue are important paths toward this end. Yet the United States cannot avoid being strong, being Western, or developing military forces to meet what are perceived to be its own security requirements. Nor can it rewrite its constitution to suit the political sensitivities of Gulf rulers. Thus, there are likely always to be limits to the willingness of Gulf rulers to cooperate with the United States on basing. Barring a fundamental change in the security situation these rulers face, the United States is not likely to get more specific conditions of access from these rulers than it already has.

CRISIS CALCULATIONS

In any case, even the best US diplomacy will not guarantee access if it lapses into incoherence or insensitivity in the heat of a crisis. Ultimately, it is in, not before, the crisis that access decisions will be made. Although the considerations noted above will affect that decision, the actual calculations involved are likely to vary substantially with specific events.

Much will depend on the threat: different threats probably will produce very different calculations associated with calling for US help. One would expect that an overt attack by the Soviet Union, for example, would legitimize a turn to the United States. By contrast, a threat from Iran, whose anti-US rhetoric and fundamentalist ideology seem to hold some appeal to Saudi citizens, might attach substantial risks to calling on the United States. The risks might not outweigh the benefits, especially if the United States seems to be the only country with forces capable of meeting the threat. Ultimately the Saudis and their neighbors are likely to take their chances with US help if the alternative is defeat or internal collapse. But most threats are likely to pose far less stark consequences, leaving the Saudis and their immediate neighbors with some room for maneuver.

Rulers in these countries must also consider the future. They are constrained by demography and geography to sharing the Gulf region with relatively stronger neighbors. US help may come and go, the neighbors stay, and the Arab Gulf states must find ways of living with them. Even successful defense may be politically dangerous if it involves US support in a way that creates political vulnerabilities inside these countries or thoroughly antagonizes the attacker. In many cases accommodation may have considerable appeal.

Consider, for example, the tanker crisis of May-June 1984.[12] Iraqi air strikes on oil tankers approaching Iran's oil terminal at Kharg Island raised fear around the Gulf (as well as in the United States) that Iran would seek to make good on its threat to close down the Gulf if its own oil exports were jeopardized. Assistant Secretary of State Richard Murphy had visited Riyadh early in April offering, among other things, US air support, but only if the Saudis opened their bases at Dhahran and their logistics facilities to incoming US air wings. As Iraqi strikes picked up in May, Iran struck at tankers, not in the Strait of Hormuz but off Kuwait's coast and, at month's end, just off the Saudi port at Ras Tanura. The Saudis responded by shooting down an Iranian F-4 early in June, yet at the same time they seemed to signal to Iran their desire to cool the conflict, and they may even have sought to pressure Iraq to lower the tempo of its air strikes.[13] Whether as a result of Saudi pressure or for their own reasons, the Iraqis in fact ceased all strikes on tankers soon thereafter, ushering in a six-week lull in the tanker war.

We will probably never know the precise contours of Saudi decision-making during this crisis. Nonetheless, the situation highlights some of the forces that probably affected—or certainly could affect—Riyadh. In particular, it is unlikely that Saudi Arabia had any desire to engage in a major military confrontation with Iran. To be sure, Saudi Arabia's small, rather sophisticated air force could probably have handled itself rather well in such a confrontation. Yet Iran has other weapons in its arsenal. It has not, for example, unleashed the kind of bombing raids and terrorist attacks against Saudi Arabia that have occasionally rocked Kuwait. Moreover, there is the issue of Iran's rearmament, which is sure to occur, and which will slowly return Iran to its position as a superior—probably the dominant—military power in the Gulf. Thus even a Saudi victory in the air war would incur serious short- and long-term risks.

Injecting US forces into the situation would have exacerbated those risks. Would not the presence of US forces at Dhahran have legitimized Iran's criticism of the Saudi regime and its Islamic credentials, with potential consequences for internal stability in Saudi Arabia? Furthermore, to have called on US forces only to have them withdrawn, say, after a series of Shi'ite-inspired terrorist attacks had undermined America's resolve (as had occurred in Beirut only months before), would have produced the worst of all possible situations. The Saudis would have exposed themselves to all the dangers that come with close ties to—indeed, military reliance on—the United States, only to have US protection withdrawn in the heat of battle.

Under the circumstances it probably was wise for Murphy to make the US offer of support, but doubly wise for him to do so in a low-key way that left the Saudis in control. A more forceful US offer would have raised the prospect of a minor crisis in US-Saudi relations in the midst of what had already become an impending crisis among the Gulf states themselves. It would also have made it more difficult to accept US help, since the acceptance would have seemed like caving-in to US pressure.

Keeping access discussions low-key so as not to complicate the real issues is perhaps the first rule of crisis diplomacy when basing is at issue. Second rules, alas, are hard to come by, and will vary with the threat. Here the Soviet threat poses the most serious problems, since this is the most demanding in terms of access, but may also be clothed in defensive rhetoric that encourages the Saudis to accommodate. There is a pressing need for advance consultation on this issue in an effort to develop common perceptions of the threat. Does it matter, for instance, if the Soviets only take the northern portion of Iran? US strategists disagree on this question, the answer to which substantially affects the nature of US military planning. We need to get our own house in order, but more importantly we need to discuss our own strategic views with those whose bases will be critical to US strategic response.

Two additional points can be made. First, if there is a *military* premium on moving quickly to meet a Soviet advance into Iran, there is likely to be a *political* premium on moving second. In short, US action must be perceived by local rulers as defensive in nature. Second, as always, the Saudis will seek to follow the consensus, and in the case of a US-Soviet confrontation, the search for consensus partners may extend beyond the Middle East proper. The position not only of Egypt, but of the European countries as well, may affect Saudi calculations. Working closely with these states thus may ultimately have a direct effect on US force projection opportunities.

CONCLUSIONS

US military planners understandably see the basing situation in the Gulf as an impasse, one of growing importance as other elements of USCENTCOM's force posture are fleshed out. It is difficult to see how the United States can avoid the need for bases in the region if it wants to protect key interests. Yet at the present time it is equally difficult to see how it can encourage local elites to be more forthcoming on the issue. Indeed, there are good security reasons for not pushing the issue any further. All that can be said is that in this region, as in few others, the projection of US force will depend on diplomacy, both before and during crises.

There are positive aspects to this situation, however, that deserve equal time. With no large and visible presence in the region, the United States is in less danger of being sucked into internal conflict it does not fully understand and perhaps would rather avoid, nor is it liable to the kind of terrorist activity that made the small US Marine Corps position in Beirut a source of tragedy in 1983. To the extent that the US presence or more obvious ties to local friends might become a source of domestic trouble for local rulers, keeping a low profile in the area implicitly helps local friends control the more likely internal threats that worry them, quite rightly, more than a Soviet invasion. Finally, it should be clear that these states, if small and weak militarily, have taken steps to protect themselves—through diplomacy, cultivation of regional friends like Jordan and Pakistan, and carefully playing the regional balances—and that a reduced US presence probably helps them do so by maximizing their flexibility.

To the extent that these arguments are correct, then the basing problem is not one that pits the United States against unwilling Gulf friends, but rather one that pits one set of US needs against another. US military planners must plan to meet the Soviet threat. But they cannot ignore a host of local and regional threats, most of them considerably more likely than a Soviet invasion of Iran, that may also endanger US interests. Meeting the first set of threats encourages an intimate embrace of local friends in an effort to construct elaborate basing arrangements. Allowing local powers maximum flexibility to meet the second set of threats, however, demands that the United States keep its distance. Since 1980 Gulf rulers have in effect *imposed* a balance on US basing efforts that is not far from the correct one. While USCENTCOM can and should continue to plan to meet the Soviet threat, unless and until the nature of Soviet activity changes fundamentally, a more forceful effort to obtain access would only undermine one set of US interests to pursue another.

ENDNOTES

1. For a recent update on the status of Oman's bases, see "U.S. Is Said to Develop Oman As Its Major Ally in the Gulf," *The New York Times*, 25 March 1985: A-1, A-8.

2. See Metin Demirsar, "U.S. Upgrades Military Links to Turkey with Eye to Soviet Union and the Mideast," *Wall Street Journal*, 12 January 1983: 32.

3. "Washington Moves to Support Its Gulf Allies," *Middle East Economic Digest*, 1 June 1984: 21.

4. Jeffrey Record gives the rapid deployment mission to the Marine Cops in part because to "stake the success or failure of an intervention force on the momentary political whims of local regimes in the Gulf serves the security interests of neither the United States nor the Western world as a whole." *The Rapid Deployment Force and U.S. Military Intervention in the Persian Gulf* (Cambridge, MA: Institute for Foreign Policy Analysis, 1981): 64. For an escalatory strategy that also minimizes regional basing requirements, see Kenneth N. Waltz, "A Strategy for the Rapid Deployment Force," *International Security*, 5 (Spring 1981): 49-73.

5. For a more detailed assessment of the local and regional security situation and the cooperative strategy local rulers have employed to meet threats, see Thomas L. McNaugher, "Arms and Allies on the Arabian Peninsula," *Orbis* 28, (Fall 1984): 489-526.

6. On expatriates and advisors in Saudi Arabia, see especially Ghassane Salameh, "Political Power and the Saudi State," *MERIP Reports* (Middle East Research and Information Project), no. 91 (October 1980): 10. On Pakistanis in particular, see Derlet Khalid, "Pakistan's Relations with Iran and the Arab States," *Journal of South Asia and Middle Eastern Studies* 5 (Spring 1982): 20-21.

7. See Maxwell Johnson, *The Military as an Instrument of US Policy in Southwest Asia: The Rapid Deployment Joint Task Force, 1979-1982* (Boulder, CO: Westview Press, 1983): 68ff.

8. *Ibid.*

9. *Ibid.* Also see Thomas McNaugher, *Arms and Oil: US Military Strategy and the Persian Gulf* (Washington, DC: Brookings, 1985): 85ff.

10. On both seaborne prepositioning and strategic lift initiatives, see Congressional Budget Office, *Rapid Deployment Forces: Policy and Budgetary Implications*, February 1983, especially pp. 32-43.

11. See US Congress, Senate Committee on Foreign Relations, *The Proposed AWACS/F-15 Enhancement Sale to Saudi Arabia*, Staff Report (1981): 13.

12. One might add that while the United States pays for basing construction or modification in the countries with which it has access agreements, the Saudis pay for their own bases, most of which are larger and more elaborate than those benefiting from US construction.

13. For a more detailed study of the May-June crisis, see Thomas L. McNaugher, "Southwest Asia: The Crises That Never Came," in Barry M. Blechman and Edward N. Luttwak, eds., *International Security Yearbook 1984/85* (Boulder, CO: Westview Press, 1985): 144-164.

CHAPTER 10

FORCE FROM THE SEA: A MODEST PROPOSAL

by

Michael Vlahos

THE PROBLEM

The importance of the Persian Gulf region to Western security emerged clearly in 1973. The inability of the United States to safeguard Western interests there did not, however, become equally clear until late 1978. The original Arab oil embargo renewed the strategic visibility of Southwest Asia (SWA). The fall of the Shah stripped away the delicate illusion that a local surrogate might be able to replace the British presence in the Indian Ocean area. Saudi Arabia proved an insufficient substitute, and the theory of regional surrogates was, in any event, incredible.

With India a hostile neutral, with an intensifying Soviet presence in Southwest Asia advertising both Soviet intentions and proximity, and with a clutch of Arab Gulf states looking ever more cowed, direct American military underwriting was required. The so-called "Carter Doctrine" enunciated both the policy goals and putative framework of an American military-naval guarantee.

Five years later, the thrust of the military commitment remains unaltered. Its capacity to intervene effectively has increased. The course of the Iran-Iraq War has diluted two local threats to Western interests. The dependence of the West on Gulf oil has lessened.

The military issue of Southwest Asian security (the US Central Command operational theater), however, has not been solved. Although less immediate in need, and under relaxed political scrutiny, the support of Western interests in the region remains highly limited:

•The United States does not deploy ground force units to South Asia. Materiel for some (SWA)-tasked units is prepositioned in-theater.

•The only in-region base under American control is Diego Garcia which is still over 2,000 miles from the Gulf. All other points of entry and operation for arriving Allied forces depend on local permission.

•Means for inserting Western forces in SWA are limited absolutely and relatively. Airlift and sealift assets can promptly insert and sustain only small increments of force into SWA. In the context of competing claims for strategic lift (in the context of a concurrent crisis in NATO or the Western Pacific), only a minor portion would be available for SWA reinforcement.

•Soviet capability to deploy ground and tactical air forces to SWA will remain superior to Western means of response, especially in important areas bordering the Soviet state (Iran and Pakistan).[1]

This chapter focuses on the root of these limitations: the necessity of defending SWA through timely reinforcement from outside the region, 90 percent of which must come by sea. It challenges the acceptance of planned arrangements for the insertion of American forces, and it suggests an alternative to the current mix of strategic sealift and in-region prepositioning.

The first issue in the defense of SWA concerns the upper limit of force necessary to achieve security. In 1983, former Secretary of Defense Harold Brown placed this force level at two to three divisions and three to four air wings in the short term (1985), with approximately twice that level as a longer-term goal (1990). Time of insertion should not exceed three weeks.[2]

To an extent, the first goal has been met. Two to three divisions and three to four air wings can be deployed to SWA in about a month. The arrangements permit this movement, provided there are developed ports and airfields prepared to accept them, and the lift required to complete the movement is available.

190

Developed ports and airfields demand steadfast, stable local allies who can deliver forward bases. Domestic political instability or strategic realignment could alter immediately the terms of bilateral basing agreements with local regimes. A swift Soviet airborne insertion, as one example of external intervention, could abruptly abridge access to provisional forward bases.

Required lift demands a SWA crisis in isolation, without distracting tensions in NATO or the Western Pacific that might claim priority in delegation of lift assets. Any potential crisis in the Levantine, Mesopotamian, or Indian arenas that would reach an intensity requiring American ground forces would likely have reached collateral levels of tension in other theaters, tension intended perhaps to forestall timely Western reinforcement to SWA.

Both requisites also assume sufficient strategic warning of crisis and political support for ground forces insertion into SWA to achieve a timely arrival in-theater. Past crises involving a US decision to commit ground forces in imminent combat operations have not demonstrated such alacrity and confidence in commission. Grenada may be the exception, Beirut the rule.

There is a potential contradiction in US force planning for Southwest Asia contingency: designated units cannot respond to an urgent and unexpected crisis, but they can deal with a relatively leisurely problem that remains locally stable. Planning concentrates on contingencies that evolve in measured fashion, and which do not disrupt delicate architectures of reinforcement.

This chapter examines the delivery and support of forces from the sea to the USCENTCOM operational theater. A specific critique will focus on several divisible issues in plans for the deployment of US ground and tactical air forces to SWA:

•Prepositioned materiel in-region sealift
•Continental US-based sealift to SWA
•The main theater base at Diego Garcia
•Delivery of ground and tactical air units to the forward operational area (FOA)

SWA POMCUS AND SEALIFT

The Near-Term Prepositioning Force (NTPF) was established in July 1980. Originally composed of seven ships, six of which held the full combat equipment and 30 days of supply (DOS) for a Marine Amphibious Brigade (MAB), it was expanded in 1981 and 1982 by 11 depot ships. These are to supply arriving Army and Air Force units with ammunition, supplies, petroleum/oil/lubricants (POL) and medical equipment. A permanent Maritime Prepositioning Ship (MPS) squadron of five vessels will be deployed at Diego Garcia in 1986, replacing the NTPF. These purpose-built or converted MPS are virtually combatants. (See chapter by Max Johnson for more detail.) They are the contemporary equivalent of the Attack Cargo Ship (AKA) of the Second World War. They are not configured, however, to transport troops.[3]

Prepositioned materiel is deployed in-region, then, to equip a MAB of about 12,500 men and several Army and Air Force units.[4] Furthermore, the materiel is preloaded on its own sealift, and can be delivered to any developed port in the Indian Ocean area within a week. At a port facility, equipment and supplies can be off-loaded in three days. It must be emphasized, however, that this materiel must be joined with unit personnel at the point of debarkation.

CONUS SEALIFT

The MPS-MAB at Diego Garcia is predeployed in-region, and some Airborne/Airmobile or "light" units designated for USCENTCOM can be inserted completely by air. In contrast, "heavy" mechanized or armor units must be transported from CONUS in their entirety by sea. In all, 90 percent of the requirements for an American expeditionary force in SWA to the level originally set by Harold Brown would be met by sealift. In current planning for global contingency, 79 percent of all military sealift is tasked for NATO. What level of sealift would be available for a SWA-first contingency?

Apart from the 5 MPS and 12 depot ships at Diego Garcia, there will be by 1990:

Atlantic:	66 ships in the Ready Reserve Force (RRF)
	17 ships in the Military Sealift Command (MSC)
	1 Hospital Ship
	1 Aviation Maintenance Ship
	4 MPS (with equipment for one MAB)
	8 Fast Logistics Ships (TAKR) operated by MSC
Pacific:	28 in RRF
	4 MPS (one MAB)
	1 Hospital Ship
	1 Aviation Maintenance Ship
	18 MSC
Gulf Ports:	22 in RRF

These 188 modern merchant hulls have the logistic capability to sustain the United States through the duration of a medium-sized conventional war: a Vietnam or Korea, or a USCENTCOM conflict to the upper level delineated by Harold Brown. How promptly, however, could this fleet deliver?

With all of these ships available (RRF activated on Day-1 and all MSC assets available within 30 days), plus all Military Airlift Command (MAC) and Civilian Reserve Air Fleet (CRAF)-activated assets, the equivalent of three Army divisions, a Marine Amphibious Force (MAF) and three tactical fighter wings could be delivered to the Persian Gulf area in three weeks. With 30 days of supply (DOS) the complete movement would require four weeks. A 30-day POL stockpile would require a month to buildup. Total: 800,000 short tons and 2.6 million barrels of POL. This notional scenario is equivalent in rate to current Department of Defense USCENTCOM reinforcement goals: six division-equivalents and seven tactical fighter wings (plus a Marine Air Wing) within six weeks.[5]

All these timetables, however, assume transit and delivery without friction.

This delivery-scenario assumes no "NATO-withholds," no interference in transit, adequate in-region port facilities, all unit equipment, ammunition, and supplies ready for loading at CONUS ports of embarkation (POE). Even with this serendipity, the entire movement takes a month. In a more time and resource-constrained scenario, the National Command Authority will have much less than a month to get significant ground and tactical air forces to SWA. It is unlikely that all air and sealift assets will be available for USCENTCOM, or that even the balance of unit equipment will be loaded and ready to go.

If two weeks is the more realistic benchmark for rapid deployment, only the 8 TAKR's stationed on the Atlantic coast (and a portion of MAC) could contribute to a SWA crisis (CRAF mobilization would be a sensitive political decision in any crisis short of an impending Soviet assault in NATO). This implies a usable capability to put a MAB,[3] or the 82d Airborne Division, and possibly one of the new light infantry divisions (LID) into SWA. At the very end of the two week response period, the TAKR's would be arriving at ports of debarkation in region with the unit equipment of a full mechanized division [the 24th]. Personnel would be flown in.

THE THEATER BASE

American military use of Diego Garcia, a coral atoll in the Chagos Archipelago, was granted by the United Kingdom in 1976. A naval support facility (NSF) was established, and a six-year construction program initiated. The result is truly a support facility. It encompasses:

- A modern communications station
- A 12,000 foot runway
- A deep-water anchorage
- Storage for fuel
- A fuel pier for loading/unloading fleet oilers
- A fuel receipt and delivery system
- An aircraft maintenance hanger and wash rack
- A limited number of warehouses
- A limited number of personnel support buildings

Since the completion of the initial construction program in 1982, there have been several improvements to the atoll facilities, "to increase the capacity of its airfield to support enroute refueling and to prepare for mooring additional MSP and ammunition ships." The facility can support, and the six-square mile lagoon anchorage can accommodate a single carrier battle group (CVBG). In addition, the airfield can stage and refuel the movement of a MAB from the Western Pacific to forward operating airstrips in SWA. Finally, aviation facilities can support the operation of B-52 and P-3 patrol aircraft.[6]

As a "support facility," however, Diego Garcia is severely constrained. It is not a real fleet base. It cannot begin to do the things that Subic Bay does for WESTPAC. There is simply too little surface area to work with. Without the atoll, however, the United States would be relatively incapable of sustaining a CVBG in the Indian Ocean area. Without the prepositioned Marine Brigade, significant military reinforcement to SWA would be equally incredible.

As a "half-base," then, the lagoon and coral strand are critical to the defense of Western interests in SWA. Its very importance, however, increases its vulnerability. The concentration of vital military stores, from the POL tank farm to the unrevetted aircraft parking ramp to the MPS and ammunition ships lined-up along the reef, is a tantalizing target. If a CVBG were to anchor in the lagoon itself, the situation would begin to resemble Pearl Harbor, with capital ships separated from the sea by a long dredged channel.

To add to its fragility, the atoll is 2,000 miles from Oman, and all incoming American forces staged through Diego Garcia must be linked with their equipment at a forward point of entry. Finally, the agreement with the United Kingdom for use of the rock runs out in 2016, although it can be extended to 2036. India has already claimed sovereignty over the Chagos Archipelago, and sometime before the agreement expires, it may have the military means to make its claims stick.

DELIVERY TO FORWARD OPERATIONS AREAS (FOA)

All ground and tactical air units to be deployed to SWA require a prepared, secure point of entry close to the FOA. This is as true for straight airlifted units, which require a developed forward airfield, as it is for incoming forces both with prepositioned and with CONUS-sealifted unit equipment. In fact, the deployment of prepositioned units is even more dependent on point of debarkation facilities.

For the MAB prepositioned at Diego Garcia, access to developed ports for the MPS squadron and nearby airfields for the combat personnel staging from WESTPAC is required. In order to form an effective battle force, men and materiel must be linked close to the operational theater, the forward operating area (FOA). If indigenous forward bases are not available, the materiel on the MPS must be landed, slowly and awkwardly "into the stream," that is, floated by barge or across pontoons over the beach. If local forward airfields are not available, MAB personnel would be unable to join their equipment. There are no modern equivalents of the Attack Transport (AP) to deliver combat personnel along with the unit equipment carried in the AKA-like MPS.

If a crisis evolved that did not permit timely—meaning effective pre-crisis—response, and forward base access were denied, American forces could be staged only so far as intermediate theater bases like Diego Garcia. Final delivery of complete combat units to FOA would be protracted. First, MPS and fast logistic ships (TAKR) would have to be reconfigured to transport personnel. Second, units would have to "close the FOA"—reach the front lines—by landing over-the-shore. This means amphibious landings. Unloading in the stream for a modern MPS requires five days. The stockpiling of POL and ammunition onshore from tankers and breakbulk vessels would increase this time by a factor of three.

The future acquisition of specialized Auxiliary Crane Ships (TACS), mobile piers, portable ramps, and POL pumps and tanks, and amphibious barges will improve this aspect of force closure. By 1990, these specialized tools, including 11 TACS, will permit amphibious landing of the SWA joint task force near the FOA if local airfields and ports are denied or damaged. The FY 1986 Secretary of Defense report to Congress declares that "our objective for SWA is to be able to deploy a major joint task force and required support within SIX WEEKS of being asked for assistance." (emphasis added) If the critical time for effective intervention is two weeks, the American expeditionary force will have missed its opportunity by about a month. Deterioration of the local situation by that time may require not only an amphibious, but an opposed landing, a rerun of D-Day or Inchon.[7]

The very conscious acquisition of amphibious unloading gear as generic equipment on all USCENTCOM sealift implies a stoic acceptance, in spite of all optimistic scenarios of reinforcement, of their ultimate and inevitable use. As one USCENTCOM planner avers: "Much of the resupply of ARCENT (Army component) and CENTAF (Air Force component) units *is planned* through the LOTS (Logistics Over the Shore) concept" (Italics mine).[8]

The problem, then, of orchestrating effective, prompt force from the sea is a mixture of (1) insufficient in-region prepositioned equipment and sealift, (2) CONUS sealift incapable of a two-week response, (3) a vulnerable, limited theater base facility, and (4) an awkward, if not unworkable method of force delivery.

AN ALTERNATIVE

What alternative conception could avoid these limitations?

If the greatest need for the defense of Western security interests in SWA is the demonstrative capability to insert sufficient ground and tactical air forces into the region within a two week period, *without the guarantee of secure indigenous forward bases*, then the United States must have its own secure forward base in-region. Such a base concept would need to fill several requirements:

•It must be US owned: whether ship or island, it must be American sovereign territory.

•It must be SWA dedicated: it should not be constructed to perform a fire brigade function in other theaters. It should be designed as a permanent US presence, an enduring statement of American political will.

•It must be regionally mobile. In order to perform as a *forward* base, it must be able to position itself in tactical proximity to the FOA.

•It must, unlike a ship or vessel, be capable of self-maintenance. A mobile, ocean-borne base will be too large for conventional docking and refit.

•It must be defensible. All fixed bases are relatively more vulnerable to effective attack-targeting than mobile bases. A survivable US regional, mobile forward base must be more than that: it must be capable of active self-defense, if only to enhance its deterrent value.

•It must be capable of performing several operational missions simultaneously: a mobile forward base should serve both ground and naval operating forces.

•It must be able to provide sufficient prepositioned materiel for a rapid deployment force, and at the same time be capable of air staging personnel from CONUS. The critical need is timely—two weeks or less— reinforcement of SWA FOA's is the delivery of complete, battle-ready combat units. Mating of personnel and unit equipment near the FOA is illusion.

•It must be able to support naval task groups in-region: any reinforcement to SWA must be covered by naval air and ASA forces. During the initial period of force insertion at the FOA, air defense and strike would be confined to organic assets on escorting CVBG's. Task groups operating for extended periods in the Indian Ocean would draw upon limited underway replenishment groups for the four main fleets. A mobile base should meet forward replenishment needs.

•It must be cost-effective: the realization of the concept should, for the course of its programmed investment, cost not more in future dollars than currently planned arrangements.

•It must be programmable over time, so that, instead of displacing current programs for SWA reinforcement, it would replace them when they reach the limit of useful operational life. A 2010 initial operating capability (IOC) should be planned.

CONCEPT BACKGROUND AND EVOLUTION

The notion of a man-made mobile base is not new. In the Second World War, Winston Churchill encouraged production of "Habakkuk," a 2000x300 foot battleship iceberg to be constructed of frozen slurry blocks.[9] More recently, in response to some of the persistent problems of CONUS force projection, several mobile base schemes have been proposed. Two of these, ISUS and MOLI, represent opposite poles in engineering solutions to the problems of designing and constructing massive sea-going structures.

The Integrated Supership System (ISUS) was developed by Stephen Liang, and presented by the Naval Ship Research and Development Center in March 1974. The system concept consisted of three catamaran modules, with flight deck dimensions of 1600x600, 1800x600, 1600x600 feet. The assembled system would present a mobile, ocean-airfield of 5000x600 feet, sufficient to handle the C-5A. The depot capacity of the ISUS was equal to 30-day mission support of a carrier battle group plus POMCUS for a MAB, and a 40,000 ton attached floating dock. Modular design was incorporated to avoid the potential hogging condition of a rigid structure under high vertical shear force from large waves. The three separate ship modules were connected with fast-acting hinges permitting vertical movement only.

The ISUS represented a thoroughly tested concept technologically feasible at the time of its proposal. A ship a mile long, however, abridged contemporary cultural receptivity, even in an era of "super-carriers."

197

The ISUS was the ultimate capital ship concept: a transcendental ship rather than a mobile base.[10]

At the other end of the conceptual spectrum was the passive, floating island. In a paper sponsored by Rand in February 1983, P.M. Dadant suggested a Mobile Operational Large Island (MOLI). A platform erected on large, reinforced concrete bottles, the MOLI would be configured for two runways, plus taxiways and parking areas, approximately 10000x4500 feet. A storage deck beneath the airfield would have sufficient volume for the unit equipment of nearly three divisional equivalents. Prepared for the US Air Force, the concept neatly sustains Air Force world view. An immobile island, shaped in the familiar "H" of a terrestrial airfield, could never be construed, nor employed, nor commanded as a ship of war.[11] The ISUS, in contrast, was so tempting a "supership" that it arguably could never have been employed as a base.

Both concepts suffered from debilitating flaws. The first was a lack of perceived need for a mobile, manmade base in preference to the acceptable, traditional, and feasible option: the land base. The second was an appearance of technological marginality combined with disproportionate costs. The MOLI, for example, was costed at $15 billion. Contrast this with the total spent on building the Diego Garcia base plus the charter costs of the NTPF: just a bit over $1 billion. ISUS would have been even more expensive, starting with the monumental docks needed to build them. The project report wisely never spoke of costs.

STRUCTURE

A reverse in this condition has made the mobile, man-made base practical. The need, especially in SWA, is overriding. Developments in ocean construction and engineering, however, have made the concept actually attractive. For more than a decade, offshore oil drilling has been conducted from platforms moored to the seabed of the continental shelf. These drilling platforms have evolved, both in capability and in sheer size. Originally moored permanently to the seabed, the incorporation of semi-submersible hull technology has lead to a proliferation of mobile platforms.

The platform itself is erected on tower-like columns that extend to the semisubmerged pontoons that ensure flotation. Typical large semisubmerged designs range from 250 to 600 feet length overall (at pontoons) and 200 to 350 feet beam overall (at pontoons), with operating displacements from 30,000-150,000 tons. These are large floating structures.

Semisub platforms have five attractive features for the mobile base concept:

- They are relatively easy to fabricate
- The technology is straightforward and proven
- Platforms can be assembled out-of-dock, to any size
- Any platform configuration and payload is possible
- Cost per ton is a fraction of conventional ship hulls

The dimensions of a mobile base built on a semisubmersible pontoon structure could be as large as 3000x1000 feet without suffering from unacceptable wave stress. The structure need not be hinged, according to naval engineers at Brown & Root, one of the major international builders of semisub platforms. A deck platform 3000x1000 feet would permit operation of C-130 aircraft and its follow-on replacement, perhaps including the C-17. The former is sufficient for intratheater staging of combat personnel, the latter is to be capable of intertheater movement as well. Three deck levels would provide nearly six million square feet of storage area for prepositioned equipment and supplies. This would be, for example, 40 times the vehicular storage area of a new Maritime Prepositioning Ship (MPS). The pontoons would provide sufficient POL tank volume to sustain both CVBG's and deployed ground and tactical air units.

The structure would, moreover, look like a base, not a floating island airfield or a mastodonic aircraft carrier. The semisub mobile structure has a no-nonsense utility of virtue that would both help to sell it to domestic political constituencies and avoid competition with "manhood" Air Force or Navy programs.

CONSTRUCTION AND COSTS

The semisub mobile base would be fabricated from components built in parallel, minimizing both cost and construction time. An innovative breakthrough in cost and construction saving has been pioneered by Brown & Root and Mitsui Engineering. The pontoon and column structure—the hull—is erected separately from the platform—or deck—and mated at sea near the yard. This approach is being adopted today for a platform of some 30,000 tons displacement. The method could be enlarged easily to incorporate simultaneous fabrication of several pontoon hulls and deck units, perhaps even at several yards. As component hulls and deck units were completed they could be joined to form a single structure. It has been suggested by naval architects that the final vessel could be developed from four to seven hull-deck components.

Based on an operational displacement of one million tons, costs of $2000 per ton could be anticipated: $2 billion for the entire bare structure, without fittings or equipment. This rough professional estimate would vary significantly depending upon choice of builder. Japan or South Korea could do it cheaper, and domestic builders would be more expensive.

It is suggested here that the structure, or vessel, not incorporate internal propulsion. This would increase cost and complexity of construction by several factors. A more utilitarian approach to mobility would be the procurement of powerful tugs (in the 50-75,000 BHP category) designed for and dedicated to the towing and maneuvering of the semisub mobile base. Speed would be sought in the 4-8 knot sustained rate range. This would help to provide continuous at-sea wind-over-deck of 15-20 knots for airlift staging.

Overall base costs—fabrication plus basic equipment, including tugs but not prepositioned unit equipment or visiting aircraft—would equal those of a large-deck carrier, about $3.5 billion. These can be compared to the total costs of alternative sealift, fleet replenishment ships, and non-US forward base investment for SWA. If a mobile base were designed to replace the current framework of SWA reinforcement, it would be highly cost-competitive.

FACILITIES

The semisub mobile base, in order to effectively perform a triple substitution mission for fleet replenishment, theater air-staging, and theater prepositioning, would require:
- Alongside refueling capability
- Hanger-shed space for aircraft maintenance
- Large electrical generating capacity
- Housing space for crew and personnel in-transit
- Ramps for vehicular loading and parking
- Workshops for fleet and POMCUS maintenance

Housing, generating, and maintenance facilities could be installed on-board in ISO-containers, up to the level of capability desired. With a platform of three decks, and six million square feet of enclosed space, the mobile base—if employed for prepositioning only—could accommodate unit equipment and 30 DOS for six MAB's, or about two division-equivalents. In order to support a CVBG, space would be divided between fleet operations and ground force staging. In a multirole configuration, the semisub mobile base could effectively serve as a depot for a MAF, and support CVBG operations for 30 days.

VULNERABILITY AND DEFENSE

The size of the semisub structure (3000x1000 feet, 1 million tons) would give it high resistance to conventional munitions. The configuration of semisubmersible vessels increases their resistance relative to conventional ship hulls, especially against torpedoes and certain kinds of antiships missiles. Finally, the choice of external propulsion in the form of specialized tugs increases this insensitivity, and ensures mobility even under conditions of widespread hull damage.

Any mobile installation is inherently less vulnerable to targeting than a fixed base. A semisub mobile base would be more resistant to attack below the nuclear threshold than any existing conventional ship or land base.

A floating base structure of this size could incorporate active defenses without mitigating its primary staging and support missions. As a caution, however, cost escalation to provide combatant capability, and the political dangers of potentially transforming mobile base into putative capital ship should inhibit this inclination.

A FINAL WORD

The successful potential deployment of American military force to Southwest Asia is perhaps less dependent on ultimate force size (although this cannot be ignored in the context of a "global war") than in the manner of its initial arrival. What is to be preferred, a brigade of the 82d in time and insufficient, or six divisions too late save for a fallback beachhead?

The realization of the mobile base concept outlined here would permit an intermediary option: delivery of a MAF or "heavy" division (plus extra airborne units) anywhere in South Asia and the Indian Ocean within a week, independent of major airfields and ports and nervous potentates.

ENDNOTES

1. See Office of the Secretary of Defense, *Soviet Military Power*, (Washington: US Government Printing Office, 1985).
2. Harold Brown, *Thinking About National Security*, (Boulder: Westview Press, 1983): 153.
3. See John Joseph Stocker, *Maritime Prepositioning Vessel: Background and Analysis of the T-AK(X) Acquisition Program*, (Washington: Congressional Research Service, 1980).

4. Office of the Secretary of Defense, *Annual Report to Congress, Fiscal Year 1986* (Washington: US Government Printing Office, 1985).

5. Based on a scenario study: "An Assessment of Strategic Sealift for Contingencies under Non-Mobilization Procedures," prepared by the National Security Industrial Association, July 1981. From unclassified sources, this study provides the following table of personnel, equipment, and supply requirements for their notional force:

	Personnel	Short Tons	30 DOS (ST)	POL (BBL)
US Army	108,000	273,600	147,000	827,000
USMC (plus Air Wing)	47,400	179,000	54,000	1,088,000
USAF	17,200	30,500	111,000	712,800

The study activated all reserve air- and sealift "assets" "under ideal conditions." It was confessed that these assumptions described a very best-case response. The actual lift planning factors were taken from "Monthly Civil Reserve Air Fleet Capability Summary," Headquarters, Military Airlift Command, 1 May 1981, and "Mobility System Policies, Procedures, and Considerations," The Joint Chiefs of Staff, Washington, DC, 2 June 1975.

6. US Congress, Senate Committee on Armed Services, "Department of Defense Authorization for Appropriations for Fiscal Year 1981:" (Washington: US Government Printing Office, 1980): 318-319.

7. Office of the Secretary of Defense, *Annual Report to Congress, Fiscal Year 1986.*

8. See chapter by LTC Max Johnson in this volume.

9. William J. Wallace, "Habakkuk," *Warship*, (V/18, 80-86).

10. Stephen T.W. Liang, "Advanced Concept Development of an Integrated Supership System," Bethesda: Naval Ship Research and Development Center, 1974.

11. P.M. Dadant, "Improving U.S. Capability to Deploy Ground Forces to Southwest Asia in the 1980's," (Santa Monica: The Rand Corporation, 1983).

CHAPTER 11

AN ALTERNATIVE STRATEGY FOR SOUTHWEST ASIA

by

Wm. J. Olson

The use of US forces overseas has become a pressing issue as military and civilian authorities have tried to come to terms with the problems of projecting force and deciding on a list of priorities for when, where, and how US forces should be used. The answer is by no means an easy one considering the range of interests, the diversity of the threats, the number of competing voices putting forward their favorite answer, and the limitations on available forces.[1]

This debate is not a recent one. The United States has been struggling since the end of World War II for an answer on how to employ its forces overseas, and over how to structure the military to meet a wide variety of challenges. In addition, the strategic context of the debate has changed. The world has become increasingly complex, and there has been both a real and a relative decline in US capabilities to deal with those complexities. Furthermore, there has been a dramatic increase in Soviet ability to project power beyond Europe and a growing ability by a number of Third World states to use military and political power to challenge the United States. This has reduced US influence and increased the need for flexibility and subtlety in response. It has also sharpened awareness that Third World issues have become more important overall, and it has forced the United States to reconsider force structure and the needs for power projection. In recent years the debate has centered on the development of rapid deployment forces to meet contingencies in the Third World, particularly in those areas identified as important to US interests. [2]

Southwest Asia has emerged as one of the areas regarded as vital to US interests. A fairly recent geographical delimitation, the designation of the area now defined as Southwest Asia grew out of an awareness of the region's importance because of oil and the Soviet threat. Generally speaking, it comprises the states of the Persian Gulf with the addition of Pakistan, and sometimes Afghanistan. In the following discussion, the terms "Southwest Asia" and the "Persian Gulf" will be used synonymously. [3]

A quick review of US policy for dealing with contingencies in the Southwest Asia region will indicate that it has been largely reactive. In one sense, all policy is reactive; that is, a response to some stimulus, in this case a response to the need to defend perceived national interests. But US policy for the Persian Gulf region has been reactive in an additional sense, in that events have driven the development of policy rather than a systematic effort to develop policy in relation to interests. Furthermore, it was not the region itself, until recently, that was at the center of concern. Since the Second World War, US interest in the region has fluctuated between neglect and overreaction, but with a basic trend toward greater interest and involvement. The main elements in this evolution have been the Soviet threat and the growing awareness of a Western dependence on oil, much of the supply of which comes from the Persian Gulf.

In both cases, however, policy for the Gulf region has been the result of shocks, a policy resulting from rude awakenings, such as those that occurred when the Soviets failed to withdraw from Iran after World War II—the first shock—or those that occurred as a result of the impact of the oil crises of 1973 and 1979, the fall of the Shah, and the Soviet invasion of Afghanistan—the latest rude awakening. Of course, no policy can be insulated from shock, or anticipate every turn of events; a policy must be flexible so that it can adjust to changing circumstances. One cannot ask or expect more of a policy than it can give, but one should not ask less than is necessary. This, however, has often been the case.

There are two basic problems, one dealing with policy, the other with strategic issues. First, the United States has tended to make policy for the region with only limited reference to the region. In other words, the region has been the object of attention and not the subject. Second, the United States has tended to ask "how" questions about what to do in the area rather than the more difficult "why" questions. The result is a policy that is often out of touch or out of sympathy with local realities, and a strategy that is fragmented, has a limited rationale or that is also unconnected to local realities. This is understandable, given the fact that the primary concern of US policy and the *raison d'etre* for US involvement in the world has been the Soviet threat. But the nature of the world and the demands on US abilities and the threats to US interests have changed significantly. The Soviet threat remains important, but the United States cannot afford to let this preoccupation obscure the fact that other threats have emerged that must be dealt with apart from the Soviets. While this is recognized in principle, it rarely forms the central theme in actual planning. This is no place more clearly demonstrated than in the Persian Gulf region.

The argument to be made in the following pages is that there needs to be a reconsideration of policy and its consequent strategy, with a new emphasis placed on developing a regional policy that both places the region at the center of the policy's concerns and puts it in perspective in relation to the importance of other interests. Policy for Southwest Asia/Persian Gulf must be both autonomous of the East-West preoccupation of the United States and subordinate to a system of priorities that will enable the United States to defend its many worldwide interests. In other words, policy and strategy for the Gulf cannot be formulated as if in a vacuum, or as if the region were uninhabited. This does not mean abandoning a key element of global US policy—namely, the containment of Soviet aggression—but it involves the development of a two-tier approach that separates the Soviet threat from regional relations, while keeping that threat an essential part of overall planning.

Many critics of US policy often make the claim that the United states does not have a policy, for the Gulf or anywhere else. The problem is not that the United States has no policy, but that it has so many, that there are so many voices involved in making or breaking policy, and that there can be conflicting interests in one region that pits policy against itself. The problem is that the United States has conflicting or contradictory interests and competing policy makers and only limited resources to respond to all the demands. The problem is that the United States has more commitments than capabilities, more opinions than wherewithal.

This means that strategy, which must be guided by policy, is developed in a confusing atmosphere of competing authorities and interests. The result can be and often is a strategy shaped not by policy or strategic necessity but by the verities of capability and bureaucratic politics—the how questions. Strategy often develops in an atmosphere where policy is paralyzed and so technical questions come to have more influence in determining responses than they should. Thus, for example, the United States has endless operational plans for how to cope with various scenarios in the Gulf, but much less of an understanding of why it is employing those plans. Although it is an exaggeration to argue, as does Kenneth Waltz in his interesting article, "A Strategy for the Rapid Deployment Force," that the "ability to act militarily carries with it the temptation to take military action," it is clear that in the absence of adequate, sustained guidance, the planning system can develop a life of its own, which in turn can come to dominate or substitute for policy.[4]

US interest in the region derives from three key factors: historic concern for containment of the Soviets, concern for the stability of the region, and a desire to see a secure supply of oil. A fourth, additional concern, part of US interest in the Middle East as a whole, is US commitment to the existence of Israel and a resolution to the Arab-Israel empasse. A key US objective in the region is to take steps to indicate US reliability and to be seen to be dealing fairly and effectively with local issues. The interplay of these interests with possible regional and extraregional threats form the context for US involvement and call for a reconsideration of strategy.

PROBLEMS IN REGIONAL STRATEGIES

US strategy for the region is outlined in several key documents, including NSDD-99, the Defense Guidance, and the Joint Strategic Planning Document with supporting analysis, which provide more detailed guidance for the military. In addition, USCENTCOM acts as a planning base for various contingencies, and numerous wargaming exercises test various assumptions and scenarios for the use of US forces in the region. The main rationale for US involvement in the Persian Gulf region today, of course, is the security of oil and its routes to the West and Japan, and the threat the Soviets pose to the supply of oil and the stability of the oil producing states.

Although the presence of oil has given the United States reason enough to be more concerned with the Persian Gulf region, per se, the Soviet invasion of Afghanistan pulled the rug from under the Carter Administration's belief in detente and demonstrated even further the type of threats that could jeopardize oil supplies. This belated realization reinforced the emphasis on the Soviet threat and the combination of these events convinced the Carter Administration to develop a more unilateral capability to defend US interests in the region. It discovered, however, that this country's ability to project the necessary force to the region was severely limited.

The formulation of the Nixon Doctrine in 1969 spelled out this country's declining ability to unilaterally defend its interests by notifying US regional allies that they would have to shoulder more of the burden for their own defense. This lead to such policies as the so-called Twin Pillar policy in which the United States gave significant military assistance to Iran and Saudi Arabia so that they could defend common interests on their own. This policy grew out of US unwillingness to use its own forces overseas as a consequence of the Vietnam War. This Vietnam syndrome also encouraged major military cutbacks that eroded US capability to project its forces. The fall of the Shah and the Soviet invasion of Afghanistan, however, exposed the dangers in such a policy.

The Carter Doctrine, that set out this country's determination to reverse the decline in US willingness to defend its interests by force if necessary, was a policy without sufficient military support. Since the Carter Doctrine identified the Soviets as the prime threat in the region, planning had to respond to the notion of a possible Soviet invasion. It became apparent very quickly, though, that this country simply did not have the projection capability to halt such an invasion. The result was an effort to develop a more realistic response capability and to improve power projection forces. The main element in this effort was the Rapid Deployment Joint Task Force (RDJTF) established in March 1980. This joint command became the planning base for US defense efforts in the Persian Gulf area, and this force became Central Command in January 1983. The creation of USCENTCOM represented the first new unified command in over 20 years and indicated the seriousness of US purpose.

The Reagan Administration accepted the imperatives of the Carter Doctrine and came to regard the security of the Southwest Asia/Persian Gulf region as vital to US interests, which means, in military terms, a willingness to resort to armed force if that extreme should be necessary to protect the region.[5] This determination was a signal to the Soviets, who were and are seen as the principal threat in the region, that the United States would not accept any more Afghanistans. The objective was to send a clear, unambiguous message, thus deterring possible Soviet aggression and reassuring our regional friends that we would stand beside them. The Reagan Administration has expanded the idea to include other forms of military assistance to local states against other forms of aggression, like internal subversion, or threats from regional powers such as Iran.

This recognition has produced greater efforts to devise plans for dealing with more purely local contingencies. In addition, there have been continuing efforts to provide military assistance to meet local problems. Recent support to Saudi Arabia by supplying Stinger antiaircraft missiles is one example, and the supply of AWACS to the Saudis is another. The Reagan Administration has also invested significant effort in strengthening US diplomatic ties in the region, particularly with Iraq, as a means of dealing with local problems and of enhancing the base for US presence in the region.

The Reagan Administration, as a consequence of accepting the Persian Gulf priority, also scrapped the notion of a 2-1/2 or a 1-1/2 war scenario developed by other administrations to give a sense of focus to defense planning.[6] The Reagan Pentagon favored a policy of strategic flexibility and horizontal escalation. The addition of the Persian Gulf to the list of defense priorities meant the United States had to be prepared to respond to the Soviets on multiple fronts.

The United States could not and would not guarantee that a confrontation with the Soviets in one area could be contained to that area. Secretary of Defense Caspar Weinberger outlined in 1983 a policy that would see the United States prepared to respond to Soviet threats in any or all theaters simultaneously; in the *Annual Report* to Congress for 1984 he once again stressed that the United States had to forego "mechanistic" assumptions about preparing to fight two wars, or one-and-a-half wars. In addition, he stressed that if there were a confrontation with the Soviets we would not necessarily confine our response to the original area of conflict but might strike at vulnerable Soviet assets in other theaters—horizontal escalation. The main vehicle for such a retaliatory doctrine was a maritime strategy. In other words, the Navy would be used to hit the Soviets in other theaters.

To implement these efforts the Reagan Administration has devoted considerable energy to improving the overall readiness of US forces and to enhancing of strategic lift capabilities that are essential to the projection of US power. Between 1982 and 1985, spending on USCENTCOM went from $871 million to $978 million not including considerable investment in air and sealift or the improvement of strategic reserves and combat supplies. Moreover, the Navy has been a key beneficiary of the new retaliatory doctrine. The active lobbying of Secretary of the Navy John Lehman for a 600 ship navy theoretically designed to take the war to the Soviets in vulnerable areas has been the major feature of this effort.

Improvements in projection capability came in two main areas: in prepositioning and in the expansion of lift resources. Prepositioning was handled in two ways, by establishing working relations with area states, such as Egypt and Oman, and by recourse to Diego Garcia, a British-owned island in the Indian Ocean. There are currently 18 ships with supplies for a Marine Amphibious Brigade and various Army and Air Force units stationed at Diego Garcia in what is called the Near Term Prepositioned Ship (NTPS) program. In addition, the Navy is in the process of acquiring eight fast cargo ships, SL-7s, able to make over 30 knots, that will be converted to Roll on/Roll off (RO/RO) ships capable of carrying significantly more supplies, as well as a number of slower support vessels that will add significantly to sealift. (See the chapter by Max Johnson in this volume for more detail.) There is also a program to develop a Maritime Prepositioning Force of 13 ships specifically designed to carry and store military equipment for long periods that will eventually replace the NTPS. In the case of ships, however, which would have to carry the bulk of supplies for any long action, there would still be a significant time lag in moving supplies to the Gulf region. Consequently, the "rapid" in the RDJTF must be supplied by airlift. Here too, there were significant shortfalls. Both the Carter and the Reagan Administrations, therefore, have devoted considerable effort to rectifying these shortcomings.

The effort has come in two main categories, improvement of the readiness, number, range and carrying capability of existing lift assets, such as the C-141 and the C-5A; and in an effort to develop a new intra/intertheater lift aircraft, the C-17. The first effort has been very successful, with programs to increase the number and extend the life of the C-5A and the load capability of the C-141, plus the expansion of the Civilian Reserve Air Fleet (CRAF) and the growth of the KC-10 tanker fleet to keep the planes in the air longer having added 40 percent to lift capabilities.[7]

Despite these improvements, however, the additional lift assets do not provide the means to lift US forces in significant numbers to Southwest Asia quickly; and in the event of a crisis elsewhere, in Europe or Asia, the demand on lift becomes intolerable. Even with projected improvements, the so-called strategy-force mismatch—more commitments than wherewithal—remains a major problem. A deployment to the Persian Gulf region would require virtually all existing air lift assets for the duration of the conflict, as resupply and reinforcement efforts would continue to place heavy demands on lift. Although the arrival of sealifted supplies, which would account for almost 90 percent of the supplies needed for a major deployment, would reduce the demand beginning after the first two-three weeks of a major deployment, even current sealift capacity and amphibious forced-entry assets are inadequate to meet regional demands in a major scenario, such as a Soviet invasion of Iran. This problem, in addition to those discussed earlier, make it doubtful that, short of full war mobilization, the United States could develop or deploy the combined lift assets to respond to multiple scenarios, or to deploy the forces necessary to confront a major Soviet invasion of Iran.

There are two basic ways to see to it that forces and equipment are available in an area of crisis. One is by moving them there by air or sea, and the other is to have prepositioned equipment or men already in the area, such as the US forces or the POMCUS sites already in Europe. In addition, one can have local allies and overflight rights or access rights to area military facilities and ports. These, along with a forced-entry capability, are the essential ingredients of power projection and in most of the areas of the world where the United States may have to send its forces, a combination of these elements will have to be used.

The situation in Southwest Asia in this regard offers a number of significant problems. First, of course, is the problem of distance. As the *Congressional Mandated Mobility Study* (CMMS) makes clear, "Mobility and logistics considerations are shaped by the extreme distances to the area from the United States. . ." It is 6,300 air nautical miles (nm) from the east coast of the United States to the Persian Gulf and 9,000 from the west coast. It is over 8,000 sea nm from the east coast if the Suez Canal is available, 12,000 if the trip must be made around the Cape; it is 10,000 nm from the west coast. Second, local facilities are limited. Although there are a number of good ports and airfields, these are not extensive and are not necessarily available for US use. In addition, road and rail networks in the region are very limited and vulnerable to interdiction. Third, local production facilities are also limited. Although oil is available in the region, this is virtually the only major commodity that US forces would find in the amounts necessary, and not all of this, of course, is militarily usable. This means that most supplies would also have to be brought in with the forces, including water and food.

Fourth, access to the region is not assured. Although the United States has several access agreements, principally with Oman, Egypt, Somalia, and Kenya, there is by no means assured access in the event of a crisis in which a local state does not want to be involved and is therefore not willing to allow US forces within its borders. There is considerable reluctance in the region to see US forces committed directly, and in some cases there is a local suspicion that the real motive for any US intervention would be solely aimed at securing the oilfields and not for local defense. This makes the regional states cautious and this attitude could easily translate into denying the US access in circumstances that it deemed necessary.

Finally, there are problems associated with refueling and overflight rights. As the United States discovered in 1973 in the airlift to Israel, even close allies may not be prepared to see their facilities used by the

United States if it means they may become involved in a regional crisis. If it had not been for access to Portuguese airfields in the Azores, the difficulty of resupplying Israel during the Yom Kippur War would have been considerably more serious, if not virtually impossible. It is unclear whether in any future crisis in the region our European allies would be any more disposed to allowing us to involve them even indirectly in the area. What these factors mean is that it will be very difficult for the United States to move forces to the region or to rely on local cooperation or facilities once they are there.

The problems do not end here, however, for the harshness of the physical environment of the region would put an incredible strain on men and materiel. The lack of water and the extremes of temperature create unique problems for both men and their equipment even if they have been acclimatized to local conditions—which is not likely to be the case since most of the forces planned for the region must serve double duty. Although US forces exercise in the region periodically and train in comparable sites in the United States, this is true for only a fraction of forces planned for a major SWA deployment and only then at long intervals. It will take considerable time on the scene for forces to acclimate to the region, and even this will deal with only part of the problem since the area will take its inevitable toll of both men and equipment.

These problems, however, are true for any deployment of US forces and the simple fact that they exist are not arguments against the use of force. The interests outlined earlier indicate that the United States cannot afford to ignore developments in the Persian Gulf, nor avoid the fact that it must be prepared to use force to defend those interests.

ALTERNATIVE STRATEGIES

It should be clear from the preceding pages that the view taken here is that the main emphasis for both policy and strategy in the Gulf region is a concentration on more regionally based threats. Such a strategy, which would tend to emphasize low intensity conflict, has implications for both policy and strategy. As currently designed, strategy holds that forces developed to counter an admittedly less likely Soviet threat in the region would be adequate to respond to the range of lesser but more likely threats. While this might be true for interventions in conventional conflicts in the region, even this type of intervention is not very likely, and forces structured to deal with such situations are not necessarily the best elements to cope with unconventional conflicts.

This is also true for strategic doctrine. If the most likely demands for involvement in the region are of the antiterrorist, counterinsurgency,

211

oilfield protection, regime support and countercoup, and hostage rescue types, then conventional doctrine and forces are not adequate to cope with these irregular situations. By organizing to deal with the least likely scenarios, then, a force structure and strategy are emerging that will not meet the most likely demands for US involvement. In addition, the development of such strategy and force structure may achieve the reverse of what is intended by needlessly overextending US capabilities and by sending the wrong signals to local supporters and opponents alike. As noted above, many local states are concerned about the motives behind current US efforts, and they are just as likely to deny US access to regional facilities out of that concern as they are to invite US support in the event of a local crisis. What is needed is a force structure and strategy that are more in resonance with local realities.

To a degree, more regionally-based approaches have gained influence in Washington and at USCENTCOM. General Robert Kingston, the former commander of USCENTCOM, has made the point that the primary responsibility for regional security rests with the regional states themselves, although the United States must be prepared to respond to requests to provide those countries with the systems and training they need to improve their own defenses. He also has reinforced the notion that the direct use of US force in a regional crisis would be a last resort.[8] The administration also has begun to move in the direction of emphasizing more regional concerns, a fact reflected in the Secretary of Defense's *Annual Report to Congress, 1985*; but the implications of a regionally-based, low intensity conflict-oriented strategy require coming to terms with a number of implications.

Much of the analysis, even that suggesting alternative strategies, remains based almost exclusively on various aspects of the Soviet threat. Thus, Keith Dunn, in his excellent study, "Toward a U.S. Military Strategy for Southwest Asia," gives lip service to the crucial importance of regional threats, but then devotes almost all of his attention to a counter-Soviet strategy.[9] Jeffrey Record, another proponent of alternative approaches, also stresses the Soviets, arguing for a naval/marine strategy of deterrence that could successfully defeat or contain them in Iran.[10] Many of these studies treat the region as if it were uninhabited, as if the local states would play little part in determining the context of intervention by either superpower. There is also endless debate over Soviet intentions and capabilities, stressing the likelihood of intervention or the constraints on such. Clearly, however, no amount of debate in the pages of *Orbis, International Security*, or the numerous monographs and conference proceedings on Southwest Asia and US policy are going to answer any of the key questions about intentions; and one could argue that many of the questions about capability and strategy will only be answered if the projected situations actually arise.

No amount of assertion will establish whether the Soviets will or will not attack; nor will assertion prove that Third World issues should join or replace the Soviets as a primary concern. These are not questions of fact. This is one reason why the debate on what to do, whether in Southwest Asia or elsewhere, is so perplexing and ultimately indecisive. Intuition and inclination will generally prevail over what facts there are even when they are clear and unequivocal; how much more so, then, when the facts themselves are ambiguous, contradictory, or irrelevant. Nor are policy and strategy, no matter how detailed, likely to provide more than minimal guidance when the situations they are designed to deal with actually develop into crisis. This is not an argument against policy making or strategic thought; it is an observation on the limitations of such exercises, and a comment on the fact that the extensive debate over strategic issues has become another complicating factor in trying to sort through the problem of defense and deterrence to discover possible courses of action.

One fact, however, is clear: US interests in the world now and for the foreseeable future exceed US capabilities. And, it is argued here, the consequent demand that this situation makes for a priority-based defense precludes a major military effort in the Gulf. The stress must not be on countering a Soviet invasion of the region, with all the consequent exaggerations in force planning and deployment strategies that this occasions, but on coping with regional threats and challenges, both political and military. If the United States recognizes that its interests are global and that Third World problems are becoming at least co-equal challenges to those interests, then there must be a shift away from seeing all local involvements through the East-West perspective. Maturity in both policy and strategy would then mean a more sophisticated effort to deal bilaterally with area states on the basis of common interests and problems, and to downplay our own necessary but unshared preoccupation with the Soviets.

This is not an argument that sees the Soviets as irrelevant. On the contrary, the challenge to US interests and to stability and peace in the world emanate largely from the Soviet Union and its mummified revolutionary doctrines. Much of the Third World, however, does not share this view, and efforts to foist it upon unwilling partners can be counterproductive, or can be used disingenuously by them to manipulate the United States. In addition, the United States cannot afford, nor should it try, to defend everything all at once in dealing with the Soviet challenge. This is a strategy for exhausting both material and psychological resources—an exhaustion that is likely to translate into a

213

strong isolationist sentiment, such as that argued by Earl Ravenal and others, that would see the United States retreat to fortress America. Instead, the United States should develop regional strategies that reflect both interests and capabilities. Such strategies should rest on military, economic, and political priorities both before and at the time of a crisis.

In this sense, the Persian Gulf area is significant economically and politically to the United States and the West, but this importance must be put into perspective. In the event of a local crisis, the United States needs to be capable of a realisitic response. A local crisis that threatens the security of oil or the stability of regional states is of significant gravity to entail a measured response. If, however, the crisis is the result of a Soviet attack, then another set of criteria must apply. The Gulf is not the place to defend the West in World War III, nor is a regional defense likely to preserve the oil fields in such circumstances. This is not to argue against a tripwire force in the region to open the possibility of escalation as a means to deterrence, or for small forces that can defend oil fields or interdict Soviet movement. Such forces, however, are a far cry from a force designed to confront major Soviet combat divisions on the plains or in the mountains of Iran.

The deterrent value of US forces lies in their escalatory potential, not in their ability to defeat the Soviets in the region. The Soviets would find the reality of the first situation a more credible deterrent than the prospect of the second. A Soviet invasion of Iran is likely to be the result of, or to create a far more significant international crisis, and in that event, the diversion of US effort to the region would only undercut the ability to deal with the Soviets in more vital theaters, particularly Europe. Even if the necessary forces and strategic lift were used for a deployment to the Gulf in the event of a pending global war—a highly unlikely eventuality—this would not be sufficient to stop the Soviets, though the diversion of US effort might be a significant force multiplier for the Soviets elsewhere. At least one key military planning document acknowledges this problem, arguing that, "Difficult choices would be necessary because planning force capabilities are insufficient to achieve simultaneously all military objectives." This position argues very strongly for sequential operations for dealing with the Soviets in the event of a global crisis.

What then, should the United States do to promote and protect its interests in the Southwest Asia/Persian Gulf region? What is the best use of force to achieve the ends of policy? How should the United States structure its responses, and what are the costs and benefits of a strategy that is more closely attuned to regional situations?

There are five key objectives for a regional strategy: promoting stability of the area; guaranteeing a secure supply of oil, which involves deterring possible Soviet political and military aggression; improving and assuring access to regional facilities in the event of crisis; improving planning and coordination with area states, and the promotion of local rapid deployment forces; concentrating on low intensity conflict; and promoting progress in the Arab-Israeli impasse. These elements, and the de-emphasis on the wisdom of making a major military effort in the region in the event of a Soviet invasion, reinforce the political and diplomatic elements of national power over the military for the achievement of national strategic goals.

Two problems complicate efforts to make strategy to promote regional stability: the first derives from the difficulties of designing forces and responses to deal with local circumstances; and the second grows out of the constraint of having to design a response in such a way as not to aggravate local sensibilities. This is a decidedly tricky problem, especially since any US involvement will excite some opposition.

The first requirement for the success of any strategy is to promote a local support environment, both politically and structurally. The effort to develop a regional infrastructure, however, is now and is likely to remain constrained. Access to local facilities will remain limited because of local concern for the destabilizing influence of an active US presence, and the prospect of a regional basing structure is remote. Over-the-horizon facilities and capabilities must take the place of major regional facilities.

This fact puts greater importance on developing an effort to build on regional friendships and partnerships, particularly with Saudi Arabia and Oman. It also means an effort to encourage the cooperative effort of the Gulf Cooperation Council (GCC) to establish a regional security system. Since the use of US forces in the region would be virtually impossible without some form of regional cooperation, it is incumbent on the United States to develop the types of relationships that would make it more possible to deploy forces if necessary. In addition, efforts to improve the stability of regional states would reduce the need to resort to unilateral effort. In the long run, regional security cannot be imposed from outside. This is a fact that US policy has long recognized, and is one reason why the United States has, in fact, encouraged local states to develop their own capabilities. Still, there are circumstances that might require a US response, and this requires the development of forces designed to deal effectively with the types of threats that are likely to develop.

As noted earlier, the best method for constructing a local response is to design forces and doctrine that will guide the use of force in the event of coups, hostage situations, limited local conflicts, counterinsurgency and counterterrorist operations or threats to oil field security—in short, for low intensity conflicts. Such forces and doctrine need to be specially tailored to deal with the local environment, physically, socially and politically. While current doctrine holds that general purpose forces with dual assignments are adequate to deal with local contingencies, this approach ignores the special requirements for local involvement, especially in low intensity situations. Such an approach reflects the preferred, though often only implied, concentration on the Soviets, with local concerns receiving short shrift, and contradicts the demands for coping with regional conflicts, which are acknowledged as the most likely scenarios.

The best force structure for dealing with low intensity conflict in the Middle East would concentrate on small, quick reaction forces, Marine and Naval forces, dedicated air squadrons, and tailored advisory missions that developed local capabilities while keeping US presence at a minimum. The mix of quick reaction forces needs to include a light infantry division (LID) trained to fight in built-up areas, in the special requirements for oil field protection and in the cultures of the region; and at least two special operations groups (SOG), one designed to provide security assistance and training—especially for low intensity conflict—and the other trained to conduct combat—particularly interdiction and sabotage—operations in the region. In addition, a command and control structure needs to be specifically designed to deal with and understand the nuances of the regional environment. Central Command provides the framework for such a structure and it is essential in any revised strategy to retain this as the planning base. Only USCENTCOM would have the flexibility, sustained interest and understanding to respond to the regional problems that are likely to develop.

The LID, or key cadres, needs to be dedicated to regional contingencies so that it has the training and the inherent capabilities to respond to the special requirements of the area. In addition, it should be air deployable and have a significant addition of integral helicopters and light, fixed-wing aircraft, as well as improved integral lift and antiarmor capability. Two special operations groups are necessary to insure that the range of missions needed to support US policy is covered. One such group is not enough because this would require it to fulfil two very different tasks—advice and actual combat. While an SOG is theoretically capable of doing both, the demands in the Middle East would place too great a burden on one group, reducing efficiency and combat readiness.

These forces would be sufficient to deal with a wide range of situations, but they need to be augmented by at least one division-equivalent Marine Amphibious Force (MAF) with at least one Marine Amphibious Unit dedicated to the region, with the necessary sea and amphibious lift to respond to local crises. The Marine force, with its integral air power and over-the-beach operations capability, is essential to support more ambitious undertakings, and could be used as a tripwire force. Once again, however, this force needs to be focused on local contingencies so that it can concentrate on training and on acquiring an understanding of the locale.

A regional response capability also needs to include at least one carrier task force in order to have available the over-the-horizon force that can display US presence from a distance, while maintaining a regional base for projecting power. The difficulties of moving naval forces into the Persian Gulf, however, preclude using just a naval force for local contingencies, and such an effort would not develop the type of on-the-ground expertise necessary to deal with the range of low intensity situations. A credible response requires a mix of forces.

The final element in a regional response capability is the dedication of at least one tactical air wing and appropriate air transport support for regional defense. This force could be used to support local regimes and it could be used as part of an interdiction/tripwire force to deter any possible Soviet moves in the area. The main purpose of such a force, however, would be to provide combat or training support to local air forces in the event of regional conflict, the current support to Saudi Arabia being one example. This effort, though, should not concentrate just on the use of sophisticated combat aircraft but should also include support for the types of air power necessary to conduct low intensity operations, particularly counterinsurgency operations.

Although this is the mix of forces that would give the United States a real capability to deal with the types of situations that are likely to develop in the Middle East, it would remain a body without muscles if adequate strategic lift were not developed to deploy the force. This means that there must also be a continuing, major effort to develop the range and type of lift assets that can deliver a US response. What this requires is significant expansion of the number and variety of amphibious assault craft and sealift ships to support a regionally dedicated MAF and a LID; increased intertheater lift, air tankers, and the development of the C-17 as a credible intratheater airlifter; the development of POL and water storage and transport-logistical facilities and equipment; and the development of prepositioning sites for outsized equipment. This latter category, however, is the most difficult to achieve, the most politically sensitive, and the least reliable means for developing deployability. It should be dealt with gingerly and no reliance should be placed on it.

The development of the force outlined above would give the United States the variety of forces needed to respond to local situations. A small force tailored to respond to the types of threats that local regimes fear most might also reassure them about US intentions and give the United States greater credibility. It would also demonstrate clearly US intentions to support its friends and it would send a message to the Soviets that we regard the region as a truly important one. Although this would not stop their efforts at subversion, US assistance in both intelligence and security operations would offset much of this activity, while a lower profile in the region would undercut much of the propaganda benefits the Soviets receive from local concerns about an all too visible US presence.

In addition, the ability to call on forces specially designed to cope with the local environment and prepared to interdict Soviet encroachments would also provide the necessary deterrent force without diverting major US forces from more important theaters in the event of a US-Soviet confrontation. The real question here is what force would constitute a tripwire. Is a large force that cannot be deployed and that would be insufficient to defeat the Soviets a more credible tripwire than a smaller force that can effectively retard Soviet advances and organize local resistance? How much is necessary to establish a credible deterrent? This is not a question that this paper can hope to answer, but it is not unrealistic to assume that any force, backed up by a corresponding will, can be a realistic deterrent. The point is not size but demonstration of intentions and thereby of the risks involved. To be effective, a tripwire must be believed. Its essence is not in its size but in the determination to follow through on the threat that is implicit in the use of a tripwire in the first place.

The final political objective for developing an effective strategy for the SWA region is to find some solution to the Arab-Israeli situation. Although this is a question of policy, dealing with or failing to deal with this problem has serious implications for strategy. To be effective, any strategy for the region must depend on local cooperation and an appreciation that the United States is capable of dealing with this most thorny local issue. Failure to cope adequately with this problem could go a long way to undermining US credibility, and could encourage local states to divest themselves of an embarrassing relationship. US credibility in the region is based to a significant degree on the perception that the United States can produce movement in resolving the Palestinian question. This perception, however, may be undergoing a change, with local elites and populations coming gradually to the conclusion that the United States not only will not work to find an equitable solution but is unable to do so.

The question that will then face policy makers is whether a successful relationship can be maintained in the region in the face of growing disbelief in US reliability and credibility. This aspect of the strategic problem underscores one of the major problems of developing a response in the region, or in low intensity conflict situations in general: political considerations are more important than military ones, and force alone is not a solution to political problems. Lebanon, for example, not only illustrates the types of conflict that could disturb the area, but also serves as an example of the limits on the use of force; and the crisis there also demonstrates the need for both policies and forces designed to deal with local problems. Although it is possible to exaggerate the dire consequences, US inability to deal with this situation will make the execution of a regional strategy that much harder and will provide an avenue for the Soviets to exploit local frustration to US detriment.

The final point that needs to be considered in the development of a strategy as outlined above is to consider the costs of embarking on the changes as suggested. The benefits have been stressed throughout, but there are significant risks as well. There are three major expenses: the first deals with the dislocations such a strategy has for US force development and planning; the second has to do with US will and the ability to develop a response to issues that do not have the imprimatur of the Soviet menace; and the third arises from the risks involved in developing a strategy that seemingly gives up on a major deterrent effort.

The creation of a regionally dedicated force as outlined would require a major shift in thinking about the use of US forces. At present, the only dedicated forces are those designed to respond to crises in Europe, and even these are multipurpose forces designed to cope with a wide variety of situations and climates. The stress in all the forces, however, is to deal with the Soviets, it being assumed that forces capable of dealing with them can be made to cope with any other situation. This emphasis helps to simplify planning and force development, and any effort to develop a response that would structure forces differently automatically runs afoul of the natural course of the system.

In addition, developing a locally dedicated force distorts the force structure, abstracts elements from the overall inventory, and raises questions about the need to develop specialized equipment and supply networks—the beginning of an almost parallel military structure. Yet, the needs of US commitments and the importance of the SWA region demand solutions; and the effort to extend the normal force structure to the region to cover the range of scenarios currently suggested is also distorting, while it threatens to overextend capabilities. Thus, there is a trade-off between the two approaches. It is hoped that the previous argument made it clear which of the two offers the best chances of giving this country a credible response capability.

The second cost of a more regionally dedicated strategy is that it removes one of the major justifications for US involvement overseas—

the Soviets. Although the proposed approach does not, in fact, do this, it does suggest that the United States has other important interests that require an effort. This smacks of *realpolitik*, and it is notoriously difficult to get the American people interested in foreign affairs short of a moral crusade. Furthermore, the emphasis on low intensity conflict has about it the aura of creeping involvement, of another Vietnam. This problem brings to the surface one of the principal dilemmas facing US policy today, the question of will. A great deal has been said about the declining will of the American people to see their interests protected through the use of force; and it is clear that lacking a clearly defined cause makes it even more difficult to justify a response involving force. There are also powerful elements in and out of government that see the world largely in terms of an immutable East-West conflict. These groups oppose efforts to develop responses that do not share this preoccupation, and without it they would lose much of their zeal for seeing US involvement overseas continue. Thus, the proposed strategy raises the costs of justifying a US response. The situation is not quite so stark, however.

Although the American people have raised questions about US overseas involvement, they have also tended to support an effective, if limited, US use of force to maintain interests. Despite intense debate, the United States has remained remarkably consistent and loyal in its obligations. Debate is part of the system and not necessarily a testimony to a collapse of will. Undoubtedly, the debate makes policy more difficult and subjects it to distorting twists and turns, but it does not preclude flexible or consistent effort. A low intensity strategy may suggest future Vietnams, but it also maintains a low-level involvement that makes it easier to justify the effort. It also makes an escalation of local effort more difficult, or it increases the number of steps involved in it. Low intensity operations also offer the prospect of being able to deal more effectively with the actual types of local situations that develop to threaten US interests. There is also no necessity to view the development of a local response capability as abandoning the commitment to contain the Soviet Union.

The development of an effective local strategy, by making the United States more able to defend its local interests as well as organize its resources to defend its global interests sequentially contributes to the overall effectiveness of US strategy. The objective is not to see the need for a response in each of its many parts, but to develop a large view and a corresponding strategy, to subordinate the parts to an overall system of priorities.

The final concern of a more regionally-based approach is that it will send the wrong signal to the Soviets. If the strategy suggests that the

United States is somehow unwilling to defend the region or would not oppose a Soviet invasion, then it opens up the prospect of the "Acheson" or "Korean" syndrome—of declaring the field open, thus inviting a response, as happened in Korea in 1950 when Dean Acheson suggested that South Korea was not included in any US defense perimeter. The proposed strategy, however, does not abandon the region to that assumption. On the contrary, it strengthens US commitment by making it more realistic, more capable. It also does not remove the tripwire. In short, despite the apparent costs, the strategy that will give the United States the most realistic and believable response capability in the Persian Gulf region is one based on local situations, one that emphasizes the demands of low intensity conflict.

THE "WHY" QUESTIONS

The principal question that strategy cannot answer is why force should be used; why the United States should expend its energy and potentially the lives of its soldiers to help to defend real estate thousands of miles from home. Nor can strategy answer with any certainty the question of when forces should be committed to best defend interests, nor at what point it is best to withdraw them, nor whether when the time comes the nation will have the will to resort to force. It can suggest limits of ability and provide the necessary support if a decision is reached, but the decision to use force or not is a political one that will be contingent upon the perceptions at the time of crisis and upon the demands that are made of the United States. Although, as General Kingston has noted, US policy sees the use of force as a last resort, local experience has taught that a policy without military support remains a hollow bluff should anyone care to challenge it. Policy cannot determine if political will or popular support will countenance the use of force, but the military must be prepared to respond, however unwelcome the use of force may be.

US interests in the Persian Gulf region are clear. The crucial importance of oil and Western dependence upon it are facts of the modern strategic picture that can only be ignored at great cost. In addition, the commitment to local friends is also important as a symbol of US reliability and as a sign to others that the United States is a willing force in the world working to hold together a system of states outside Soviet domination or influence. The convergence of Western dependency on oil and the growth of Soviet power in the oil-important regions has only exacerbated the problems for policy and strategic planning. This convergence has added significantly to the defense burden and has strained already overstretched resources, both physical and mental. It has created another major contradiction for US policy to deal with: how to defend important interests without giving up something else or destroying the object of interest. The response in such circumstances is usually a compromise, a tendency to hedge with temporizing solutions that often satisfy few of the critics and do not necessarily respond to the actual needs. This has been the case in Southwest Asia. The importance of the interests in the region, however, require more.

Answering the question of why the United States should reconsider its position in Southwest Asia and organize more for low intensity conflicts is easier to deal with. First, low intensity situations are far more likely to be the types of situations that the United States will face in the region, and it is important to have forces configured and indoctrinated in the realities of such conflict in this particular region. Second, it increases US flexibility to respond with a range of forces to a significant range of scenarios, including a tripwire force to deter the Soviets. Third, such a approach reduces the pressure on regional states to accept the kind of commitment that they find politically embarrassing. Finally, it establishes a force that can concentrate its energies on preparing for this region, while not subtracting from other priorities.

One of the central difficulties that US policy has had to deal with in recent times is how to respond to the multiplication of demands with diminishing resources. The habit has been to try to continue to cover all the bases; to torture the force structure into all the contortions necessary to meet every challenge or potential threat that fertile imaginations can conceive; to speak of the need of priorities but then to avoid dealing with the implications of such a position, a situation outlined with clarity by Ambassador Robert Komer in his study, *Maritime Strategy or Coalition Defense*? The result is neither increased peace of mind nor adequate forces to meet the various contingencies. This form of denial of reality will not, however, give the United States the force it needs to protect its interests and it could wear down US resolve to defend anything. As Stuart Perkins has noted in his *Global Demands: Limited Resources*,

> Few people enjoy thinking about the difficult decisions that will be required in a major crisis....But strategy involves making the tough choices....If our resources are inadequate, some important tasks will remain undone because the limited forces available will be committed to regions deemed more important.

What remains to be done is to accept that reality and make the necessary adjustments.[11]

ENDNOTES

1. The literature on this debate, on the balance of forces, their distribution and rationale for use, is now legion. A sampling includes the following: Kenneth Oye, *et. al.*, eds., *Eagle Entangled: US Foreign Policy in a Complex World* (New York: Longman, 1979); W. Scott Thompson, *et al.*, eds., *National Security in the 1980s: From Weakness to Strength* (San Francisco: Institute for Contemporary Studies, 1980); Robert Komer, "Maritime Strategy vs. Coalition Defense," *Foreign Affairs* 61, (Summer 1982): 1124-44 and *Maritime Strategy or Coalition Defense* (Cambridge, MA: Apt Books, 1984); William Staudenmaier and Keith Dunn, eds., *Military Strategy in Transition: Defense and Deterrence in the 1980s* (Carlisle, PA: US Army War College, 1984); Joshua Epstein, "Horizontal Escalation: Sour Notes On A Recurrent Theme," *International Security* 8 (Winter 1984): 19-31; John Gaddis, "Containment: Its Past and Future," *International Security* 5 (Spring 1981): 71-102; Aaron Wildavsky, *Beyond Containment: Alternative American Policies Toward the Soviet Union* (San Francisco: ICS Press, 1983); Jeffrey Record, *Revising US Military Strategy: Tailoring Means to Ends* (New York: Pergamon-Brassey's, 1984); John Mearsheimer, *Conventional Deterrence* (Ithaca, NY: Cornell University Press, 1983); Kenneth Rush, *et. al.*, eds., *Strengthening Deterrence: NATO and the Credibility of Western Defense in the 1980's* (Cambridge, MA: Ballinger Pub., 1981).

2. The debate over rapid deployment capability has been equally fierce. A brief survey of some of the contestants include the following: Robert Haffa, Jr., *The Half War: Planning US Rapid Deployment Forces to Meet a Limited Contingency, 1960-1983* (Boulder, CO: Westview, 1984); Uri Ra'anan, *et. al.*, eds., *Projection of Power: Perspectives, Perceptions and Power* (Medford, MA: Archon Books, 1982); Sherwood Cordier, *US Military Power and Rapid Deployment Requirements in the 1980s* (Boulder, CO: Westview, 1980); Maxwell Johnson, *The Military As An Instrument of US Policy in Southwest Asia: The Rapid Deployment Joint Task Force, 1978-1982* (Boulder, CO: Westview, 1983); Jeffrey Record, *The Rapid Deployment Force* (Cambridge, MA: Institute for Foreign Policy Analysis, 1981); Stuart Perkins, *Global Demands: Limited Forces* (Washington, DC: Nov Press, 1984); and Kenneth Waltz, "A Strategy for the Rapid Deployment Force," *International Security* 5 (Spring 1981): 49-73.

3. There is a cottage industry on works on SWA as well. Some of the relevant works are as follows: Shirin Tahir-Kheli, ed., *US Strategic Interests in Southwest Asia* (New York: Praeger, 1982); Alvin Rubinstein, *The Great Game: Rivalry in the Persian Gulf and South Asia* (New York: Praeger, 1983); Lenore Martin, *The Unstable Gulf: Threats from Within* (Lexington, MA: Lexington Books, 1984); Hussain Amir Sadeghi, ed., *The Security of the Persian Gulf* (London: Croom Helm, 1981); and *Security in the Persian Gulf,* 4 vols (London, International Institute for Strategic Studies, 1982).

4. Waltz, "Strategy," 49.

5. Numerous public statements make this clear, but the testimony of administration officials before Congress spell out the details. In addition, the *Annual Reports* of the various Secretaries of Defense to Congress use strong language to outline US views on defense of the Gulf.

6. See Haffa.

7. See Cordier, Johnson, and Haffa.

8. Interview with General Kingston, *Armed Forces Journal International*, July 1984, 67-73; *Army*, Oct. 1984: 159-60.

9. See Dunn in Rubinstein, *The Great Game*, 209-37.

10. See Record, "Jousting with Unreality: Reagan's Military Strategy," *International Security* 8 (Winter 83/84): 3-18; and his testimony before the US Senate, *Department of Defense Appropriations, Fiscal Year, 1987*, Part II. There is, however, considerable inconsistency in Record's position. In his article he maintains that the Reagan horizontal escalation strategy jeopardizes US defense by not concentrating on Europe, while in his testimony, more or less during the same period, he maintains that the United States should reduce commitments in Europe and place greater emphasis on defense elsewhere. A little more consistently, he does argue that the Soviets are the chief threat in any event.

11. See Komer; and Perkins, 95.

LIST OF CONTRIBUTORS

DR. RIAD AJAMI is currently a Visiting Professor of International Management and Strategy, the Wharton School, University of Pennsylvania, on leave from Ohio State University, College of Business Administrative Science, where he is an Associate Professor of International Business and Policy. He has had appointments as a visiting scholar at the Harvard Center for International Affairs, Harvard University, and at American University, as well as having been a distinguished visiting scholar at the American University in Beirut. Dr. Ajami received his Ph.D. from Pennsylvania State University. He is the author of the book *Arab Response to the Multinationals*, among others, and is a frequent contributor to books and journals.

DR. ROBERT FREEDMAN is Peggy Meyerhoff Pearlstone Professor of Political Science and Dean of Graduate Studies at the Hebrew College, Baltimore. He received his Ph.D. from Columbia University, 1969. He is the author of *Soviet Policy toward the Middle East since 1970* (Third Edition), and is editor of *The Middle East since Camp David*, *The Middle East since the Israeli Invasion of Lebanon*, and numerous other books.

DR. JERROLD GREEN is currently an Associate Professor of Political Science and Director of the Middle East Center, University of Arizona, Tucson. Formerly he was an Associate Professor at the Univeristy of Michigan, Ann Arbor. He received his Ph.D. from the University of Chicago, 1981. He has held numerous grants, including awards from the National Endowment for the Humanities, the Ford Foundation, and the

Fulbright Senior Research Fellow program. He is the author of *Revolution in Iran: The Politics of Countermobilization* and numerous articles on Middle East politics.

LTC MAXWELL ORME JOHNSON is a serving Marine. An armor officer, he has commanded tank companies in CONUS, NATO, and Korea. He has an M.A. in Middle East Studies from the American University of Beirut and a Ph.D. in Foreign Affairs from the University of Virginia. He is the author of *The Military as an Instrument of U.S. Policy in Southwest Asia: The Rapid Deployment Joint Task Force, 1979-1982.*

DR. THOMAS MCNAUGHER is a Research Associate at the Brookings Institution. His works include *The M16 Controversies: Military Organizations and Weapons Acquisition*, and *Arms and Oil: US Military Strategy and the Persian Gulf*.

DR. LENORE MARTIN is an Associate Professor and chairperson of the Department of Political Science at Emmanuel College in Boston. She received her Ph.D. from the University of Chicago and is a Faculty Associate of the Center for Middle Eastern Studies at Harvard University. She is the author of *The Unstable Gulf*.

LTC AUGUSTUS RICHARD NORTON is currently an Associate Professor of Comparative Politics in the Department of Social Sciences, United States Military Academy, West Point. He is an expert on Shi'ism and has traveled extensively in Lebanon and the Middle East. He is the author of *The Emergence of a New Lebanon* and numerous articles on Middle East politics and religion.

DR. WILLIAM OLSON received his Ph.D. from the University of Texas, Austin. In 1977-81 he was the Leverhulme Post-Doctoral Fellow at the University of Aberdeen, Scotland, and then a University Fellow at the University of Sydney, Australia. In 1981 he was a research associate at CSIS, Georgetown University. He then became a research analyst on Middle Eastern affairs at the Library of Congress. He joined the Strategic Studies Institute of the US Army War College in 1983. Dr. Olson is the author of *Britain's Elusive Empire in the Middle East*, and *Anglo-Iranian Relations During World War I*.

DR. RICHARD REMNEK was Visiting Professor at the Strategic Studies Institute, US Army War College and is currently Director of Soviet Area Studies at Berkeley. He received his Ph.D. from Duke

226

University. From 1970 to 1977 he was Assistant Professor of Political Science at Memphis State University. He is the author of *Soviet Scholars and Soviet Foreign Policy* and editor of *Social Scientists and Policy Making in the USSR.*

DR. MICHAEL RYAN is currently Chief of Programs Analysis Division, Plans Directorate, Defense Security Assistance Agency. He was a military-political analyst for DoD dealing with the Middle East, 1979-1984. He received his Ph.D. in Middle Eastern studies from Harvard University in 1981. He is the author of a number of articles and government studies on security assistance and Middle Eastern affairs.

DR. MICHAEL VLAHOS is currently Research Professor and Co-Director of Security Studies at the Johns Hopkins School of Advanced International Studies. He received his Ph.D. from the Fletcher School of Law and Diplomacy. From 1977-1979 he was a strategic analyst for the CIA dealing with Soviet naval doctrine. He is the author of *America: Images of Empire* and *The BLUE Sword: The Naval War College and the American Mission, 1919-1941.*

INDEX

Abu Musa, 16, 18, 35
Abu Nidal, 63
Acheson, Dean, 221
Achille Lauro, 38
Aden, 11, 88, 93, 96-97
Afghanistan, 9, 14, 19, 44-45, 47-50, 52, 54, 56, 58, 68, 72, 74-75, 92-93, 110, 112-113, 119, 136-137, 173-175, 204, 206-207
Agency for International Development, (AID), 150
Ahwaz, 18
Algeria, 45, 49, 52
Algiers agreement of 1975, 12, 16
Algiers Conference, 18
Amal, 35
Andreasyan, Reuben, 58
Andropov, Yuri, 60, 63, 65, 75-76
Angolan Civil War, 91, 94
Annual Report, 167-168
Arab League, 11, 31, 34, 65
Arab-Israeli, 2, 29-32, 37-40, 45-46, 72, 111, 161-162, 215, 218
Arabian Peninsula, 10, 15, 18, 140, 157, 166
Arabian Sea, 85, 88, 90, 93, 96
Arafat, Yasir, 33, 35-37, 60-61, 65, 73
ARCENT, see Commander, US Army Central Command
Arms Export Control Act (AECA), 145, 149, 159, 196
Asir, 22
al-Assad, Hafiz, 65
Aswan Dam, 44
Auxiliary Crane Ships (TACS), 195

AWACS, 51, 54, 59, 67-69, 75, 126, 140-141, 160, 208
Azerbaijan, 20
Azeris, 13, 19
Aziz, Tariq, 55, 61, 63, 73
Azores, 211
Ba'ath, 45
Ba'athism, 14-15
Ba'athist, 11, 15, 21
Bab el Mandeb, 99
Baghdad, 2, 12, 47-49, 54-55, 62-63
Baghdad Conference, March 1979, 47
Baghdad Pact, 2
Bahrain, 10-11, 13, 18, 21-22, 49, 51, 61, 117
Bakhtiar, Shahpur, 48
Baluchis, 14, 20
Bangladesh, 89, 127
Bani-Sadr, Hassan, 48, 55-56
Begin, Menachim, 54
Beheshti, Ayatollah Mohammed, 56
Beirut, 35-36, 60, 64-65, 72, 113-114, 184-185, 191
Belyayev, Igor, 58
Berbera, 93, 95
Bill, James, 115
Bin Sultan, Bandar, 67
Boldryev, V.K., 57
Bovin, Alexander, 57
Brazil, 123
Brezhnev, Leonid, 52-53, 60, 62, 74-76
BRIGHT STAR, 143
Brown, Harold, 190, 192-193, 199
Brown & Root, 199
Bubiyan, 11, 17-18, 21

229

53, 60, 62, 71, 74, 87, 92, 107, 109-110, 113-116, 136, 160, 164, 173, 189, 204, 207
Mokri, Mohammed, 56
Morocco, 45, 49, 60, 65
Moscow, 43-75, 85, 89-90, 92, 94-101, 108, 112, 175, 181
Mossadeq, Mohammed, 15
Mousavi, Hussain, 57, 73
Mozambique, 88, 98
Mubarak, Hosni, 59, 65, 174
Mujahidin, 56, 71, 112
Multinational Force and Observers, 141
Murphy, Richard, 183-184
Nasserism, 19
National Command Authority, 140, 145, 193
National Democratic Front (NDF), 14, 22
National Security Council, 136
NATO, 16, 46, 70, 136, 161, 165-166, 174, 176, 180, 190-193
Navy Special Warfare Group (SEALS), 142
Near Term Prepositioning Ships (NTPS), 137, 209
Near-Term Prepositioning Force (NTPF), 137, 142, 145, 179, 191-192, 198
Nixon Doctrine, 48, 207
North Korea, 71
North Yemen, 10-11, 14, 16, 19, 22, 44-45, 49
NSDD-99, 206
NTPF, see Near Term Prepositioning Force
NTPS, see Near Term Prepositioning Ships
October 1973 Middle East War, 90-91, 211
Ogaden War, 90, 93-95, 97, 99-102
Ogarkov, Nikolai, 66
oil, 1, 3, 12-13, 19-21, 23-25, 38, 44-47, 49-51, 54, 58-60, 63, 66-67, 74, 83-85, 89, 92, 100, 115, 117, 121, 123-124, 126, 128, 130-131, 139, 151, 157, 162, 167, 173-174, 176-178, 180-181, 183, 189-191, 198, 204, 206, 210, 214-216, 221
Oman, 10, 14, 16-17, 22-23, 48-49, 51, 84, 97, 99-100, 114, 130, 146, 173-174, 176, 178-179, 182, 194, 208, 210, 215
OPEC, 38, 59
Orbis, 212
Ottoman empire, 11
Pakistan, 14, 21, 24, 58, 89-90, 96, 98, 109-111, 113, 175, 178, 186, 190, 204
Palestine Liberation Organization (PLO), 32-39, 46-47, 49, 60, 111

Palestine National Council, 73
Palestinian, 2, 32-37, 39, 60, 63, 111, 118, 181-182, 218
PDRY, see People's Democratic Republic of Yemen
Peace Shield Program, 126
Pearl Harbor, Hawaii, 141
People's Democratic Republic of Yemen (PDRY), 12, 88, 97
Perkins, Stuart, 222
Persian Gulf, 1, 3-4, 9-25, 29-30, 32-33, 38, 43, 46-48, 50-54, 58-60, 63-64, 66-68, 70, 72-75, 83-85, 88-89, 92, 100, 107, 110, 113-119, 124, 128-130, 135-137, 139-147, 149, 157-161, 165-168, 170, 173-186, 189-190, 192-193, 204-211, 213-215, 217, 221
PLO, see Palestine Liberation Organization
Polaris, 85
Ponomarev, Boris, 61
Popular Front for the Liberation of Bahrain, 61
Popular Front for the Liberation of Oman (PFLO), 97, 99
Poseidon, 85
Pravda, 57, 59-60, 62
Qadaffi, Maummar, 110
Qaru, 16
Qashqais, 14
Qasim, Abd al-Karim, 11
Qatar, 10, 22, 49, 51
Quinton, Anthony, 69
Rafsanjani, Hashemi, 71
Rajai, Mohammed Ali, 55-56
Rajavi, Massoud, 56
Ramadan, Taha Yasin, 66
Rapid Deployment Force, 19, 23-25, 59, 70, 114, 136, 196, 206
Rapid Deployment Joint Task Force (RDJTF), 136-138, 147, 173, 179, 207, 209
Ras al-Khaymah, 10, 16
Ras Banas, 174
Ras Tanura, 184
ar-Rashid, Rashid, 68
RDJTF, see Rapid Deployment Joint Task Force
Ready Reserve Force (RRF), 192
Reagan, Ronald, 9, 19, 24, 36-38, 52, 54, 56, 60-61, 64-65, 67-69, 73-75, 111, 114, 119, 139, 143, 153-154, 159, 207-209
Reagan Corollary, 8, 19
Reagan plan, 60-61, 64-65, 73-74
Record, Jeffrey, 212
Red Sea, 22, 67, 72, 88-89, 99

232

Reunion, 84, 89
Revolutionary Guard (Pasdaran), 75
Riyadh, 126, 141, 181-184
Romberg, Alan, 67
Ruhani, Ayatollah Sadiq, 11
Rumsfeld, Donald, 63
Ryabov, Yaacov, 66, 68
Sabra and Shatila, 36
Sadat, Anwar, 30, 46, 54, 59, 111, 113, 116, 119, 164
Saddam Hussain, 12, 16, 18, 55, 60-61, 63, 75, 110, 115
Saudi Arabia, 3, 9-10, 13-17, 19-23, 43, 47, 49, 51, 53-55, 58-59, 61, 63-64, 67-68, 70, 72, 74-75, 109-111, 113-114, 116-117, 121, 124-127, 130-132, 157-158, 160-161, 166, 177-178, 180-182, 184, 189, 207-208, 215, 217
Second World War, see WW II
Senate Foreign Relations Committee, 55
7th Infantry Division, 141
7th Marine Amphibious Brigade (7th MAB), 137, 142
Seychelles, 88, 96
SHADOW HAWK, 143
Shamir, Itzhak, 64
Sharja, 16
Shatt, see Shatt al Arab
Shatt al Arab, 12, 16, 165
Shaw AFB, South Carolina, 141
Sheik Sabah, 53-54
Sheik Salem as-Sabah, 68-69
Sheikh Sabah al-Sabah, 68
Shi'ism, 14, 18
Shi'ite, 11-14, 18-19, 21, 35-36, 113, 131, 184
Shultz, George, 63, 67
Sinai, 47, 141
Sinai I, 47
Sinai II, 47
SL-7, 145, 179
Socotra Island, 88
SOG, see special operations group
Somalia, 44-45, 49, 94-97, 99-100, 146, 174, 179, 210
South China Sea, 90
South Korea, 200, 221
South Lebanon, 35-36
South Yemen, 10-12, 14, 16, 18-19, 22, 29, 44-45, 49, 65, 97
Southwest Asia, 135-137, 139, 146, 149-152, 154, 156, 161-163, 166-167, 174, 189-198, 200-201, 203-205, 207, 209-214, 218-219, 222
Soviet, 1-4, 9, 11-12, 14, 16-24, 30, 38, 43-75, 83-101, 108, 110, 112-114, 119, 130, 135-137, 139-140, 142, 146-147,

150-151, 155, 161-164, 166-167, 173-178, 180-186, 189-191, 193, 203-215, 217-221
Soviet Middle East Plan, 74
Soviet Union, 9, 12, 16-23, 30, 38, 44-53, 55-58, 61-63, 65-66, 68, 69-73, 75, 83-86, 89, 92, 96-99, 112-114, 130, 135, 140, 150, 155, 159, 161-164, 166-167, 174, 176, 180, 183, 213, 220
special operations groups (SOG), 216
Spetznaz, 85
Sri Lanka, 127
Steadfastness Front, 49, 52
Stinger missiles, 67-68
Stoddard, Philip, 38
Straits of Hormuz, 19, 50-51, 66, 84-85, 90, 114, 173-174
Sudan, 30, 45, 49, 109-110, 113, 119
Suez Canal, 67, 89, 139, 179, 210
Sultan Qabus, 174
Sunnis, 12, 13-14, 116, 131
Super-Etendard, 62, 66, 74
SWA, see Southwest Asia
Syria, 18, 31, 35-36, 44-45, 47-49, 51, 60-61, 64-65, 74, 109-110, 112, 139, 162
Tehran, 48, 53, 56-57, 62-63, 71-72, 110, 139
Third World, 47, 86, 89, 91-96, 100, 126, 136, 151, 154-155, 159, 164, 204, 213
36b notification, 159
Thumrait, 22
Tikhonov, Nikolai, 66
Tripartite Agreement, 163
Trucial States, 15
Tudeh, 45, 48, 50, 57-58, 61-62, 70-72, 75
Tunbs, 16, 18
Tunisia, 49
Turkey, 24, 58, 123, 174, 176, 179-180
24th Infantry Division, 137, 141
Twenty-Nine Palms, 142
twin pillars, 19
UAE, 10, 14-16, 22
Ulema, 131
Umm al-Maradim, 16
Umm Qasr, 11
ummah, 115
UN, see United Nations
United Arab Emirates (UAE), 10
United Nations, 34, 54-55, 152
United States, 1-5, 9-10, 15, 17, 19-20, 22-25, 30, 32-33, 38-40, 44-56, 58-61, 63-70, 72-75, 83, 85-96, 98-102, 110-111, 113-119, 124, 128, 130, 135-144, 146-147, 149-152, 154-170, 173-186, 189-192, 194, 196, 198, 200, 203-222, 220-222
US, see United States

233

US Central Command (USCENTCOM),
19, 22-25, 114, 136, 138-146, 173-174,
176, 178-180, 185-186, 190-193, 196,
206-208, 212, 216
US Readiness Command, 136
US-Saudi, 1, 59, 67, 75, 162, 181, 184
USCENTAF, 141
USCENTCOM, see US Central
Command
USSR, see Soviet Union
Velayati, Ali Akhbar, 72
Vietnam, 113-114, 192, 207, 220
Vinogradov, Vladimir, 56
Vladivostok, 87-88, 91
Volsky, Dimitry, 72
Wahhabism, 14
Waltz, Kenneth, 206

Warba, 11, 17-18, 21
Warsaw Pact, 72
Washington, 38, 52, 55, 63, 65-67, 69, 75,
94, 111, 212
West Bank, 36, 60, 118
World War I, 11
World War II, 14, 29, 71, 159, 192, 197,
203-204
World War III, 214
XVIII Airborne Corps, 137, 141
Yamani, Mohammed Abdul, 61
Yassan, Taha, 61
Yom Kippur War, see October 1973 war
Zagros Mountains, 137, 140
Zia al-Haq, 109
Zionism, 45
Zubara, 10